Modernism to the present

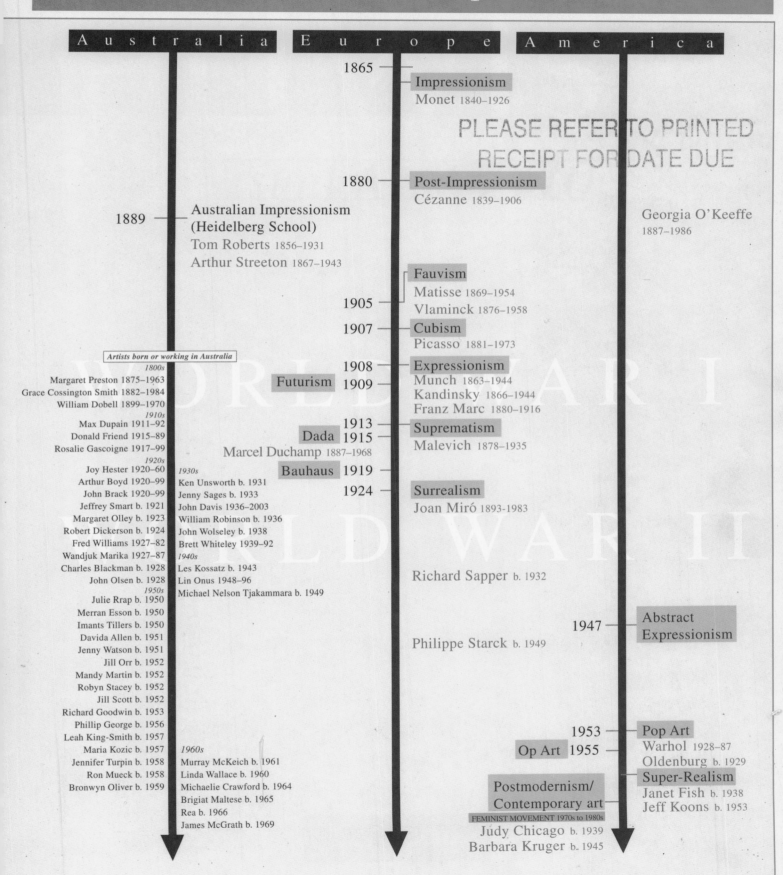

Australia	Europe	America

1865 — Impressionism
Monet 1840–1926

1880 — Post-Impressionism
Cézanne 1839–1906

Georgia O'Keeffe 1887–1986

1889 — Australian Impressionism (Heidelberg School)
Tom Roberts 1856–1931
Arthur Streeton 1867–1943

Fauvism
Matisse 1869–1954
1905 — Vlaminck 1876–1958

1907 — Cubism
Picasso 1881–1973

Artists born or working in Australia

1800s
Margaret Preston 1875–1963
Grace Cossington Smith 1882–1984
William Dobell 1899–1970

1908 — Expressionism
Futurism **1909** — Munch 1863–1944
Kandinsky 1866–1944
Franz Marc 1880–1916

1910s
Max Dupain 1911–92
Donald Friend 1915–89
Rosalie Gascoigne 1917–99

1913 — Suprematism
Dada **1915** — Malevich 1878–1935
Marcel Duchamp 1887–1968

1920s
Joy Hester 1920–60
Arthur Boyd 1920–99
John Brack 1920–99
Jeffrey Smart b. 1921
Margaret Olley b. 1923
Robert Dickerson b. 1924
Fred Williams 1927–82
Wandjuk Marika 1927–87
Charles Blackman b. 1928
John Olsen b. 1928

Bauhaus **1919** —

1924 — Surrealism
Joan Miró 1893-1983

1930s
Ken Unsworth b. 1931
Jenny Sages b. 1933
John Davis 1936–2003
William Robinson b. 1936
John Wolseley b. 1938
Brett Whiteley 1939–92

1940s
Les Kossatz b. 1943
Lin Onus 1948–96
Michael Nelson Tjakammara b. 1949

Richard Sapper b. 1932

1950s
Julie Rrap b. 1950
Merran Esson b. 1950
Imants Tillers b. 1950
Davida Allen b. 1951
Jenny Watson b. 1951
Jill Orr b. 1952
Mandy Martin b. 1952
Robyn Stacey b. 1952
Jill Scott b. 1952
Richard Goodwin b. 1953
Phillip George b. 1956
Leah King-Smith b. 1957
Maria Kozic b. 1957
Jennifer Turpin b. 1958
Ron Mueck b. 1958
Bronwyn Oliver b. 1959

Philippe Starck b. 1949

1947 — Abstract Expressionism

1953 — Pop Art
Warhol 1928–87
Op Art **1955** — Oldenburg b. 1929

1960s
Murray McKeich b. 1961
Linda Wallace b. 1960
Michaelie Crawford b. 1964
Brigiat Maltese b. 1965
Rea b. 1966
James McGrath b. 1969

Super-Realism
Postmodernism/ Janet Fish b. 1938
Contemporary art Jeff Koons b. 1953

FEMINIST MOVEMENT 1970s to 1980s
Judy Chicago b. 1939
Barbara Kruger b. 1945

This edition published 2004 by
John Wiley & Sons Australia, Ltd
33 Park Road, Milton, Qld 4064

Offices also in Sydney and Melbourne

Typeset in 11/13 pt Times

First edition published 1997

© Glenis Israel 1997, 2004

National Library of Australia
Cataloguing-in-publication data

Israel, Glenis.
  Artwise 1: visual arts 7–10

  2nd ed.
  Includes index.
  For secondary students.
  ISBN 0 7314 0108 5.

  1. Art, modern — Juvenile literature. 2. Art criticism
  — Juvenile literature. 3. Art — History — Juvenile
  literature. I. Title.

701.18

Artwork on cover:
James McGrath
Votum #3, 2003
Lambda print face mounted to plexiglass
152 × 101 cm
James McGrath is represented by
Michael Carr Art Dealer
124A Queen St Woollahra NSW 2025

Printed in China by
C & C Offset Printing Co., Ltd

10 9 8 7 6 5 4 3 2 1

Contents

Introduction

How to use this book

This second edition of *Artwise* has been updated to reflect developments in the 2003 NSW Visual Arts Syllabus due for implementation in 2004/5. The Conceptual Framework already included in the *Senior Artwise* series had been adapted to develop the 7–10 students' understanding.

Additions include more recent examples by artists in the original text as well as some new artists, including designers and artists working in digital media. In the *Studying art* questions students are encouraged to use information technology, thus using the computer as a research, presentation and writing tool. *Making art* exercises have also been updated with new tasks employing digital media.

Artists have been grouped together in chapters according to the subject matter of the artworks, for example, 'Other living things' (chapter 2). Within each chapter there are sub-headings, for example 'Plant life', 'Animals/birds' and 'Sea life'. The artists within each sub-heading have been organised in a chronological way; that is, they have been looked at in an historical order. This allows you to see any influence from one artist to another. The table on pages vi–vii provides alternative ways to locate artists in this book.

Artists work in a variety of forms such as drawing, painting, sculpture, photography, ceramics, performance and electronic media. The text discusses these and other forms and explains techniques and art terms. In the box next to the artist's name, you are given the frame or frames from which the artist is working and the form of the media or artwork. The relationship between the artist, his or her world, the artwork and the audience is also explained (the conceptual framework, explained further on page xii).

The *Critical study* and *Historical study* sections (see page viii) contain information about the artwork and the artist. This will help you understand the different types of activities or tasks an art critic and an art historian undertake. The art critic explains what the artist has created and how. The art historian investigates the historical evidence, and looks at the development of an artist's work and the influences on it. The art historian is particularly concerned with the intention of the artist.

The *Studying art* sections will help you understand the information in the earlier sections and will challenge you to form your own opinions. They are organised in 'frames' under further *Critical study* and *Historical study* headings. By looking at an artwork from different frames or approaches you are able to get different types of information (see page ix). You will not be asked to consider each frame for every artwork, as the frames have been selected to suit the main approaches of the artist. Although it is possible to write critically and historically about one artist using all the frames, this would have made the book too long!

Two-dimensional

Art forms	Artists	Dates	Culture	Page no.
Two-dimensional				
Printmaking	Edvard Munch	1863–1944	Norwegian	140
Photography	Max Dupain	1911–92	Australian	82
	Barbara Kruger	b. 1945	American	164
	Julie Rrap	b. 1950	Australian	166
	Robyn Stacey	b. 1952	Australian	182
	Leah King-Smith	b. 1957	Australian	176
Digital media	Julie Rrap	b. 1950	Australian	166
	Yasumasa Morimura	b. 1951	Japanese	88
	Phillip George	b. 1956	Australian	184, 188
	Murray McKeich	b. 1961	New Zealand	66
	Rea	b. 1966	Australian	174
	James McGrath	b. 1969	Australian	157
Montage	Barbara Kruger	b. 1945	American	164
	Murray McKeich	b. 1961	New Zealand	66
Three-dimensional				
Sculpture	Polykleitos	c.480–350 BC	Greek	2
	Bernini	1598–1680	Italian	10
	Pablo Picasso	1881–1973	Spanish	14
	Marcel Duchamp	1887–1968	French	90
	Rosalie Gascoigne	1917–99	New Zealand	92
	Claes Oldenburg	b. 1929	Swedish	98
	Ken Unsworth	b. 1931	Australian	94
	John Davis	1936–2003	Australian	62
	Les Kossatz	b. 1943	Australian	54
	Richard Goodwin	b. 1953	Australian	68
	Jeff Koons	b. 1955	American	56
	Ron Mueck	b. 1958	Australian	20
	Bronwyn Oliver	b. 1959	Australian	60
Ceramics	Greek pottery	6th century BC	Greek	72
	Merran Esson	b. 1950	Australian	64
	Brigiat Maltese	b. 1965	Australian	34
Installations	Rosalie Gascoigne	1917–99	New Zealand	92
	Ken Unsworth	b. 1931	Australian	94
	Judy Chicago	b. 1939	American	162
	Lin Onus	1948–96	Indigenous Australian	172
	Julie Rrap	b. 1950	Australian	166
	Robyn Stacey	b. 1952	Australian	182
	Jennifer Turpin	b. 1958	Australian	134
	Michaelie Crawford	b. 1964	Australian	134
Designed objects	Richard Sapper	b. 1932	German	74
	Philippe Starck	b. 1949	French	76
Four-dimensional				
Performance	Jill Orr	b. 1952	Australian	18
Video works and video installations	Jill Scott	b. 1952	Australian	180
	Linda Wallace	b. 1960	Australian	186

The *Further research* sections contain more difficult questions and require you to do further research in the library or on the Internet. Many are essay-type questions.

The *Making art* sections will help you to get ideas for your own art-making by looking at other artworks. Your understanding of the practices of art criticism and art history will broaden and support your artmaking.

Terms which are in bold type in the text are explained in the *Vocabulary* at the beginning of the discussion about the artist, and in the *Glossary* at the end of the book.

Art criticism and art history

This book deals with the two basic approaches to interpreting or gaining information from artworks: the critical and historical. The stance of both art critics and art historians depends on their frame of working. The four frames — subjective, structural, cultural and postmodern — are discussed on page ix.

Critical study

The critical study approach reveals knowledge to be gained and understood by looking carefully at and analysing the artwork. It involves a personal response. This type of study includes describing, interpreting and judging an artwork. A. D. Coleman, in explaining his method of criticism, says 'I merely look closely at ... and attempt to pinpoint in words what they provoke me to think and feel and understand'.[1] Roberta Smith says that sometimes her criticism is 'just like pointing at things'.[2] Alloway defined the art critic's function as 'the description, interpretation, and evaluation of new art'.[3] This last definition suggests that art criticism can only be applied to recent art; it can, however, be a useful tool to interpret past works if only the artwork itself is considered (not the artwork's place in art history).

The example on page x shows the type of information that can be gained by a critical approach. Through questions in the *Studying art* section, students will be encouraged to use critical skills to personally respond to and evaluate artworks.

Quotes from art critics are included as a stimulus for discussion as well as a way of helping students understand the role of the art critic.

Historical study

The historical study approach is an explanatory approach. It defines, compares and explains the artwork's meaning or function within the social, cultural, political and historical time in which it was created. It involves looking at what others have said about an artwork. This historical approach adds extra information to that gained by a critical study of the artwork. It creates a deeper understanding, particularly of the intention of the artist.

Information is given about the artist and their artistic style. The section also contains statements by the artists themselves, writings in manifestos and catalogues, and comments by art historians.

Further research will be suggested.

Note to the teacher

Although artworks will be looked at using both the critical study and historical study methods, there is sometimes an overlap, as these disciplines do inform each other, and create a synthesis of interpretation. However, the overall approach of this text is to help students understand critical and historical study in order to be able to identify them and use the appropriate methods and skills. It is also intended that students become familiar with contemporary art critics and art historians to prepare them for senior work.

The frames

The frames — subjective, structural, cultural and postmodern — provide a basis for interpreting the making and studying of the visual arts. Frames are a device or process which help us to understand what the artist was trying to achieve. Using the frames helps us to understand not only the attitude of artists but also the stance or approach of critics and historians.

The frames are four models or ways of approaching art and asking questions about art. Below is a brief, simplified definition of each frame.[4]

Subjective frame: This involves an immediate response based on the senses. We can make an expressive, personal response that draws on the imagination, the unconscious, intuition, and shared human experiences.

- *Critical study*
  Ask yourself: What do I see and feel about the artwork?

- *Historical study*
  What do others see and feel about the artwork, considering its historical time?

Structural frame: This looks at the codes, symbols and signs used in the artwork; at the use of elements — line, shape, texture, and so on; at organisation and relationships, composition, scale, materials and techniques.

- *Critical study*
  Ask yourself: How has it been organised and what symbols are used and why?

- *Historical study*
  What do others say about the techniques and use of signs and symbols?

Cultural frame: This requires you to examine cultural identity — race, class, gender, place; art movements and styles; the influence of politics and economics; and symbols relating to culture.

- *Critical study*
  Ask yourself: What does it show you about the culture or society?

- *Historical study*
  What do others say about the artist, influences, style or meaning?

Postmodern frame: Within this frame, you look at whether words or images from the past have been used for a new purpose or in a new way; at mass media, technology, popular culture; at new, non-traditional media and methods, and at diversity.

- *Critical study*
  Ask yourself: Have past artworks been used in a new way (appropriated)? Is it a new form of art?

- *Historical study*
  What do others say about the ideas, appropriations, art form, meanings?

An example of the use of frames

The frames are used to provide a viewpoint when making and studying art. The term 'frames' has been used in this book to represent the different approaches or attitudes that can be taken by art critics, art historians and artists. Thus, if you use the four different frames to look at a particular artwork you are going to find four viewpoints or types of information.

TOM ROBERTS
Shearing the Rams 1889–90
Oil on canvas, 121.9 × 182.6 cm
National Gallery of Victoria
Felton Bequest 1932

STUDYING ART

Critical study

Subjective frame

What do I see?
Shearing of sheep is taking place on a country property.
All ages are involved in this event. It seems hard work.

What do I feel?
It appears exciting since many people are actively involved in the shearing.
A warm, friendly atmosphere has been created. I am drawn into the space.

What does it remind me of?
I am reminded of visits to farms, and of Australian poetry.

Structural frame

What form is it?
It is a painting.

What materials and techniques have been used?
It is a realistic oil painting on canvas. There are free brushstrokes and an interest in light.

Composition
My eye has been carefully led from the young boy in the foreground back to the shaft of light in the background. It is a lively composition with a sense of space.

Art elements
- Direction: There is a strong diagonal direction leading backwards.
- Colour: A warm, rich colour scheme has been used, creating an atmosphere of friendship. It also reminds me of the dryness of the country.
- Tone: Tone has been used to emphasise the effect of light coming through the openings. It also helps to unify the work.
- Texture: Roberts has skilfully painted a wide range of textures, for example the soft fleece, rough timber.
- Symbols: The sheep was a symbol for Australia and country life.

Cultural frame

What country and time does it belong to?
Australia, around the time of centenary celebrations. It belongs to a time of nationalistic feelings.

Does it belong to an art movement or style?
Heidelberg School.

How does it reflect a culture — class, race, gender, politics, economics, technology?
Roberts was attempting to portray a unique Australian identity — hard work, country life, mateship, courage. Wool at the time was our most important export. It reflected the Australian politics of the time.

Postmodern frame

Does it still have the same meaning and value for us today? What is missing?
This does not symbolise the present Australia, with the majority of our people living in cities, our multicultural nature and our changing economy. There are no women in this painting. Aboriginal people, who have played an important part in this industry, have also been omitted.

Artmaking practice

An artist's artmaking practice is a reflection of how they investigate and communicate their ideas, responses, values and beliefs. Through their media choices and techniques they reveal their intentions — what they wish the audience to experience and how they go about it. Artmaking practice involves the artist's methods of working, their research, influences, experiments, decisions, approaches, methods of display and whether they work alone, in collaboration or have technical assistance.

Quotes by artists have been included to help students understand their practice — the how and why of their artmaking.

Conceptual framework

The conceptual framework refers to the components of the art world — the artwork, the artist, the audience or viewer and the world.

- We consider what is an *artwork*, and how an artwork now can take many forms. An artwork used to be in the form of a drawing, painting, sculpture or architecture. This was later broadened to include photography, and then the ready-made. Now we have installations, and technology-based artworks such as video, hologram and computer-generated works. Some artworks exist for only a short period of time, so the documentation of them by video or photograph also becomes the artwork. This is particularly true of performances and earth art. We also consider the purpose of an artwork.

- What is the definition of an *artist*? Historically it was someone skilled in art media and its techniques. We thought of an artist as a creative person whose perceptions of the world were heightened or more sensitive. Artists created original works. Now it is acceptable to appropriate (copy) past artworks if the meaning or context is altered. Artists now are often the performers in their artworks, particularly video works. We have artists who work together on a project (collaborative artists) and artists who have the ideas but employ skilled people to help create them. The definition changes with changes in our culture.

- The role of the *audience* or *viewer* is also changing. Sometimes the meaning of an artwork is left to the viewer to interpret, according to how it relates to their own experiences and ideas. Artworks have become more accessible to a wider public — for example, you no longer have to visit an art gallery to experience art. The mass media have also made us more aware of art. Perhaps the biggest recent change is interactive art, where the viewer actually determines what happens with an artwork.

- What aspects of the *world* does the artist choose to comment on? How does the world affect the viewpoint or emotional reaction of the artist? What social, political and technological changes have made an impact on the artist or artwork?

The conceptual framework is concerned with looking at these components as well as the relationships between them. Statements by artists can help us to understand which components of the art world are of concern to them.

Acknowledgements

The author and publisher would like to thank the following copyright holders, organisations and individuals for their assistance and for permission to reproduce copyright material in this book. (The following acknowledgements are in addition to any copyright information contained within the caption for each artwork.)

Images

• Scala Group SPA, page **xiv** (bottom left), *Doryphorus*, Roman marble copy of a lost Greek bronze by Polykleitos, Museo Nazionale, Naples; page **xiv** (bottom right), *The School of Athens* 1509–11, wall fresco, 579 × 807 cm, Signature Room, Vatican, Rome • AAP Image, page **xiv** (top right), *Boy* 1999, mixed media, 490 × 490 × 240 cm/AAP Image/AFP/Gabriel Bouys • The Bridgeman Art Library: pages **xiv** (top left), **4**, **78**, **102**, **104** (top right), **114**, **138** (centre right & bottom), **144**, **146**/Giraudon/Bridgeman Art Library, London; pages **6**, **15**, **46**, **110**/Bridgeman Art Library, London; pages **38** (bottom left), **48**/Christie's Images/Bridgeman Art Library, London • Art Gallery of New South Wales, pages **38** (top left), Bronwyn Oliver *Unicorn* 1984, mixed media sculpture, 700 × 70 × 270 cm, gift of the artist under the terms of the NSW travelling scholarship 1986; **138** (top right), Arthur Merric Bloomfield Boyd *The Expulsion* 1947–48, oil on hardboard, 99.5 × 119.6 cm, reproduced with the permission of Bundanon • Photograph John Wiley & Sons Australia, Ltd, pages **38** (bottom right), **55** (top & bottom) • Merran Esson, page **38** (top centre), *Starfish*, from series *Beneath the Surface*, 1993, height 40 cm, ceramics, coloured slips, dry glazes, metallic leaf • Courtesy of the artist and Roslyn Oxley9 Gallery, Sydney, page **38** (top right), *Tracing the Wallace Line: wing leaf and land* 1999, watercolour on paper, 136 × 205 cm; page **104** (bottom) *Lake Julius* 1994, oil with ochres and pigment on linen, 152 × 275 cm; page **158** (bottom right), *Coogee Paul* 2003, from the series *Fleshstones*, digital print, 150 × 126 cm • Art Resource, pages **40**, **41** • Anna Schwartz Gallery, Melbourne, page **70** (bottom left) *Masterpieces* (Warhol) 1986, synthetic polymer paint on wood, 182 × 122 cm, collection of Museum of Contemporary Art, Sydney, courtesy of the artist and Anna Schwartz Gallery, Melbourne • Courtesy Boutwell Draper Gallery, page **70** (top right) *Sundry Appearances* 1995, piano, wood, 136 × 148 × 62 cm • Luhring Augustine Gallery, page **70** (bottom right) *Criticism and the Lover* 1990, coloured photograph, transparent medium, 180 × 225 cm © the artist, collection Iwaki City Art Museum, photograph courtesy of the artist • Phillippe Starck, page **70** (top centre) courtesy Phillippe Starck • VISCOPY, page **70** (top left) *Gordon's Gin Bottles* 1972, oil on canvas, 183 × 112.4 cm, © Janet Fish, licensed by VISCOPY, Australia, 2004 • Di Palma Associati, page **75** • Walker Art Center page **99**, *Shoestring Potatoes Spilling From a Bag* 1966, canvas stiffened with glue, filled with kapok, painted with acrylic, 274.3 × 132.1 × 106.6 cm dimensions variable, collection Walker Art Center, Minneapolis, gift of the T.B. Walker Foundation 1966, © Claes Oldenburg and Coosje van Bruggen • Ashmolean Museum, Oxford, page **104** (centre), *Landscape with Ascanius Shooting the Stag of Sylvia* 1682, oil on canvas, 120 × 150 cm, presented by Mrs WFR Weldon in 1926 • Stephen Rogers, page **104** (top left) *Underground Car Park* 1993, oil on canvas, 76 × 110 cm • Dickerson Gallery, page **124** • National Gallery of Australia, page **138** (top left), *The Birth of the Djang'kawu Children at Yalangbara* 1982, ochres on eucalyptus bark, 147.5 × 66.0 cm, © Aboriginal Artists Agency, Sydney • National Gallery of Victoria, page **138** (top centre), *The Death of my Father* 1981–82, oil on canvas, 165.3 × 271.9 cm • Linda Wallace, page **158** (top left) © Linda Wallace • Courtesy Mary Boone Gallery, New York, page **158** (centre left), untitled (We have received orders not to move) 1982, photograph, 182.9 × 121.9 cm • Phillip George, page **158** (bottom left), *Mnemonicon 4* from *Mnemonic Notations* 1992, mixed media on paper on canvas, 130 × 288 cm, photograph courtesy the artist • Through the Flower, page **158** (top right), *The Dinner Party* © Judy Chicago 1979, mixed media, 1463 cm × 1280 cm × 91 cm, collection of the Brooklyn Museum of Art, gift of the Elizabeth A. Sackler Foundation, photo © Donald Woodman • Ancient Art & Architecture, page **191** (top)

Text

• Jenny Sages, page **31** • Linda Wallace, page **187** • Random House Group UK, pages **59**, **103**, **114**, **115** from *Nothing Not Critical* by Robert Hughes, published by Collins Harvill, reprinted by permission of The Random House Group Ltd • Sarah Donnelly, pages **203–5** • VISCOPY, page **93**, © Rosalie Gascoigne, Licensed by VISCOPY, Australia, 2004

Every effort has been made to trace the ownership of copyright material. Information that will enable the publisher to rectify any error or omission in subsequent reprints will be welcome. In such cases, please contact the Permission Section at John Wiley & Sons, who will arrange for the payment of the usual fee.

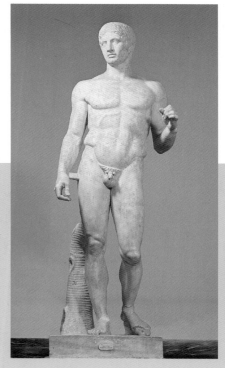

one

PEOPLE

DISCUSSION

1. Subjective frame

Choose two artworks from this chapter, each one showing a different emotion, for example sorrow and joy, or courage and fear. Compare and contrast how the position of the body, hand gestures and facial expressions have been used by the artist to reveal this emotion.

2. Postmodern frame

Choose two artworks from this chapter which include a female. What is the role of the female in each work? Has this role changed in any way with the ideas of feminism?

3. Class debate

Choose one of the artworks opposite and debate its value. One group should make its judgement from an historical study approach, the other group from a critical study approach.

Polykleitos

(Classical Greek sculpture c.480–350 BC)

Frames: structural; cultural
Form: sculpture — marble
Conceptual framework: This sculpture of a spear-bearer is the artist's interpretation of the perfect human form. In a world where warriors and athletes were revered, its perfection also linked it to the gods.

Vocabulary

contrapposto: sculpture of the human body in which shoulders and chest are turned slightly one way, hips and legs another

idealised: presented in a perfect or ideal form, without imperfections

in the round: describes a three-dimensional sculpture that you can view from all sides

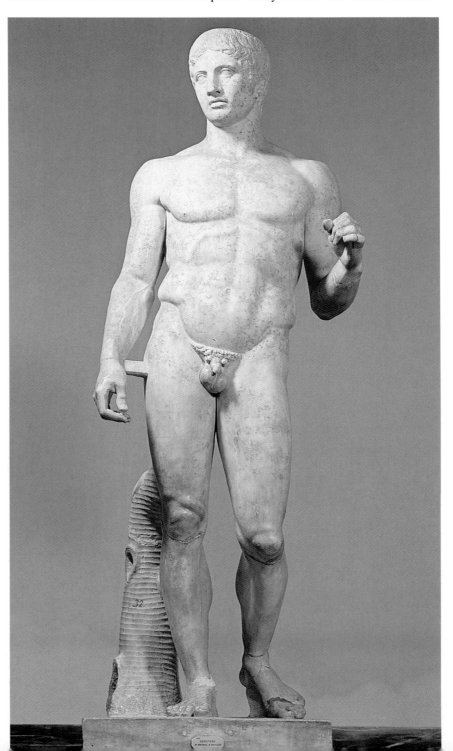

DORYPHORUS
Roman marble copy of a lost Greek bronze by Polykleitos
Museo Nazionale, Naples

Here we have a sculpture **in the round** of a nude male in a relaxed pose, with his weight on one foot while the other knee is bent. He is a youth with an athletic, well-proportioned body. The feeling created by the sculpture is one of calm. There is no emotion on the face.

HISTORICAL STUDY

Polykleitos belonged to the Classical style of Greek art, often called the Golden Age of Greek art. At this stage the Greek sculptors achieved mastery over all technical aspects of sculpture. They created relaxed figures of ideal physical beauty and correct anatomy. The sculptures thus appear perfected or **idealised**. Polykleitos developed a system or rule for representing the human body. His rule was that the head should be one-seventh of the figure's height. The foot should be three times the length of the palm of the hand. The length of the leg from the foot to the knee and the distance between the knee and the centre of the abdomen should be six times that of the palm of the hand.

The figures often had their weight on one foot, thereby raising one hip and dropping a shoulder (an S-bend). When this weight shift causes a slight turn to the body it is generally termed **contrapposto**. This technique was later adopted by the Renaissance artists. To the Greeks, physical perfection was a link with the gods. Athletics was a favourite pastime, with competitive games taking place as part of religious festivals. Of these, the most important was the Olympic Games, held at Olympia every four years in honour of Zeus (God of the heavens and father of all the gods and goddesses). Sport was also considered important training for warfare. Greek sculptors were moving towards naturalism, but they were less interested in individuals than in a universal way of represention. Thus all young men at the time were portrayed as tall, slender, perfectly proportioned, firm and muscular, and the young women as sturdy and healthy. They all appear serene and calm.

The naturalism of Greek art was not suited to the aims and ideals of Medieval art. Naturalism was to re-emerge during the Renaissance.

STUDYING ART

Critical study
Subjective frame
1. Stand in the position of the figure in the sculpture, then describe how you feel.

Cultural frame
2. Athletes performed in the Olympic Games in the nude. What effect do you think that would have had on their ideas of nudity? How might it have influenced what they considered to be the perfect human figure?

Historical study
Cultural frame
3. List three characteristics of Classical Greek sculpture.
4. In what ways is Greek sculpture a reflection of the beliefs, values and lifestyle of the ancient Greeks?

FURTHER RESEARCH

1. Look at Greek art in more depth to see evidence of the development of Greek sculpture. How did the representation of the figure change from the early Archaic to the Classical period and finally through to the Hellenistic period?
2. Find an example of a work by the Renaissance sculptor Donatello. In what ways do you think Donatello was influenced by the work of ancient Greek sculptors such as Polykleitos? In what ways is the work of Renaissance sculptors different to the work of ancient Greek sculptors?

MAKING ART

1. Draw from life a person (perhaps one of the pupils in the class) in the position of the figure in the sculpture. Move around the figure and draw it from several viewpoints.
2. Create a sculpture of a figure in action. Suggested materials to use are wire and wax; wire and plaster; or clay.
3. Using computer graphics software, draw a person using the rules for measurements developed by Polykleitos as described in the text above. Write a paragraph commenting on your results.

Giotto

(c.1267–1337, Italian)

Vocabulary

Classical: describes ancient Greek and Roman art

composition: the placement of figures and objects; the organisation of an artwork

dramatic: like a play; containing drama, emotion or conflict

expression: indication of emotion on the face

humanism: belief system that stresses human, not spiritual, concerns

perspective: way of making objects appear to recede into the distance. In *aerial perspective* distant objects are lighter and bluer in tone, with softer edges. *Linear perspective* is a geometrical method of representing depth on a two-dimensional surface by drawing lines going to a vanishing point.

Discussion

In what ways is this painting stiff, unnatural and symbolic, and in what ways is it natural and humanistic?

The Lamentation of Christ 1303–05
Fresco, 184 × 200 cm
Scrovegni (Arena) Chapel, Padua

CRITICAL STUDY

This artwork is obviously a religious painting with its symbolic haloes and angels. It tells a religious story, and it is being told with emotion and human sympathy. People are crouched around Christ and women are crying. Each face is individual and shows **expression**. Hand gestures are also important. Beneath the robes the figures appear solid. Giotto has not painted the background the usual flat gold but has added objects from nature, including rocks and trees. This makes it seem a part of real life even though the background looks like a shallow stage setting.

Critical study

Subjective frame

1. Giotto was able to show human emotions. Describe the emotions you see in this artwork. Don't forget to look at the angels.
2. Why do you think his paintings are called 'dramatic'?
3. One of the ways in which Giotto added emotion to a painting was to have two faces confronting each other. Which two faces are facing each other in this painting and how does it make you feel?

Structural frame

4. Symbols are used to represent a religion or its teachings. For example, the shape of an upturned begging bowl represents Buddhism; a cross or fish represents Christianity; a dove represents peace. List any symbols of religion you can see in *The Lamentation of Christ*.
5. How have the figures been arranged to give importance to Christ (make him the focus) and thus help tell the story?
6. How has Giotto made the figures appear to have weight and solidity?
7. Why do you think Giotto has cut off the figures at the edges?

Historical study

Cultural frame

8. What social changes were taking place in the fourteenth century? What were the changes in attitude towards religion?
9. Acrylic and oil paint were not available in Giotto's time. Giotto painted the walls of the Arena Chapel using the fresco technique. How do you think this affected the style of his work? What other differences in artmaking practice would there have been for Giotto compared with today's artists?

Giotto di Bondone from Florence, Italy, is usually acknowledged as the founder or originator of Renaissance painting. His painting style is thus usually termed Proto-Renaissance (before-Renaissance). Giotto's style of naturalism and the emotional or **dramatic** power of his works were new at the time. For the first time in Christian art, people are shown as individuals in natural poses. Previously, figures were unrealistic and faced the front. They generally had haloes and were set against a gold or one-colour background, and represented important religious figures. Giotto has attempted to include a natural background, with a sense of space. His work led to the development of a new style of painting based on realism.

While still only a boy Giotto was apprenticed to an artist in Florence called Cimabue who was the first painter to absorb into his work the influence of **Classical** art (Greek and Roman). The term 'Renaissance' means 'rebirth' and has come to be applied to a cultural period (and group of artists) which began in Italy in the fourteenth century. The Renaissance period showed an awakened interest in people's relationship with each other rather than just their relationship to God. People began to look carefully at themselves and the world around them.

The Renaissance style of art was partly a result of a new interest in human values and a belief in one's freedom through the powers of reason or thought. There was a new concern for people as individuals. This way of thinking, which existed in Classical writings but which was not prominent until the fourteenth century, is usually called **humanism**. Giotto's work shows the beginnings of the main characteristics of Renaissance art:

(a) natural poses of figures
(b) feeling of depth by using **perspective**
(c) natural light and shade to model figures (solidness)
(d) observation of nature
(e) balanced **compositions** — often in a triangular shape.

The Lamentation of Christ is one scene from the overall decoration on the walls and ceiling of the Arena Chapel. Giotto's theme was the 'redemption of mankind'. The story runs clockwise along the walls and down in three tiers or levels. It was painted in fresco technique. Artists painted on wet plaster so that the pigment soaked into the surface. Because the fresh plaster dried quickly, artists had to carefully plan their work. New plaster was applied for each day's painting session, so the work proceeded in sections.

Subjective frame

1. Look at the expressions on the faces in this fresco. The people are in mourning for the dead Christ. How do you think they feel? Take a digital photograph of your face or a friend's face. Using software such as Adobe Photoshop, experiment with the features and manipulate the image to change the facial expression. Add captions to each expression, describing the emotion that is expressed.

Postmodern frame

2. Copy the positions of the figures in *The Lamentation of Christ* but put them into a contemporary setting such as the aftermath of a street fight.
3. Scan this artwork and use Photoshop to change its setting to a contemporary one.

Masaccio

(c.1401–28, Italian)

Frames: structural; cultural
Form: fresco painting
Conceptual framework: This is the artist's own interpretation of a story. Having the figures so close to the front causes a strong link with the viewer.

Vocabulary

aerial perspective: technique that makes distant objects lighter and bluer in tone

linear perspective: technique that represents depth by drawing lines going to a vanishing point

model: to blend light to dark to create solidity

narrative: a story

Renaissance (art): art in which the emphasis was on humankind and nature. 'Renaissance' means rebirth. It was a time of rediscovery of Roman classical ideals, and covers the period from about the fourteenth to the sixteenth century.

unify: work as one, bring together

The Tribute Money c. 1427
Wall fresco, 640 × 1463 cm
Brancacci Chapel, Santa Maria del Carmine, Florence

CRITICAL STUDY

This is a further development in realism from the work of Giotto (see page 4). Masaccio's clothes are not just simple robes but reflect the fashion of the day. The figures are relating to each other by look and hand movements. The faces show individual character and various expressions. Masaccio has used light and shade, giving the figures a feeling of solidity. By using a single light source from one side he has been able to **model** his forms and **unify** his composition. A major change is the new sense of depth in the painting. No longer are all the figures at the front of the painting. There is now a figure in the middle distance. Our eye is led backwards by the lines in the architecture (**linear perspective**) and the trees getting smaller in size. The deep space in the painting is created by softening the edges of objects in the distance, leaving out detail and using a bluish-grey colour. This method is called **aerial perspective**.

HISTORICAL STUDY

Masaccio is termed an Early **Renaissance** Florentine painter. Florence was the main artistic centre of Italy during the fifteenth century. This was a reflection of its prosperity as an emerging merchant city, based on textiles and banking (leading to the growth of the upper middle class). There was a new feeling of civic pride. Artists were commissioned by the church and by wealthy patrons to paint private chapels and to paint portraits.

This painting is of the New Testament story of Christ requesting Peter to take a coin from the mouth of a fish (on the left) to pay the tax collector (on the right). It is in the form of a continuous **narrative**, representing three stages of the one story.

Masaccio has represented a religious story using real figures in an everyday environment. In this painting we can appreciate that Masaccio has taken one step closer towards the illusion of reality in painting that is achieved with perfection by High Renaissance artists such as Raphael and Leonardo Da Vinci.

STUDYING ART

Critical study

Structural frame
1. Compare Masaccio's faces with those of Giotto's (see page 4). Can you see any differences in the degree of naturalism or solidity?
2. What device has the artist used to lead the viewer's eye from the left to the right of the painting?

Cultural frame
3. How can you recognise this as an Italian painting of the fifteenth century and not an Australian painting of the present time?

FURTHER RESEARCH

Historical study

Cultural frame
1. How does this painting reflect society during the fifteenth century? Read the notes on Giotto and consider such things as dress, people as individuals (humanism), new interest in people's surroundings and new attitudes in religion.
2. Describe the work of one other early Renaissance painter who experimented with perspective.

MAKING ART

Postmodern frame
1. Borrow the image of the two people shaking hands on the right of Masaccio's painting *The Tribute Money*. Transform this into a meeting of two people in our present time in your neighbourhood or city.

Structural frame
2. Use the two methods of aerial and linear perspective to create a street scene with a sense of depth. Create a particular time of day and mood through your choice of colours and tone. Scan your drawing and use graphics software to add different colours and tones in order to create different moods.

Raphael

(1483–1520, Italian)

Frame: cultural
Forms: oil painting; wall fresco
Conceptual framework: Raphael reflects his world, conveying to the viewer a sense of peace, calmness and harmony. His artworks were highly respected at the time as creations of a master painter, and as objects of beauty.

Vocabulary

foreshortening: drawing/painting technique in which parts of the body that are closer to the viewer appear larger, and limbs appear shorter

symmetrically balanced: describes an image in which each side has equal weight, equal balance

The School of Athens 1509–11
Wall fresco, 579 × 807 cm
Signature Room, Vatican, Rome

CRITICAL STUDY

In *The School of Athens* we see various groups of figures in a large area of a classical building. The painting is basically **symmetrically balanced** with the central arches and the figures fairly evenly divided on each side. This creates a sense of *harmony* and unity. The main arch helps to hold the painting together, creating a feeling of *balance*. The architecture cleverly leads the eye back in space to a central focal point; and the pattern on the floor joins in the middle.

Even though there are some sixty figures in this painting in various positions there is still a sense of order and naturalness. Raphael has used the method of **foreshortening** that was being experimented with in the Early Renaissance. Raphael also displays his knowledge of anatomy. The figures are alive and animated with emotion; they bend, twist, think and converse with others. Each is an individual.

HISTORICAL STUDY

Raffaello Sanzio (Raphael) is a typical High Renaissance artist. His work reveals the main characteristics of this style, having:
(a) a feeling of harmony and balance
(b) calmness and serenity
(c) an ideal world without imperfections
(d) an understanding of perspective, resulting in the creation of deep space
(e) an understanding of the proportions of the human figure.

Raphael was born in Urbino. He was taught to paint, first by his father, then later by Perugino. In about 1504 he went to Florence, then in 1508 on to Rome, the centre of High Renaissance art. In Rome, at the age of twenty-five, he was asked by Pope Julius II to decorate the papal rooms in the Vatican.

Raphael worked in one part of the Vatican, in the Signature Room, at the same time as Michelangelo was working on the Sistine Chapel, which is also part of the Vatican.

The School of Athens actually symbolises philosophy and the search for truth. Raphael has depicted Greek philosophers such as Plato and Aristotle. Greek philosophy was a strong influence on Renaissance thought.

Raphael's work relates strongly to the *cultural frame* since it reflects the ideas, beliefs, achievements and society of its time.

Raphael is also known for his tender, peaceful paintings of the Madonna, which reflect a sense of grace and beauty. He painted more than 100 Madonna paintings, including *The Alba Madonna*. He was a popular, well-liked artist in his time and, as a result, quite wealthy.

The Alba Madonna c. 1510
Oil on panel transferred to canvas
95 cm diameter
© 1996 Board of Trustees
National Gallery of Art, Washington
Andrew W. Mellon Collection

STUDYING ART

Critical study

Subjective frame

1. Describe your reactions to the way Raphael has painted the Madonna in *The Alba Madonna*. What type of mother does she appear to be?

Structural frame

2. Explain how Raphael has used light in *The School of Athens*.
3. How has Raphael shown more depth in this painting than Giotto did in *The Lamentation of Christ*?
4. Explain the composition (the arrangement or organisation) of *The Alba Madonna*.
5. What clues, or symbols, are you given to tell you that this is not just any mother, but the Madonna?

Historical study

6. Discuss the development of naturalism in Renaissance painting by referring to the work of Giotto, Masaccio and Raphael.

MAKING ART

Postmodern frame
Copy the positions of three of the figures in *The School of Athens*, change their clothes and put them in a contemporary setting. (They could be on the steps of your school hall or outside a building in the city perhaps.)

This activity should help you understand the Postmodern method of appropriation. Appropriation is the taking of images from past artworks and putting them in a new context to alter their meaning.

Bernini

(1598–1680, Italian)

Frame: subjective
Form: sculpture
Conceptual framework: The audience cannot help but respond to the realism of the figures (the art object) and the emotion expressed.

Vocabulary

Baroque: style of art (c.1700s) that set out to impress with dramatic emotional effects and strong tonal contrasts

Mannerism: style of sixteenth-century European art, mainly current in Italy

The Rape of Proserpina
1621–22
Marble, height 255 cm
Borghese Gallery, Rome

In this sculpture Bernini has created a sense of movement and heightened emotion. Proserpina struggles, pushing Pluto away. The positions of the figures form two opposing arcs. The muscular strength of Pluto contrasts with the smooth flesh of Proserpina. Pluto has a firm grasp, his hand pushing into the flesh of Proserpina's thigh. The figures are extremely *tactile* (you want to touch them to see if they are warm flesh rather than hard, cold marble) and anatomically correct. Bernini has demonstrated great skill in carving the marble to resemble the different textures of flesh, hair and cloth. The drapery wraps around the figures and adds to the overall movement. The way Bernini has carved the drapery with deep undercutting creates shadows, leading the eye around the figures and adding to the theatrical effect (they almost appear spotlit). It is as if Bernini has caught Pluto and Proserpina at a split second of time, a dramatic moment. We can almost imagine Proserpina calling out, her mouth open. This heightens the emotional effect.

Gian Lorenzo Bernini was an Italian artist of the Baroque period. The calm harmony of Renaissance art was followed by the tension and uncertainty of **Mannerism**, which arose during the Reformation — a time when the authority of the Church was being questioned. In the Counter-Reformation of the seventeenth century, the Church was trying to win back followers through emotional displays of splendour that we know as the **Baroque** style. Bernini's artmaking practice was diverse. He was an architect, painter, sculptor, playwright, stage designer and composer of music. Some of his projects combine many of these talents into the one flamboyant creation. Such a project was the Cornaro Chapel. It contains a sculpture, *The Ecstasy of St Theresa*, set on a cloud, among fluttering robes, in a deep architectural setting with columns on either side. Light pours down (from a hidden source), and gilt bronze rods suggest heavenly rays. Life-size marble figures sit in theatre boxes on either side as if observing the miracle.

STUDYING ART

Critical study

Subjective frame
1. What is your reaction to the sculpture *The Rape of Proserpina*?
2. Give your opinion of this sculpture.

Structural frame
3. Marble is a material that looks hard and inflexible. Describe how Bernini has used the marble to look like another texture.

Cultural frame
4. Look at *A Lion Hunt* by Rubens (see page 48). Bernini and Rubens both belong to the Baroque period of the seventeenth century. What similarities can you see in their approach?
5. How has Bernini suggested that Pluto is a mythological god?

Postmodern frame
6. Does the sculpture portray a believable situation in our present world?
7. What might Proserpina be calling out?

FURTHER RESEARCH

Historical study

1. Research Bernini's works *The Ecstasy of St Theresa* and *Apollo and Daphne*. Write a one-page essay explaining the dramatic nature of his Baroque style.

Cultural frame
2. Research a Baroque architect such as Francesco Borromini to find similarities in approach during the Baroque age.
3. Access a website that provides examples of the works of a range of Baroque artists, for example, http://witcombe.sbc.edu/ARTHbaroque.html. Choose three Baroque artists and compose a handout advertising a local exhibition of their works. Present this as a desktop published document.

MAKING ART

Structural frame
1. Create a sculpture, in clay or papier-mâché, of a figure caught in a moment of dramatic movement. Take inspiration from Bernini's methods of creating realism and drama.

Postmodern frame
2. Draw the struggle between Pluto and Proserpina in charcoal but make it a present-day interpretation. You will need to change the hair and clothes, and add a background.

Henri Matisse

(1869–1954, French)

Frame: subjective; structural
Form: painting — oil on canvas
Conceptual framework: Matisse's paintings are 'art for art's sake' — a modernist concept in which artworks are created not only to represent reality but also to be objects of value in their own right.

Vocabulary

aesthetic: relating only to beauty, and not to other aspects of art

avant-garde: new, modern, different, experimental

medium: the material used by an artist

FAUVISM

a modern French art movement that began around 1905, and which was interested in bold, pure colour and decorative line

CRITICAL STUDY

Lady in Blue shows clearly defined bold colour areas. Lines have been used as outlines as well as to create pattern. The body appears flat: there is no gentle modelling with tone, no blending light to dark to create a three-dimensional effect (solidity) as was seen in the paintings of Giotto and Raphael. The face has been simplified, and is represented only by freely drawn black outlines. The curved shape is dominant.

The surfaces remain flat. There is no attempt at depth or perspective. The painting on the wall, which should be behind, appears as close as the figure itself.

HISTORICAL STUDY

Matisse can be categorised as a Modernist. Modernism (late 1800s to the 1970s) strove to be original, to seek the new (**avant-garde**). Modernism was a period of innovation, of new ways of expression, either through ideas or emotion. The traditional aim of painting was to create the illusion of reality and three-dimensional space. The avant-garde artists, who included Matisse, wanted to break free from this. The avant-garde artists wanted the canvas and the paint to be seen in their own right (what is now referred to as 'art for art's sake'). They thus explored the art **medium** itself and how it could be used for **aesthetic** effects. Matisse concentrated on the art elements of line and colour, and tended to flatten objects and spaces.

In 1905 the first true Modernist exhibition, the Salon d'Automne, took place in Paris, and included works by Matisse, Derain and Vlaminck (see page 112). An art critic at the time, Louis Vauxcelles, upon catching sight of a sculpture of a figure surrounded by Fauvist paintings, remarked: 'The honesty of these busts astonishes in the midst of the orgy of pure tones: Donatello among the wild beasts'.[1] (*Note*: Donatello created realistic sculptures during the Renaissance period.)

'Wild beasts' in French is 'les fauves' and the style came to be known as **Fauvism**. The Fauvist style was characterised by vibrant, clashing colours and obvious vigorous brushstrokes. Colour was used for its own purity or intensity, its emotional impact, rather than to imitate reality. Art critic John Russell suggests that the hostility towards Matisse's art at the time was 'because his new methods were applied not only to landscape and still life, but to the human face'.[2]

To appreciate why this art was so new and shocking we need to look at what existed previously. It is perhaps hard for us now to see why the public at the time was so outraged. We are familiar with unnatural colours, the bright, flat, decorative colours of posters, abstract art and even distortions of the face created by computers, whereas patrons of the 1930s were not.

Lady in Blue 1937
Oil on canvas, 92.7 × 73.6 cm
Philadelphia Museum of Art
Gift of Mrs John Wintersteen
© Henri Matisse, licensed by VISCOPY, Australia, 2004

Pablo Picasso

(1881–1973, Spanish)

Frame: structural
Form: painting — oil on canvas
Conceptual framework:
Consideration needs to be given to the art world's view of the art object as a unique creation of a 'master' artist.

Vocabulary

Cubism: a modern art movement. The Cubists were seeking a new way to represent reality by using multiple viewpoints and fragmenting form.

distorted: twisted or out of shape

semi-abstract: not quite abstract; containing some reference to the real world

Les Demoiselles d'Avignon
June–July 1907
Oil on canvas, 243.9 × 233.7 cm
The Museum of Modern Art, New York
Acquired through the
Lillie P. Bliss Bequest.
Photograph © 1996 The Museum of
Modern Art, New York
© Pablo Picasso, licensed by VISCOPY,
Australia, 2004

CRITICAL STUDY

Les Demoiselles d'Avignon is a painting of five nude women. It is quite different from previous paintings of the female figure. The forms have been broken up into sharp angles and curves, as if the artist had changed his mind about what position they should be in. Although we can tell the forms are female, they are certainly not realistic. They have been **distorted** to become what we now term **semi-abstract**; that is, they have been simplified but are still recognisable. It is as if the figures have been analysed, dissected and rearranged. As we look across the painting from left to right we can see the faces becoming progressively distorted. The fruit and table have been treated in a similar way. The background has also been broken up (fragmented). The shading appears haphazard in that the light is not coming from a single direction. The figures seem to be on the same level as the background, rather than in front of it.

STUDYING ART

Critical study
Subjective frame
1. What is your reaction to Picasso's figures? Explain why you feel like that.
2. What is your opinion of this artwork? Art critic Norbert Lynton has written that Picasso 'left it unfinished' and 'can't believe he intended to leave the painting like that'.[5]

   Where do you see any evidence or suggestion in the painting that this statement is correct?

Structural frame
3. Describe Picasso's method of breaking up the forms or shapes.
4. In one sentence, describe Picasso's use of tone.

Cultural frame
5. What similarities can you see between Picasso's painting and the African mask?

FURTHER RESEARCH

Historical study
Locate works by the Cubist Georges Braque as well as other works by Picasso, and make a list of four characteristics of Cubism that you can see.

MAKING ART

Structural frame
Cut out five pictures of female models from magazines. Arrange them into a composition across the page. Draw these figures from left to right and progressively distort each figure as Picasso has done in his painting *Les Demoiselles d'Avignon*. Alternatively, you may wish to scan the images into a computer and use graphics software to manipulate and distort their shapes and expressions.

Picasso is typically Modernist in his constant striving to be original, seeking new ways to express his ideas. This painting, created just two years after Fauvism began, was another attempt to create a new way of seeing. The style, which is slowly developing from left to right in this painting, came to be known as **Cubism**. Like Fauvism, the aim of the Cubists was to break painting's traditional role of creating an illusion of reality. Traditionally, artists recreated the appearance of people and objects from one viewpoint, setting them in a deep space. Picasso tried to create a new way of interpreting reality by looking from different viewpoints at once. He fragmented the forms, breaking them up into planes. He used flat, angular, almost geometrically shaped segments.

Picasso's borrowing of ideas from 'primitive cultures', such as African and ancient Spanish, and from Iberian sculpture, was rather radical at the time. Picasso was particularly influenced by their bold lines, simplified shapes, and horrific expressions. This abstraction of the figures was the beginning of Cubism. The picture appears flattened, and we have no sense of looking through the painting into a world as we do in Renaissance art (see pages 6 and 8).

African sculpture — Fang, Congo mask
British Museum, London

Charles Blackman

(b. 1928, Australian)

Frame: subjective
Form: drawing
Conceptual framework: There is a close relationship between the artist and his artwork, and viewers are left to interpret the work according to their own experiences.

Vocabulary

domestic: to do with home life

Colette at the Piano (from 'Colette' series) 1976
Crayon, pastel, charcoal and synthetic polymer paint on woven paper
176.8 × 147 cm
Purchased 1978
Reproduced by permission from the collection of the Queensland Art Gallery, Brisbane

CRITICAL STUDY

This intimate **domestic** scene of a young girl practising at the piano has been shown to us in a unique way. The tenderness of the subject itself, the gentle curve of the girl's face and the long plaited hair have been contrasted by the bold line work and the harsh shapes of the piano and chair. Lines have been used freely as outline and to add pattern, as in the dress and background. The mood is one of mystery. Why the blank sheet of music? It seems to act as a stimulus to the viewer's imagination.

HISTORICAL STUDY

Charles Blackman was the only boy in a fatherless, underprivileged family of four. His relationship with his mother and sisters created a sensitivity and awareness of emotions. Another influence on his life and painting was his wife Barbara, who had failing eyesight. This made Blackman more aware of human feelings and actions. It also helped foster his love of reading, as he read aloud to his wife. He read mainly fantasy and poetry. The influence from the books he read can be seen in his *Alice in Wonderland* series of paintings. Blackman created many paintings of domestic scenes such as mother and child, picnics and children playing. Many expressed loneliness. Blackman often mixed together elements of the real world and his dreams or fantasies.

Art critic James Gleeson wrote in the *Sun* newspaper, in July 1969, that 'Blackman opens up the doorway from the world of ordinary events into the world of the artist's imagination, where children play or dream or float unfettered by the bonds of everyday realities'.[6]

STUDYING ART

Subjective frame
1. Many of Blackman's paintings have heads turned away or eyes downcast. What effect does this create? Can you suggest why Blackman would do this?

Structural frame
2. Can you see any symbolism in this work?

Historical study
3. What does Charles Blackman reveal about his personal history in his paintings? You may need to research other works of his.
4. Look at the work of Dickerson (page 124). What similarities with Blackman can you see in mood or subject matter?

FURTHER RESEARCH

1. Look at what was happening in art in America in the 1950s and 1960s. What were the main styles or movements?
   Was the work of the Antipodeans, including Blackman, Boyd (see page 154) and Dickerson (see page 124), following American trends or were they creating a unique Australian style at this time?
2. Art critic Bernard Smith has written that 'Blackman is a painter of women but not of flesh'.[7] What do you think this statement means? Do you agree? You will need to find other paintings by Blackman to help you form your opinion.

MAKING ART

Create an artwork about children, using collage (images cut out of magazines and stuck on). Alternatively, use scanned images and graphics software. Include words from a poem or story.

Jill Orr

(b. 1952, Australian)

Frame: postmodern
Form: performance art
Conceptual framework: Orr herself is the artwork. Her work is meant to shock the audience.

Vocabulary

performance art: art in which the artist is part of the work, the action of creating is important, and which is presented to an audience

site-specific: designed for a particular place

DADA

a modern art movement that was anti-art and tried to shock its audience (from a French word meaning 'hobby horse')

Images from *Bleeding Trees* 1979
Performance work
National Gallery of Victoria

The placement of the figure draped over the tree suggests a ritual or sacrifice (crucifixion?). In this piece of **performance art**, Orr has used her body in an expressive way as a piece of sculpture. It is suspended from the tree in a position of careful balance. Balance is usually an important part of sculpture. The body is acting as the soul of nature. She has connected the body to the environment by its position and nudity. Her body is coloured and textured so that it blends in with the soil and rocks.

Ten colour photographs document this performance work for the 1979 Sydney Biennale. The whole work was concerned with the destruction of the rainforests. At the end of the performance Orr was half buried in rocks and soil letting out a scream.

In her work Jill Orr comments on aspects of human and cultural behaviour. Other work includes *Walking on Planet Earth* (1989), in which the body is a link between the elements of nature, earth and fire. Orr's background is in sculpture but she has extended into performance work.

Performance work began with the **Dada** artists but became an art form in the 1960s. American Allan Kaprow was largely responsible for its development. Performance work became popular in Australia in the 1970s. It often combines theatre, dance and ritual.

Performance art frequently makes social or political comments. The artist uses his/her own body to express an idea. Orr's art is Postmodern in the way it explores the concept of what art is and uses non-traditional materials. Her works combine acting, ideas, language, photography and sculpture. Her work is closely linked with the environment, so it is **site-specific**. This sometimes limits the size of her audience, so documenting the performance in the form of photographs is important.

STUDYING ART

Critical study
Postmodern frame
1. How is performance art closer to the real world than a painting on a wall?
2. Jill Orr's performance work lasts only for a short time. How is this different from more traditional forms of art?
3. A painter decides on a subject and sets up their paints. What does Jill Orr have to consider in creating her form of art?
4. Have a class debate on this topic: 'Performance is a more powerful medium than painting when conveying a controversial issue'.

Historical study
5. Why is Jill Orr's work classified as Postmodern?

FURTHER RESEARCH

1. Locate other examples of Australian performance work. What do they have in common? What modern technological development has helped establish performance work as a documented artform?
2. Research the work of one other artist concerned with environmental conservation, such as Jan Senbergs or Ruth Waller. Do an Internet search by typing the artist's name into the search engine. Find information for a brief profile of the artist and present this as a word-processed report, including images.

MAKING ART

1. Taking one of the themes of peace or war, create a group performance work. Document the piece with photographs or a video.
2. Create your own artwork concerned with the issue of the destruction of the rainforests. Consider making it an installation or performance piece.

Ron Mueck

(b. 1958, Australian, working in London)

Vocabulary

armature: a framework on which a sculptor builds

slurry: semiliquid mixture of clay and water

Discussion

What do you think makes Mueck's creations artworks rather than models for a film or exhibits in a wax museum? To answer this, you will have to consider the difficult question of the purpose or role of an artwork.

CRITICAL STUDY

The viewer wonders why the boy is in such a frightened, vulnerable position. Who is he hiding from? Who is he waiting for? His look is wary and intense. The boy's huge size seems to overwhelm the gallery audience.

Boy 1999
Mixed media
490 × 490 × 240 cm

Mueck omits no detail. His sculptures imitate life so closely that the audience is left feeling the sculptures have the possibility of motion. This work is powerful and definitely confronting.

The huge face in *Mask II* is flawless in its precise realism, from the creases in the forehead to the stubble of facial hair. The way the cheek is flattened and the mouth pushed slightly off-centre makes us aware that the face is deep in sleep. With all of Mueck's works, including this one, the illusion is so real that the viewer wants to touch them — to check the softness of the skin, to make sure it does not have the warmth of a living person. Yet even when we come back to reality, accepting them as sculptures (partly because of their scale), we still sense the emotion they represent.

HISTORICAL STUDY

Ron Mueck first worked as a model-maker for television and film. He was recently elevated into the contemporary art world as a result of recognition by advertising expert and art collector Charles Saatchi. Since 2001, he has been artist in residence at the National Gallery in London.

Mueck's artmaking process is quite tedious and labour- and time-intensive. He works from photographs as well as from models. He sculpts his figures in clay on **armatures** made of metal and chicken-wire.

Subtle details such as moles and goosebumps are added by using clay **slurry** applied with a brush or damp cloth. He then casts a mould of fibreglass around the clay. The fibreglass mould must be removed with great care but, even so, the original clay sculpture is generally destroyed in the process. Next, he paints the skin colour and textures on the fibreglass mould, and applies freckles, veins and so on. The face is made separately from silicone so that hair can be inserted — a slow process because each hair must be inserted separately.

Mask II 2001
Mixed media
77 × 118 × 85 cm
© the artist
Courtesy the artist and Anthony d'Offay, London

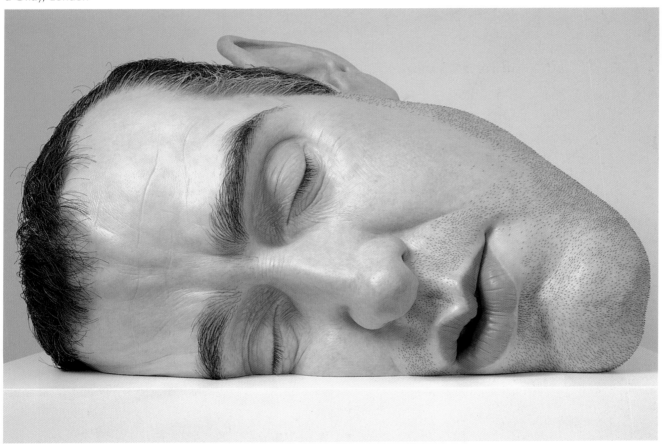

Boy took nine months to create and had to be brought to the Venice Biennale in pieces, then assembled. As with all Mueck's sculptures, the realism of this piece is extreme. Great attention has been given to the skin texture, lifelike lashes and folds of skin. Another artwork, *Old Woman in Bed*, has been shrunk to the size of a baby to show the vulnerability and frailty of the woman about to die. This work is actually a portrait of his wife's grandmother in the final days of her illness. However, a personal, intimate work such as this becomes a public object when displayed.

Boy with Mirror is a reflective piece, the boy marvelling at his own perfection in a mirror. He crouches, bringing his whole body into the smallest possible space. The impression is one of innocence, the mirror a symbol of his inner thoughts.

The manipulation of scale is one of Mueck's techniques that has a profound impact on the viewer. It jolts us into realising that these sculptures, despite the realism of their appearance, are not actually human. This forces us into seeing these states of humanity in a fresh way. The avoidance of eye contact, and the fact that the subjects seem to be totally immersed in their own world, leaves us to wonder and anticipate. Mueck's talent is in the portrayal of emotional states.

STUDYING ART

Conceptual framework
1. Why do you think onlookers at a Mueck exhibition stare in amazement at his sculptures of humans of various ages?
2. Mueck's sculptures are realistic in every way except their size. Why do you think Mueck chooses to make them smaller than life-size or a lot larger? What could his intention be?

Practice
3. Describe three steps in Mueck's artmaking practice.

William Dobell

(1899–1970, Australian)

Frame: subjective
Form: painting — oil
Conceptual framework: Dobell does not just paint people as they appear, but adds his reactions to them, his interpretation of their personality, thus adding meaning for the viewer.

Vocabulary

Archibald Prize:	an annual prize set up by a bequest in the will of Jules Francois Archibald in 1919. The bequest stipulated that first prize was to be awarded to an Australian artist for the best portrait of a man or woman distinguished in art, letters, science or politics.
caricature:	painting or drawing that exaggerates the features of the person depicted
elongated:	stretched, made longer, distorted
exaggerate:	emphasise or magnify certain physical aspects
portrait:	individual likeness of a person
voluptuous:	well-rounded, sensuous

Joshua Smith 1943
Oil on canvas, 122 × 81 cm
Private collection
© William Dobell, licensed by
VISCOPY, Australia, 2004

Margaret Olley 1948
Oil on hardboard, 114.3 × 85.7 cm
The Art Gallery of New South Wales
© William Dobell, licensed by VISCOPY, Australia, 2004

Dobell tried to capture the personality or character of the person he was painting. This is why these two **portraits** are quite different. The portrait of Joshua Smith is quite angular and **elongated**. The look on his face is determined. He gazes not at us, but at some far-away point as if he is lost in his own thoughts. The starkness of the background and the limited colour scheme suggest a harshness, particularly in comparison to the painting of Margaret Olley.

Dobell has also **exaggerated** the features of Margaret Olley, making her quite round, even **voluptuous**. We get the impression that Olley is a jolly, pleasant, friendly person. The emphasis is on delicate textures and curved shapes. Olley appears to love to dress up and collect things. In comparison to Joshua Smith, she looks like someone who enjoys life. Interestingly, both these portraits are of fellow artists who were friends of Dobell. Dobell painted not only what he saw but also what he felt about his sitters.

Interestingly, Margaret Olley did not wear this dress to Dobell's studio to sit for her portrait. She had, in fact, worn it the week before to an opening and party with Dobell. Dobell had obviously remembered the dress and thought it reflected her flamboyant style of dress and essential character.

Both these portraits were winners in the **Archibald Prize**. This is one of Australia's most famous art competitions, held annually and judged by the trustees of the Art Gallery of New South Wales. There has always been great public interest and debate over the winner.

The portrait of Joshua Smith won the Archibald Prize. This caused an uproar, and the matter went to the Supreme Court. Some believed that the distortion and exaggeration in Dobell's painting made it a **caricature** rather than a portrait. Many people were called to give evidence on whether it was indeed a 'portrait'. They included fellow entrants, art critics, including James MacDonald (then director of the National Gallery of New South Wales), and even a medical doctor. After two days in court and much comment in the papers, the judge agreed that it was a distortion. The judge also thought it bore a strong likeness to the subject and thus was a portrait. Dobell had won the case. Both Dobell and Smith suffered over the case. Dobell lost confidence. Joshua Smith himself was awarded the prize the following year.

Although Dobell's technique was traditional — building up the painting using layers of thin paint to create rich, glowing colours — he introduced new ideas to Australian painting. His art was a move away from strict realism. He believed portraits should include an artist's feelings or reactions to a subject.

STUDYING ART

Critical study

Subjective frame

1. How would you describe Joshua Smith's personality and mood?
2. What evidence do we see in these works that Dobell believed in the freedom of expression of the artist?
3. Personality is often shown by the way the hands are held and by the expression on the face. Compare the facial expressions and hands of each portrait.

Structural frame

4. Where has Dobell used distortion or exaggeration in the portrait of Joshua Smith?
5. What words would you use to describe Dobell's style in his portrait of Margaret Olley?

6. Look carefully at different areas of both paintings — clothes, faces, backgrounds. Describe the areas and the different approaches or techniques used (for example, thin washes of colour, thickly applied paint, fine delicate lines, use of palette knife).
7. What colours has Dobell used to create shadows in *Margaret Olley*?
8. What effect has been created by the use of tone (light to dark) in each portrait?

Historical study

Cultural and structural frames

9. Compare and contrast the portrait of *Margaret Olley* by Dobell with *The Alba Madonna* by Raphael (see page 9).

FURTHER RESEARCH

Critical study

1. Write your own critical review of the current Archibald Prize winner. Use desktop publishing software to present this as a news article. Include an image of the prize winner. (Go to www.artgallery.nsw.gov.au and search for 'Archibald'.)
2. Collect two examples of caricature from newspapers. Evaluate their success at portraying personality.

Cultural frame

3. Look up other examples of portraits by Dobell, such as *The Strapper, Billy Boy, Boy at the Basin, Mrs South Kensington, Dame Mary Gilmore*, and explain how he has portrayed the Australian way of life and its various social levels.

MAKING ART

1. Create a portrait, either by drawing or using digital media, of someone you have strong feelings towards. Try to show their personality.
2. Create a caricature of one of the following: football player, scientist, pop singer.
3. Using a computer graphics program, and possibly a scanned photograph, include text and symbols to create a self-portrait.

Joy Hester

(1920–60, Australian)

Frame: subjective
Form: drawing
Conceptual framework: There is a close relationship between Hester and her artworks because of their personal nature and the way she explores her world and experiences. They also evoke strong feelings in the audience.

Vocabulary

emotive: causing us to feel emotion
spontaneous: quickly done, unplanned, instinctive, unconstrained

CRITICAL STUDY

Joy Hester has used brush and ink in a rapid, **spontaneous** way to show her feelings. She has distorted some shapes and left out others. Both works remain powerful, **emotive** images. There is something disturbing about her images, apart from the obvious distortion of the boy's eye. Hester has used large, bold areas of black on white, balancing them with her expressive lines and areas of texture or pattern.

**Woman in Fur Coat
(Self-portrait)**
c. 1950
Ink and brush on
cartridge paper
37 × 26 cm
© Joy Hester, licensed by
VISCOPY, Australia, 2004

Boy with Yellow Bird 1957
Ink and watercolour on paper
39.1 × 57.5 cm
Reproduced by permission of the
National Gallery of Australia, Canberra
© Joy Hester, licensed by VISCOPY,
Australia, 2004

HISTORICAL STUDY

Joy Hester worked in Melbourne in the 1940s and 1950s. She used drawing and painting as a way to express and understand her feelings and emotions. These included her worries, fears and joys, and also her experiences and ideas on love, relationships, death and violence. To Hester, emotions were never simple. Her father had been an alcoholic. She was tormented by her desire to be an artist as well as a wife and mother. Not being accepted as a serious artist also frustrated her. This was partly because she was a female and perhaps because she chose to do drawings on paper. Her work gave her no success or recognition during her lifetime. She died from cancer at the age of forty, having produced several hundred drawings and poems and a handful of oil paintings. Her originality and talent are now recognised. We can appreciate her intense reactions to states of mind and emotions such as loneliness and love. Her works have not lost their impact and are quite relevant to our times.

STUDYING ART

Critical study
Subjective frame
1. What is the mood of each of these works?
2. Why do you think Hester has enlarged one of the boy's eyes?
3. Although an exact likeness was obviously not her intention, what has she described about each person? What do you know and feel about each person?

Structural frame
4. How has Hester shown the texture of her hair and fur coat?
5. How has her choice of working in ink with brush affected her work?
6. Which art element is most important in Hester's work?
7. Explain Hester's use of balance.

Historical study
Subjective frame
8. Some artists have revealed their perceptions of themselves in their self-portraits. Many, like Joy Hester, have revealed their pain, joy, fear and passions. Research a self-portrait by Frida Kahlo and one by Van Gogh. How effectively does each work express the artist's emotions?

Cultural frame
9. Which other female Australian artists were working at this time? What were their main themes or subject matter? What can we learn from their art about life for females in the 1940s and 1950s?

MAKING ART

1. Look in the mirror and decide on your essential features. What is your most typical mood — friendly, sad, grumpy, lonely, agitated, wishful? Create a self-portrait in ink which expresses your main characteristics, both physical and emotional. Don't be afraid to distort certain features.
2. Create a linoprint or monoprint of you in front of your dressing table. You may like to include words of a poem or a song around the edge that explains your mood or interests. (Don't forget that the words have to be written backwards for printing.)

Jenny Sages

(b. 1933 Shanghai, arrived in Australia 1948)

Frame: subjective
Form: painting
Conceptual framework: Sages works from her own experiences of places and people, considering the surface of the artwork in particular. Viewers are drawn into the work, to contemplate and consider their own experiences.

Vocabulary

austere: severely simple, without ornament

diverse: varied; having many different kinds

impregnated: saturated, thoroughly mixed with, absorbed

innovative: new, different, ahead of its time

muted: toned down, softened

prestigious: regarded as important; bringing success and fame

transcend: rise above or beyond; exceed

CRITICAL STUDY

True Stories — Helen Garner 2003
Encaustic and pigment
© Jenny Sages
Photograph: Jenni Carter for AGNSW

The impressive portrait of writer Helen Garner reflects Jenny Sages' admiration and respect for Garner as a woman 'distinguished in letters'. The painting is **austere** yet sensitive. Sage has used a limited colour scheme of cream, flesh and **muted** lemon yet the inner strength of the author is evident. Garner stares at the viewer as if caught unawares. There is a determined set to her face, one eyebrow raised in curiosity. Her brown-green eyes are the focus and her quizzical expression is captured beautifully. The artist has created a rich surface of smeared layers, the artist using her fingers rather than a brush for most of this. Outlines of olive and red define and add interest but do not dominate the image. The writer's right arm goes to her face, giving the face emphasis and reminding us of her profession.

The artist admits that after 37 research drawings, the actual portrait took only a week. The result is a portrait that has an immediacy of feeling and a sensitive perception of the sitter's character.

Jenny Sages stated about Helen Garner: 'She is as spare and as honest as her work. I wanted so much to acknowledge that in her work'. In this aim, Jenny Sages has been highly successful. Helen Garner has been honoured as a forceful personality, a notable Australian identity as well as a person of note in her creative profession. The viewer is both intrigued and in awe of the person portrayed.

The simplicity and directness of this portrait makes it both eye-catching and memorable. It **transcends** styles and time to make it appealing to a wide range of viewers.

The painting *Renewal* (2003) was exhibited as a finalist in the 2003 Wynne Prize (a **prestigious** prize for landscape art) at the Art Gallery of New South Wales. At first glance, it appears to be an abstract work with an all-over textured surface. Closer inspection reveals the minute, subtle arrangement of tiny flowers or seeded grasses. The surface has been applied with wax **impregnated** with pigment that has then been delicately scratched. The colour range is limited to beiges and warm, muted tones, reflecting the dry, harsh vegetation typical of Australia. The title suggests the life that emerges after a period of drought.

HISTORICAL STUDY

Jenny Sages was born in Shanghai to Russian–Jewish parents. She has been painting full-time since 1985. Her signature style uses sensitive linear patterns that create a rich textural background. The works are basically abstract yet suggest landscape and nature in their irregularity within a repeated format. Sages has entered the Archibald Prize several times, being highly commended in 2000 for her self-portrait *Every Morning I Wake Up I Put On My Mother's Face*. In 2001, the judges were quoted as being 'extremely impressed' with her double portrait of Kerryn Phelps and Jackie Stricker.

The Archibald Prize is unique and sought-after for a variety of reasons. One is that it is a non-acquisitive prize, so the winning artist is awarded $35 000 but also gets to keep the painting (with the chance of selling it at a later date). Also, the Archibald Prize brings with it prestige, providing the artist with recognition from a wide Australian audience. The exhibition of short-listed artworks is an important attendance drawcard for the gallery because it appeals to a **diverse** audience, not only those who are knowledgeable about art. People come because they are curious to see images of people who are considered to be notable Australians 'distinguished in art, letters, science or politics' — a condition for the choice of subject for the painting. Some people enjoy guessing names and seeing how many they recognise; others simply like to vote for the 'People's Choice'. The Archibald exhibition is also notable in that it appeals to a wide age group.

It is interesting to note that the accompanying Wynne Prize for landscape painting does not draw the same interest or debate from the public. Perhaps this is partly because of the historically controversial nature of the Archibald Prize (see William Dobell, page 22).

The Archibald Prize provides a forum for the traditions and high standards of Australian portraiture while also providing a venue for **innovative** works. The three main purposes of the prize are: to foster portraiture, to support artists and to perpetuate the memory of great Australians. However, it also stimulates public interest in art and strengthens our visual cultural identity.

Renewal 2003
Encaustic and pigment on board
180 × 122 cm
Courtesy the artist and king street
gallery on burton

There are several other important annual art prizes awarded in Australia. These can be very important in an artist's career, although many of them have restrictions. The Moët & Chandon Prize, for example, is open only to artists under 35 years of age.

Likewise, the Portia Geach Memorial Award is open only to women. This prize, for the best portrait of a person distinguished in arts, letters or sciences, is worth $18 000. Sages won this prize in 1992 for her double portrait of artist Nancy Borlase and her husband, trade union leader Laurie Short, who are depicted at opposite ends of their kitchen table. This work now forms part of the permanent collection of the National Portrait Gallery in Canberra. Sages won the Portia Geach Memorial Award again in 1994 with her portrait of artist Ann Thomson. Another of her portraits, *Emily Kame Kngwarreye with Lily*, captures the dignity and serenity of the artist Emily Kngwarreye. This was added to the National Portrait Gallery's collection in 1998.

Artist's practice

While preparing to work, Sages likes to listen to classical music and jazz. She is inspired by travelling inland and recording the daily lives of people. She finds portraits easier than her abstract work because, to her, portraits are more skill based. Yet each portrait is done differently and she finds it essential to know the subject well. 'Because I have a certain facility in drawing, which is part of my past commercial work [she was a magazine illustrator], I am very suspicious about portraits', she says. 'I didn't touch them for seven, eight years. I didn't want the portraits to be facile; portraits are a lot more.'[8]

With her landscape-based abstract work, forms are hinted at, while symbols and images float and fade across surfaces. Her colours are generally restricted to earth-browns, blacks and ochres, with an occasional bright green or orange. For these works, Sages' wide reading often provides inspiration, one series being based on the Russian poet Anna Akhmatova. Sages works on board that is first prepared with gesso. To this she applies encaustic — a wax medium whose use dates back to the fourteenth century. The artist must heat it until it melts and then work quickly. Sages also uses dry pigments, oil paints and Flashe, which is a strong, dense water-based medium. She often works on the floor, particularly because the pigments she uses are very fine powders. Working on the floor also allows her to manipulate the surface of the artwork by scratching back and rubbing pigment into it, and to see the images from different perspectives.

When asked the question 'In your eyes what is an artist?' her reply was: 'It's the celebration of an individual's voice. The recording of one's time on earth'.[9]

Critics' statements

Bruce James, referring to the Archibald entries of Julie Dowling and Jenny Sages, wrote:

'They are surely, if very differently, two of the most significant paintings to have been exhibited in the 80-year history of the Archibald Prize ... And Sages — what an admirable artist Sydney has in her, as diligent a worker as any apprentice, yet in her full maturity. It is hard to think of a more industrious professional, or a more various one. Her distinguished Wynne Prize entry is realised in a representational shorthand at conscious odds with the photographic naturalism of **Jackie and Kerryn.***'[10]*

Edmund Capon reported on the 1994 Mosman Art Prize:

'Jenny Sages' work has distinctive and individual qualities — the maturity of the texture, the subtlety of the textures and colours, the sense of the organic as if images and instincts were metamorphosing on the canvas before our very eyes. Hers are pictures of deeply evolving instincts, which, in those processes, engage our intellectual and emotive attentions. They are pictures of individuality and personality, and yet they are vehicles of universal communication. To my mind a worthy winner of the 1994 Mosman Art Prize.'[11]

STUDYING ART

Critical study

Subjective frame

1. What is your personal response to the portrait of Helen Garner? Having seen this portrait, how would you describe her as a person?

Structural frame

2. In *True Stories — Helen Garner,* Sages has included very few objects and has kept the background fairly simple. What effect does this have?

3. Comment on Sages' artmaking practice: her working methods, her choice of media, application, subjects and so on.

Cultural frame

4. Why do you think the Archibald Prize is important to the Australian culture?

MAKING ART

Create your own portrait of an Australian man or woman you consider to be important or famous. You may like to use digital media or include text.

William Robinson

(b. 1936, Australian)

Frame: subjective
Form: painting — oil on canvas
Conceptual framework: The artist expresses his own feelings towards his local area, inviting the audience to share his personal experiences and sense of humour.

Self Portrait With Goose Feathers 1989
Oil on canvas
198 × 138 cm
Reproduced courtesy of the artist

Self Portrait With Stunned Mullet 1995
Oil on canvas
197 × 164 cm
Reproduced courtesy of the artist

CRITICAL STUDY

Both of these paintings are realistic self-portraits but are approached with a sense of humour. The expressions on the faces show little emotion.

In *Self Portrait With Goose Feathers*, Robinson has portrayed himself as a simple fisherman/farmer wearing on his head a comical feedbag printed with the words 'bran mash'. He is wearing gumboots. The face, hands and feathers are painted with realistic detail. The legs and background have been painted in a naive, childlike approach. There is an element of fantasy. We seem to be looking from above at the background but straight at the figure. When we look at the painting we are confronted by a number of questions. Why is the figure holding two feathers? Why is he standing on an isolated rock? Are we seeing the white foam of surf or is it the clouds reflected in the water, or is it meant to be both? Who is he looking at? This is the challenge and intrigue of his work. It is not a simple picture.

Self Portrait With Stunned Mullet won Robinson the 1995 Archibald Prize for portraiture. *Self Portrait With Goose Feathers* was runner-up for the same prize in 1989. His 1991 entry, *Self-Portrait for Town and Country*, in which he painted his face to look like his loyal pug dogs, was runner-up also (four votes to five). Robinson's entries in the Archibald have all been unusual. They almost mock the terms of the competition, which is to portray some man or woman distinguished in art, letters, science or politics. Although Robinson is an established, respected artist, his self-portraits do not show him in that role. Each is a humorous, if not satirical, comment on the pomp and ceremony of the Archibald Prize itself and the tradition of portrait painting throughout history. Robinson himself calls his entries 'a bit of light entertainment' among his more serious landscape work.

Robinson's interpretations of the Australian landscape are unique. They often contain a sense of fantasy. (See page 194 for another example of his work, *Dawn* (1985).) He uses unusual multi-viewpoints, as if he is looking up at the sky at the same time as he is peering into a creek. He and his wife Shirley are sometimes depicted as tiny figures within the landscape, sitting on a log or swimming in a creek.

When you look at a Robinson rainforest you experience it with all of your senses. He paints particular localities from experience, being concerned in particular with humanity's place in the landscape.

'[Robinson] thinks of the extraordinary fact that the world has a molten centre and is spinning in space and he paints what he sees of a tiny portion of it. He paints the rainforest as timeless but also as ephemeral [short-lived]. He documents some of its myriad life forms. He conveys its silence and mystery, its translucent and iridescent light.'[12]

STUDYING ART

Subjective frame
1. What is your response to the four questions about *Self Portrait With Goose Feathers* in the 'Critical study' section on page 32?
2. Why do you think Robinson has chosen to paint himself dressed in this way in the two self-portraits?
3. What can you tell about Robinson's life and personality from these works?

Structural frame
4. In his portraits Robinson has used areas of different texture (smoothness or roughness of the surface). Choose three areas of different texture in the paintings and describe which areas they are and how you think the paint has been applied to create them. (You might like to try creating the texture yourself with paint.)

5. Robinson has said of his painting style that he is a slow painter, uses small brushes, and is fascinated by colour. Look carefully at his paintings and explain what effect his methods have on his work.

Historical study
Cultural frame
Research three portraits from different times and places. Suggestions are: Roman portrait; Botticelli (Renaissance); Dürer (Northern Renaissance); Rembrandt (seventeenth century, Dutch); Albert Tucker (Australian). What does each portrait reveal about the status/wealth, beliefs and interests of the person portrayed? Draw up a table on computer and enter your findings for each artist under these three column headings.

MAKING ART

Subjective and cultural frames
1. Create a humorous portrait of someone famous to create a social comment. Incorporate Robinson's method of areas of heavily textured surfaces.
2. Transform a hero of your choice into an anti-hero through humour.

Brigiat Maltese

(b. 1965, Australian)

Frames: subjective; structural
Form: ceramics
Conceptual framework: There is a close link between the artist and the artwork, as the pots reflect the artist's personality and interests.

Vocabulary

bisque:	first firing of clay
contemporary:	belonging to the past decade; modern
motif:	ornament or distinctive feature
narrative:	a story
symmetrical:	able to be divided into parts of equal shape and size; same both sides
utilitarian:	having a use or purpose; for example a jug or cup

From *Animal, Vegetable, Mineral* (series) 1994
Front and side views
Hand-built terracotta, stains and matt glaze
78 × 48 cm

CRITICAL STUDY

The pot shown is a self-portrait. Looking from a structural viewpoint, we can appreciate how this pot shows a love of decoration, colour and pattern. Line is prominent. The shapes and pattern have been cleverly linked to the shape of the form.

Maltese's pieces are constructed using the traditional hand building technique of coiling and joining. It appears that the surface of the pot has not been completely smoothed, so that the use of the human hand is apparent. 'Handmade things have a sense of soul',[13] says Maltese.

When the pot is dry but still unfired (that is, greenware) she decorates it with a combination of stains and underglazes. After being **bisque** fired at 1100°C, the works are covered in a clear matt glaze and fired at 1050°C to seal the decoration.

HISTORICAL STUDY

Maltese has said, 'The pots mark my own journey and also key into the lives of others'.[14] Each work is an expression of her feelings and interests at the time. Her work is therefore a personal **narrative**.

Culturally, her work reflects her Slovenian background and early childhood.

'My parents' house was full of ornaments and every piece of material was embroidered or decorated in some way. Eastern Europeans seem to have this thing for decorating **utilitarian** objects. I guess I have always been interested in the surface of things and had the desire to decorate that surface.'[15]

Brigiat Maltese has carefully researched the **motifs** for her pots from a wide range of historical sources. These include classical Greek and Roman patterns used on vases and wall paintings, and traditional Italian and Spanish craft objects. She has blended these with her own symbols based on her experiences. Her shapes also have a strong link to traditional clay vessels, jugs and Greek amphoras (pots for carrying water). Therefore, her pots are generally **symmetrical** and have handles. She has often adapted these traditional shapes in whimsical ways; for example, handles become wings or ears. Maltese has also made these old forms **contemporary** by decorating them with personal symbols.

STUDYING ART

Critical study

Subjective frame
1. What is your reaction to Maltese's pot? How does it make you feel?
2. What do you discover about Brigiat Maltese from her pot?
3. What do you see, other than faces, in the pot?

Structural frame
4. Artmaking practice: Explain the stages or processes Brigiat Maltese goes through in creating her pots. (Hint: Start with research.)

Historical study
5. Research Greek amphoras to see their influence on the work of Brigiat Maltese. How does Maltese add her own interpretation to the amphora form?

MAKING ART

Create a hand-built coil pot and decorate it with your own personal symbols.

Frame: cultural
Forms: oil painting; murals
Conceptual framework: Artists reflect their society and its attitudes towards religion at that time.

FOCUS WORK
HISTORICAL STUDY

Tintoretto
(1518–94, Italian)

CLASS ACTIVITY

Divide the blackboard into two columns, headed 'Leonardo Da Vinci' and 'Tintoretto'. Students on one side of the room will suggest things they notice about Leonardo's painting. Students on the other side of the room will respond to those comments, comparing them to Tintoretto's painting.

QUESTIONS

1. What three words would you use to describe the positions of the figures in Tintoretto's work?

2. Compare the figure of Christ in each painting.

3. What do you think will happen next in Tintoretto's painting?

4. Compare the strong diagonal direction of the table in Tintoretto's painting to that in Leonardo's. How does this affect the mood?

5. Follow the outflung limbs and body angles in Tintoretto's painting to see where your eye is being led. Where is the focal point (main interest) in Leonardo's work? How has Leonardo led your eye there?

6. How has Tintoretto created a sense of mystery?

7. Describe the way Tintoretto's use of light adds to the excitement of the painting.

8. It is obvious that a spiritual experience is occurring in Tintoretto's work. What religious symbols have been used? How does the image of people using real, everyday objects add to the mood?

HISTORICAL REPORT

Cultural frame

How does Tintoretto's *The Last Supper* reflect the time in which it was painted?

Discuss the feeling of heightened emotion, anxiety and frenzy that Tintoretto has created with this figure composition.

Before you begin your report, read through the following historical information and quotes by art historians.

Historical information

Jacopo Robusti ('Tintoretto') was a Venetian Mannerist painter. *Mannerism* (sixteenth century) follows on from the later stages of the High Renaissance and is a link with the later period, the Baroque. Its main qualities are a feeling of anxiety or disquiet, strong lighting effects, exaggerated colour and a feeling of tension. Figures are often placed in exaggerated poses, with obvious hand gestures. Gone is the quiet calm and order of the Renaissance; instead Mannerists used distortions and a feeling of unease. Figures are often crowded together, particularly near the edge of the picture. This art style reflects the tensions of society at the time. Things were changing. On the one hand, there were favourable conditions for bankers and merchants, as manufacturing increased and trade expanded due to new sea routes. On the other hand, the peasants and working class were disadvantaged and angry, which led them into violent conflict with their feudal and bourgeois masters. The early sixteenth century was a time of scientific questioning of religion and religious conflict. In 1510 the German Augustinian monk Martin Luther visited Rome, where he became disillusioned by what he felt was the extravagance and corrupt ways of the Catholic Church. This led to the Reformation — a split of Christianity in northern Europe into the Catholic Church and the Protestant faith.

After Mannerism came the Baroque period. Its main characteristics are strong lighting effects, split-second moments, emotion and dramatic movement.

There were some major scientific discoveries during the 1400s to the 1600s:

- Galileo (1564–1642) was an Italian astronomer and physicist. He was asked by Pope Paul V to relinquish his statement that the sun was the centre of the universe, and that the Earth moved around it. Galileo was brought before the Inquisition, and the sale of his writings was forbidden. Theologians at the time preferred the view that the Earth was the centre of the universe.
- Columbus (1451–1506) was the Italian–Spanish explorer who discovered America.
- Magellan (1480–1521) was the first person to circumnavigate the globe, proving that the world was not flat.

Art historians speak

'Mannerist dismay and perplexity at the beginning of the Counter Reformation are found in Tintoretto's religious paintings.'[16] *Graham Hopwood*

Mannerism (1525–1600) was 'a time of crisis that gave rise to several competing tendencies... a time full of inner contradictions, not unlike the present and thus peculiarly fascinating to us'.[17] *H. W. Janson*

TINTORETTO (Mannerism)
The Last Supper 1592–94
Oil on canvas, 365 × 569 cm
S. Giorgio Maggiore, Venice

LEONARDO DA VINCI 1452–1519 (High Renaissance)
The Last Supper 1497
Mural, 420 × 910 cm
Santa Maria delle Grazie, Milan

two

OTHER LIVING THINGS

DISCUSSION

1. By looking at the selection of works opposite, what do you think are some of the purposes of using 'living things' as subject matter for artworks?

2. As a class activity, discuss what particular birds, sea life, animals or plants symbolise to you. (Hint: Think of different countries, religions, emotions or issues.)

3. Discuss how the representation of nature and its relationship to humans has altered over the centuries. How have available media and changes in artmaking practice altered the art object?

Georgia O'Keeffe

(1887–1986, American)

Frame: subjective; structural
Form: painting
Conceptual framework: O'Keeffe creates her own sensitive and simplified vision of the natural world around her.

Vocabulary

abstract: not representing anything from real life; non-representational
subjective: exhibiting personal feelings; not objective

MODERNISM

a twentieth-century art movement that broke away from the traditions of realism, eventually reaching abstraction. It included many different styles, such as Cubism, Fauvism, Expressionism and Surrealism.

Discussion

'Much of the excitement of O'Keeffe's work lies in the tensions between the real and the abstract, nature and the spirit. The abstract element is due not so much to actual distortion as to a stark revelation of the latent harmony in nature — an art that strongly implies a form of nature worship.' Discuss this quote by art critic Jack A. Hobbs, 1980.

CRITICAL STUDY

Jimson Weed is one of O'Keeffe's more realistic paintings of flowers, but even here we can see her concentration on curving, simplified forms and on gentle gradation of tone. The view is close up, which draws the viewer into the image. In *Corn No. 2* (opposite page) the emphasis is on the movement created by the sharp edges of the form, the color bolder yet softly blended.

To O'Keeffe it was the shapes and tonal gradations that were of importance rather than the subject and its precise, detailed representation. In some of her works she moved the focus even closer, magnifying and softening the image, and eliminating the edges of the petals or leaves; these became **abstract** symbols for nature. Her gently spiralling, unfolding shapes suggest growth, while the delicate colours create a mood of intrigue. Her paintings are intimate, personal responses to nature.

Jimson Weed 1932
Oil on canvas, 121.9 × 101.6 cm
Gift of the Burnett Foundation. © Georgia O'Keeffe Foundation.
© Georgia O'Keeffe, licensed by VISCOPY, Australia, 2004

Georgia O'Keeffe was an American artist. Her career as an artist began in the 1910s and extended into the 1970s. She was best known for her work in the 1930s and 1940s based on flowers, bones and New Mexico landscapes.

Corn No. 2 1924
Oil on canvas, 69.2 × 25.4 cm
Georgia O'Keeffe Museum
Gift of the Burnett Foundation and the
Georgia O'Keeffe Foundation
Photograph: Georgia O'Keeffe Museum,
Santa Fe/Art Resources, NY
© Georgia O'Keeffe, licensed by
VISCOPY, Australia, 2004

O'Keeffe's style was unique, bordering on pure abstraction. Her work expressed her feelings. Her paintings became visual symbols of her emotional state at the time. Her approach was **subjective** but with strong consideration for the structure of her paintings. She created mood by the balance of shapes and the soft modelling of her forms.

O'Keeffe was greatly influenced by her husband, Alfred Stieglitz, who was an innovative photographer. Stieglitz created fascinating photographs of skies and clouds. He was an early supporter of Modernism in America.

O'Keeffe produced more than nine hundred works of art. Nature was a major inspiration for her. She painted the same subject (such as ears of corn, flowers, a skull or a pelvic bone) over and over, trying to capture its essence in spirit and form. She captured an object's mood through colour and line. Her form, which was gently modelled, was a result of extreme simplification of shape and detail. She had a strong, individual style. Along with her Modernist approach, this led to her being recognised as one of the important American artists of the century.

STUDYING ART

Critical study
Subjective frame
1. What does this painting suggest to you other than a realistic representation of a flower?
2. What mood has been created in this painting?

Structural frame
3. Where is the main weight or dark tone of this painting?
4. The composition could be said to be organised within a geometric shape. What is it?
5. What art elements (line, direction, shape, size, tone, texture, colour) have been used?

Historical study
6. When was it painted? Find two other artworks (one Australian) in this book that were created around the same date. Was O'Keeffe modern for her time? How?

FURTHER RESEARCH

Look at the influence of the photographer Imogen Cunningham on the work of O'Keeffe. Discuss any similarities that you can see between these two artists' works.

ESSAY

Compare and contrast the art practice of Georgia O'Keeffe with the next artist in this book, Margaret Preston. Consider the similarity of their subject but their different approaches to it. Examine their techniques and choice of media.

MAKING ART

Subjective and structural frame
Draw a natural object in an exciting way by imagining you are an ant crawling on either a piece of bark, rocks by the sea, a seed pod, a leaf, a flower or a feather. You should be looking at your object from an unusual viewpoint or in close-up focus. Be guided by Georgia O'Keeffe's method of concentrating on shape, tone and texture. Look at the way her main shapes extend past the edge of the page or canvas. You may like to work in pencil, pastel or inks.

Margaret Preston

(1875–1963, Australian)

Frame: structural; cultural
Form: woodcut painting
Conceptual framework: Preston wished to create artworks that showed her awareness of modern art (the world art situation) yet reflected an Australian identity (her immediate world).

Vocabulary

composition: the placement of figures and objects; the organisation of an artwork
gouache: opaque water-based paint, similar to poster paint
Modernism: a twentieth-century art movement that broke away from the traditions of realism, eventually reaching abstraction. It included many different styles, such as Cubism, Fauvism, Expressionism and Surrealism.

Discussion

'Art, to fulfil its destiny, requires to be accepted by a nation or race and not by a few only.' [1]

Do you agree with this statement by Preston and how did she try to achieve this aim?

CRITICAL STUDY

Two main qualities are apparent in *Anemone*: a simplification of shapes with a flattening of the picture plane (no attempt at depth) and a love of rich colour and decorative line. Her bold asymmetrical arrangement with its patterned border is balanced by the decoration on the jug and the positions of the flowers.

Preston seems to have analysed the flowers and carefully considered the **composition**. The woodblock method ensures that the shapes are severe. This way of printing is similar to linocut printing in that areas to be printed are left raised while others are carved away. Preston has adapted this technique by adding hand-painted flat colours in **gouache** to the final print. Preston has taken as her main subject the domestic world of flowers. Another example of her work, *Protea*, shows her interest in the decorative qualities of Australian flora.

Pink Jug 1925
Woodcut, black ink, hand coloured with gouache on ivory laid Japanese paper
38.1 × 35.7 cm
Gift of Mrs Alison Brown 1968
The Art Gallery of New South Wales
© Margaret Preston, licensed by VISCOPY, Australia, 2004

HISTORICAL STUDY

Margaret Rose Macpherson decided early in life to become an artist. In 1893 she enrolled at the National Gallery of Victoria Art School and in 1898 she became a student at the South Australian School of Design, Painting and Technical Arts in Adelaide. In 1919 she married wealthy businessman William Preston, and settled in Mosman, Sydney.

Margaret Preston's art shows her commitment to the Australian environment, through her still lifes of native flowers, harbour views and rural landscapes. Her attention to colour and almost geometric shapes were influenced by **Modernism** (the work of the Post-Impressionists as well as Picasso and Matisse).

Protea, 1925 completed 1939, Berowra, New South Wales
Woodcut, hand-coloured with gouache on paper
24.8 × 24.5 cm
Art Gallery of South Australia, Adelaide
David Murray Bequest Fund 1939
© Margaret Preston, licensed by VISCOPY, Australia, 2004

Preston wrote: 'I design with the utmost care, the exact position of every tiny detail in leaf and flower, bowl or pot... when I have the exact position engraved on my mind, I set the model up, pot and flowers, leaves and background, and begin work.'[2]

Margaret Preston was trying to create a distinctly Australian art, a national style. She wished this style to be up-to-date with modern overseas trends in advertising, design and art. She had, in fact, gone to France to study modern art between 1904 and 1907. Preston also studied in Japan to learn their methods of woodblock printing.

From 1932 to 1939 Preston lived at Berowra. Here her prints became simpler, larger and less reliant on bright colours. Flowers were no longer arranged in vases. There were Aboriginal rock carvings near her property and from then on she developed a lifelong interest in Aboriginal art. This can be seen in her change in colours, patterns and the use of aerial views in her landscape work.

Preston was a highly original and dedicated artist. She worked within both the *structural* and *cultural frames*. She produced over 400 prints and many paintings during her lifetime. She made constant attempts through lectures, discussions and writings to encourage Modernism in Australia.

STUDYING ART

Critical study
Structural frame

1. How does the design on the jug in *Anemone* form a link between the anemone flowers and the border on the left?
2. If you were to 'rearrange' *Anemone* so that the border was the same on all sides, what would you need to alter to maintain the sense of balance?
3. Which areas have been printed?
4. If Preston had created this work by only using woodblock, instead of hand painting areas, she would have had to carve a separate block for each colour. How many blocks would she have needed?
5. Which design elements does Preston concentrate on? How are they used?
6. In what ways is Margaret Preston's work similar to the work of Matisse (see page 12)?

Cultural frame

7. Do you think the fact that Margaret Preston was a female could have had any effect on her work?

Historical study

8. At the time Preston was working, Australian art concentrated on landscapes of the bush, painted by men. How was she trying to change this image and why?
9. In her essay 'From Eggs to Electrolux', printed in the 1927 edition of *Art in Australia*, Preston explained her love of modern design, particularly new vacuum cleaners (because they freed women). She also explained what she considered to be art's first aim: 'to delight the mind, not the eye... the mind must rule the eye'.[3] How does she achieve this aim in her work?

MAKING ART

Structural and cultural frames
Using photographs from magazines, create a still life of objects that you think represent Australia in the 1990s.
Simplify these objects, and add pattern to create a design suitable for a linoprint.

ESSAY

Cultural frame
Explain how Margaret Preston tried to create a national style of art in Australia. Refer to at least three of her artworks.

John Wolseley

(b. 1938 England, working in Australia)

Frame: structural
Forms: drawing; painting
Conceptual framework: Wolseley's artworks represent his interpretation and exploration of certain places.

Vocabulary

aesthetic: relating only to beauty, and not to other aspects of art

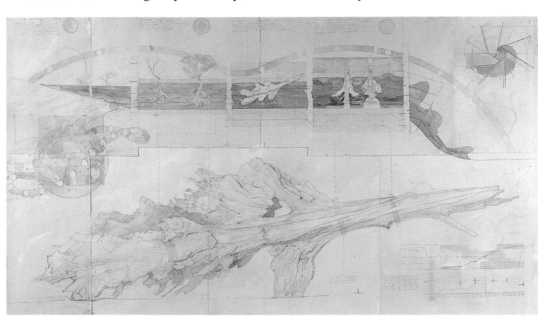

Tidal Almanac with Mangrove Trunk
1988–90
Watercolour on paper, 128 × 208 cm
Collection Lowenstein's Arts Management
© John Wolseley Licensed by VISCOPY, Australia, 2004

CRITICAL STUDY

John Wolseley's art is not really landscape art. It is more a record of his wanderings and observations. His images record in minute detail aspects of the environment he has experienced.

He has blown up details, jotted down information and included diagrams. He does this to show the structure of natural things as well as the delicate balance that exists in people's relationships to the land.

He shows the flora, animal and insect life, soil types and the imprint of human habitation. Wolseley's art suggests a form of mapping or survey.

In *Tidal Almanac with Mangrove Trunk* we are shown the patterns of nature's life cycles. His drawings are faithfully observed and recorded with meticulous care. Wolseley's paintings are more than a naturalist's record or an environmentalist's view of nature as fragile and in danger. His work reflects his **aesthetic** vision of Australia. The drawing is sensitive. The colour is delicate and the composition is well thought out. He has created a sense of unity. Wolseley's unusual way of structuring his information and images informs us about nature and his own emotional response to it.

The drawings in the series *Tracing the Wallace Line* capture the diverse life forms that have evolved along the Wallace Line, where the Australian bio-geographical region meets the Asian region. Wolseley spent four years travelling in Indonesia and Malaysia, documenting the transformations of the diverse flora and fauna. His drawings feature leaf forms from both sides of the Wallace Line, as well as bird plumage, insects and forest mosses. The drawings are exquisite, with fine pencil work and free areas of brilliant watercolour. For the exhibition, the gallery floor was marked with a dotted line to represent the Wallace Line, and cabinets were devoted to extinct species.

John Wolseley says: 'I am trying to give form to my obsession and fascination with the way every living species is part of the huge dynamic movement of the Earth and its evolution. If one looks at the frond of a fern say, in its design and structure, there lies the history of the Earth'.[4]

Born in England in 1938, Wolseley came to live in Melbourne in 1976. He is fascinated with the Australian interior, particularly the desert areas, and is keen to show the 'Australian-ness' of his imagery. He has stated: 'I hold the desert in great awe and I respect it. If you find a way into it, it isn't as hostile as other artists say it is... I seek to find out what the desert does to me rather than what I can do to it'.[5]

On each day of his walking trips, Wolseley records where he spent the day, the campsites, waterholes, vegetation and creatures he observed, all drawn in fine detail. These will often be stuck onto larger pieces of paper or hardboard when he returns to his studio. This forms the basis of a larger work. These larger works record what it is like to be moving within a landscape, stopping here and there to look more carefully.

Wolseley's work is a kind of extension of the early explorer painters like von Guérard (see page 178). He has links with the early botanists in his scientific approach to the structure of natural things. He goes further than that, however, to show the whole ecological view: how each form of nature impacts on the whole system.

STUDYING ART

Critical study

Subjective frame

1. What else can you see in this work besides drawings of natural objects? Try and explain why you think Wolseley might have included these.
2. Art critic Lee Fergusson has written that 'Wolseley's message seems straightforward: everything in creation forms, no matter how obscure or small, a vital part in an interconnected web of ecological relations'.[6] What evidence do you see in this artwork by Wolseley that this is the message of his work?

Structural frame

3. Why do you think Wolseley has divided up his page into different sections, to form a type of grid? What effect does it have?
4. The relationship between sizes — the scale — is an important aspect of Wolseley's drawings. What does this changing of scale allow him to do? What does it suggest to you of his aims and methods of working?
5. What else have you discovered about Wolseley's art practice? (Consider his methods, techniques, choice of media, type of research and the way he creates his artworks.)

Historical study

6. In what ways is Wolseley's work a link with early botanists and the early colonial artists? In what ways does his work reflect our contemporary society?

Tracing the Wallace Line; Wing Leaf and Land 1999
Watercolour on paper
136 × 205 cm
Courtesy of the artist and Roslyn Oxley9 Gallery, Sydney

MAKING ART

Subjective frame
Look at a one-metre square section of the playground and meticulously draw four images of nature that you observe (use a magnifying glass).

ESSAY

Wolseley says he should be referred to as a 'land artist' rather than a 'landscape artist'. Discuss the difference between these two labels by looking at Wolseley's work and the work of other artists in chapter 4.

Albrecht Dürer

(1471–1528, German)

Frame: structural
Form: painting
Conceptual framework: This is an objective, realistic interpretation of the artist's world, requiring only recognition and appreciation of the artist's skill from the audience.

Vocabulary

humanism: belief system that stresses human, not spiritual, concerns

The Young Hare 1502
Watercolour, 25 × 22.5 cm
Graphische Sammlung Albertina, Vienna

The realism of this work is impressive, particularly since there would have been no photograph to work from. Dürer displays an acute objective observation of the subject. He has depicted its solidity through careful use of light and shading. He also concentrates on fine detail in order to show the texture of the hare's fur. We can almost imagine its nose twitching, so lifelike and vital is the image. This is not the stereotyped hare we might see in children's storybooks, nor is it merely a copy as in a photograph. Dürer observes nature with precision and an awareness of beauty.

HISTORICAL STUDY

Travel between countries increased in the fifteenth century, allowing for exchange of ideas between artists. Dürer was born in Nuremberg, Germany. He visited Italy and was impressed by the work of the Renaissance artists, particularly Mantegna. Dürer brought back to Germany the new Renaissance way of searching for ideal realism. The **humanism** of the Italian Renaissance meant a concern for the individual and their natural surroundings. Philosophers of the Renaissance wished to understand and even control their world. Renaissance artists investigated in detail how things looked. Dürer linked this with his imaginative interpretation and northern European love of minute detail. He was trained as a goldsmith and in the crafts of painting, drawing, woodcuts and engraving. He is best known for his ability as a graphic artist, and his engravings and woodcuts, in particular the 'Apocalypse' series.

STUDYING ART

Critical study
Subjective frame
1. What was your first impression of this work? Are you impressed by it? Why?
2. If you were asked to create the perfect room to display this work, what would it be like?

Postmodern frame
3. What is missing from this work? Where would this animal be sitting if it belonged to you?
4. Artist's practice: Describe Dürer's approach to his artmaking; that is, what he is trying to do and how he achieves it.

FURTHER RESEARCH

Historical study
1. Compare and contrast Dürer's depiction of animals with examples by Australians Brett Whiteley or John Olsen. Consider in your essay the cultural background, technique and media.

Structural study
2. How is this work similar in technique and approach to that of Raphael's *Alba Madonna* on page 9?

MAKING ART

Subjective frame
1. Using pencil, do a detailed drawing of your pet in your Visual Arts Process Diary.
2. Using tissue paper and cut-out masonite or cardboard, create a painted relief sculpture of your pet in its 'house'.

Cultural frame
3. Create an artwork with a social comment (for example, cruelty to animals, extinction of a species) in any media, titled 'Caged Animal'.

Peter Paul Rubens

(1577–1640, Flemish)

Frame: subjective
Form: oil painting
Conceptual framework: Rubens evokes an emotional response from the viewer through his use of colour and tone, and the detailed, dramatic way he paints the subject.

Vocabulary

clientele: customers
mythological: belonging to a traditional myth or legend, usually to do with gods and goddesses
narrative: a story

A Lion Hunt c.1616–21
Oil on canvas, 249 × 375.5 cm
Collection: Alte Pinakothek, Munich

CRITICAL STUDY

Here we see a **narrative** of man's strength being tested against the strength and grandeur of the king of the beasts — the lion, a symbol of power. It is a crucial moment in a wild, violent battle for existence. This painting displays vigour and passion.

Structurally, colour, tone and light have been used to create a sense of movement and drama. Animals and humans are intertwined in writhing movement, heightened by the strong use of diagonal direction. Although the main action takes place at the front of the canvas, there is still a great sense of space.

Rubens, a Flemish artist, generally produced his work for the rich nobility and the Catholic Church. He painted **mythological**, biblical and historical subjects, as well as landscapes and portraits, with great technical skill and a sense of vitality, emotion and drama. His works also reveal his understanding of anatomy.

Rubens is known as a Baroque artist. Baroque art is generally recognisable by the strong contrasts of light and shade and the dominance of diagonal direction, which creates a sense of movement. Images are often caught in a split second of time (with subjects often showing open mouths as if they are calling out). Baroque art expresses emotion, and there is an overall sense of the dramatic.

Rubens spent ten years studying in Italy and while there was influenced by Michelangelo, Tintoretto (see page 36) and Caravaggio. This can be seen in Rubens' paintings of muscular, straining bodies, powerful, often violent action and the use of a dramatic light source.

Rubens painted with rich, vibrant colours, applying his paint thinly. He used walnut oil to create glowing, transparent glazes of colour.

Rubens was assisted in his painting by many associates and apprentices. He turned out large numbers of paintings for an international **clientele**. He was the court painter to dukes of Italy, a friend and adviser on art to the king of Spain, painter to the queen of France, painter to Charles I of England and permanent court painter to the Spanish governors of Flanders.

STUDYING ART

Critical study

Subjective frame

1. How does this painting make you feel?
2. Who do you have sympathy for — the lions, the horses or the men? Why?

Structural frame

3. List how many men, lions and horses are in the painting.
4. What symbols of power or violence are present?
5. Describe the different textures Rubens has carefully rendered.
6. This painting has an 'open composition'. What do you think this could mean?

7. How has Rubens created a sense of movement?

Historical study

Cultural frame

8. List three characteristics of Baroque art.
9. Rubens did not paint animals only. What else did he paint?
10. Two animals — the lion and horse — have been used as symbols in this painting. What do you think they symbolised in the seventeenth century? Cultural changes have altered their symbolic meaning for us today. How and why?

11. Artist's practice: How does the art practice of Rubens differ from that of an artist working now in Australia? Consider working conditions, available materials, type of subject, how artworks are exhibited and sold and how an artist's reputation was made then and now.
12. While Rubens is often referred to as the master of Baroque painting, Bernini (page 10) is called the master of Baroque sculpture. Look at the work of these two artists and write a one-page comparison on their treatment of the human figure.

MAKING ART

Subjective frame

Using charcoal, create a drawing of a fight in the playground. Use a sense of drama and diagonal lines to create the same mood as in Ruben's painting *A Lion Hunt*.

Franz Marc

(1880–1916, German)

Frame: subjective; structural
Form: oil painting
Conceptual framework: Marc applies his theories on life to his artworks in order to convey meaning to the audience.

Vocabulary

naturalistic: presenting nature in an accurate, lifelike way
schematic: simplified like a diagram

EXPRESSIONISM

a modern art style that emphasises emotion and the projection of inner feelings.

Yellow Cow (Gelbe Kuh) 1911
Oil on canvas, 140.5 × 189.2 cm
Solomon R. Guggenheim Museum, New York
Photo © The Solomon R. Guggenheim Foundation, New York
FN 49.1210

Here we have a lively, lovable cow which seems to be kicking with happiness as it frolics in the landscape. It seems to be in harmony with nature.

The shapes of the cow seem to be mirrored in the shapes of the mountains and plant forms at the front. The surface has been broken up into clearly defined areas, yet there is a flattening of the space, a lack of depth. The choice of colour for both the cow and the landscape seems to set them apart from what is normal. The colours and the use of diagonals create a sense of strength and passionate emotions.

Along with Kandinsky, Franz Marc helped form the second movement of German **Expressionism** called the Blue Rider. The earlier movement was called the Bridge. *Yellow Cow* was shown at the first Blue Rider exhibition in Munich in 1911. Marc, at this time, was developing his personal theme of the noble nature of animals and their union with the universe.

Marc once wrote: 'Very early I found people to be "ugly": animals seemed more beautiful, more pure. But then I discovered in them, too, so much that was ugly and unfeeling — and instinctively, by an inner compulsion, my presentation became more **schematic** or more abstract'.[7]

Yellow Cow was painted during Marc's transition stage between his earlier, more **naturalistic** treatment of animals and his later work which is more fragmented and geometric, suggestive of the Cubists and Futurists. At this time he was also working out his theories on the symbolic emotional equivalents of colour. In his correspondence with August Macke in December 1910, Marc wrote: 'Blue is the male principle, severe, bitter, spiritual and intellectual. Yellow is the female principle, gentle, cheerful and sensual. Red is matter, brutal and heavy, the colour which must be fought and overcome by the other two'.[8]

Marc used various types of animals, including the deer, horse and tiger, as symbols to make his statements about life.

STUDYING ART

Critical study
Subjective frame
1. List three words that describe how this painting makes you feel.
2. Can you think of a poem or nursery rhyme that would match this painting?
3. Do you find this painting realistic? Why or why not?

Historical study
4. What are the two movements of German Expressionism called?
5. What is the basic idea behind Marc's theories on art?

Cultural frame
6. Discuss the role of farmhouse animals as symbols in the work of Franz Marc and Les Kossatz (page 54), considering the different media and social situations.

MAKING ART

Subjective frame
Use your knowledge of Marc's symbolic use of colour (yellow, red, blue) to paint how you feel about an issue that means a lot to you.

Joan Miró

(1893–1983, Spanish)

Frame: subjective
Form: oil painting
Conceptual framework: Miró does not depict the real world but works from his own inner world of dreams and imagination. Viewers are free to interpret his work in their own way.

Vocabulary

irrational: not what is normally expected; unreasonable, illogical
organic: based on native, on living things
semi-abstract: not quite abstract; containing some reference to the real world

SURREALISM   **a modern art style interested in dreams and the subconscious**

Discussion

What do you find *irrational* about this painting?

Hirondelle/Amour Winter 1933–34
Oil on canvas, 199.3 × 247.6 cm. The Museum of Modern Art, New York
Gift of Nelson A. Rockefeller. Photograph © 1996 The Museum of Modern Art, New York
© Joan Miró, licensed by VISCOPY, Australia, 2004

Miró's imaginary, whimsical shapes suggest creatures, animals, birds or parts of figures that seem to belong to the dreamworld. The fanciful forms and shapes float in space and remind us of children's drawings. They stir our imagination in that they seem to belong outside or beyond reality.

Miró's **semi-abstract** shapes, **organic** forms and flowing lines are painted in bright, pure, decorative colours. His forms are suggestive rather than realistic. Miró's shapes are symbolic. They act as some kind of personal language.

Miró's dreamlike images belong to the Surrealist style. André Breton, a former Dadaist (member of a movement which tried to discover new meaning and methods for art), helped establish **Surrealism**. Surrealism carried further the Dada ideas of spontaneity and unconscious associations. Breton's 1924 manifesto states that the purpose of Surrealism is 'to resolve the previously contradictory conditions of dream and reality into an absolute reality, a super reality'.[9] This concept of the Surrealist escaping from the world through fantasy and dreams can clearly be seen in the work of the painter Joan Miró.

The Surrealists were reacting against the ordered and restricted ways of civilization. They were influenced by a psychoanalyst, Sigmund Freud, who studied dreams. Surrealists aimed to produce spontaneous imagery and automatic forms which came from the subconscious. They were trying to break away from the constriction of reason and the need to depict reality. They worked mainly within the *subjective frame* of art.

STUDYING ART

Critical study
Subjective frame
1. Which of the following words would you use to describe this painting?
   - magical
   - joyful
   - crazy
   - dull
   - rich
   - cold
2. Imagine you could hop into this painting. Where would you be? Under water? On the moon?
3. The title of this painting means 'Swallows/Love'. Does this help your understanding of the painting? What does it suggest to you?
4. What might happen next?

Structural frame
5. Are the colours real or imaginary?
6. What parts of the human body can you see?

7. How many eyes can you find?
8. What creatures other than birds can you see?
9. Count how many red shapes there are. What does the colour red add to the painting?
10. What are three characteristics or aims of Surrealism?

Structural frame
11. Miró once said 'a picture had to be right to a millimetre — had to be in balance to a millimetre'.[10] What instance can you see in this work of his concern for balance?
12. Miró also said 'for me form is never something abstract; it is always a sign of something. It is always a bird, or something else. For me painting is never form for form's sake'.[11] What does this tell you of Miró's method of painting and his use of symbols?

FURTHER RESEARCH

Historical study
Subjective and cultural frames
Compare and contrast the work of another Surrealist, Yves Tanguy, with that of Miró. Consider their use of imaginary living forms, the mood created, colours, tone and how their artworks reflect the social conditions at the time.

MAKING ART

Subjective frame
Create your own fantasy world. Perhaps you could look for inspiration from images under a microscope: amoeba, bacteria or cells. Do three small drawings in pencil in your Visual Arts Process Diary, then choose one of these to develop into a larger work using colour. Work in pen and ink with watercolour or washes of coloured ink. You may find it interesting to work within a circular shape.

Les Kossatz

(b. 1943, Australian)

Frame: cultural; structural
Form: sculpture
Conceptual framework: Kossatz makes comments on his world and involves the audience by encouraging them to experience his life-size works by walking around them. Kossatz's sense of humour also attracts the audience.

Vocabulary

tableau: (plural — tableaux) group of people or objects arranged to represent a striking scene

CRITICAL STUDY

These life-like bronze sheep appear to be going through a ritual. We are reminded of the way sheep are dipped. At first they appear comic: one is flying through a curtain as on a stage; another behind the curtain has slipped and is using the third sheep as leverage to get up. We gradually become aware of a deeper meaning — perhaps the sheep are not just representations of animals but are being used to symbolise human behaviour. We, too, are often on show and we also struggle mindlessly at times to keep up with the mob. These sheep at Darling Harbour make us aware of the predicaments which characterise the insecurity of humanity as a whole.

HISTORICAL STUDY

The sheep in Kossatz's **tableaux** undergo a series of tortures and indignations. They in fact are symbolising humans in various social situations. It is usual in Kossatz's sheep sculptures for the sheep to be in motion or at a point of action, as in *Hard Slide* in the National Gallery of Victoria where the sheep are poised to slide.

In the past sheep have been used as sacrificial beasts in many different cultures. They are perceived as 'dumb animals', and are shown this way in the work of Kossatz. They blindly follow each other to their fate.

Kossatz's sculptures are powerful images revealing the ironies of life and death.

STUDYING ART

Critical study
Cultural frame
1. Does this work make any comments to you about race, class or gender?
2. What is the relationship of the sheep to the Australian national identity? Can you think of any other artwork where a sheep has been used as a symbol?
3. Do you think this is a good choice of artwork for a public place? Why? (It was sponsored by Leighton Contractors Pty Ltd.)
4. What contribution to its meaning does the scale and the choice of materials make?

FURTHER RESEARCH

Historical study
Find one other artwork which contains an image of a sheep. What does it symbolise and how does it relate to society at the time it was created?

MAKING ART

Cultural or Postmodern frame
Can you think of another situation in which you could place sheep to create a social message? You may use any media to communicate your comment. You may like to appropriate (borrow) an image from past art to create a Postmodern work.

Curtain Call 1988
Timber and bronze, life-size
Darling Harbour, Sydney

Jeff Koons

(b. 1955, American)

Vocabulary

appropriation: the act of putting a familiar image in a new context to change its meaning

contemporary: belonging to the past decade; modern

kitsch: pretentious, sentimental or in bad taste

parody: a humorous, exaggerated imitation

Discussion

Koons argued, in relation to a court case concerning *String of Puppies*, that his *appropriation* of the image was fair use since his sculpture was both a *parody* and a form of legitimate social criticism.[12] Do you think this is a fair reason for breaking copyright?

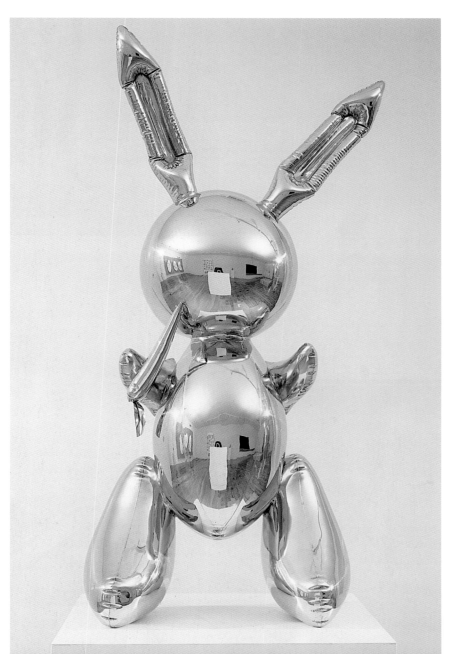

Rabbit 1986
Stainless steel, 104 × 48.2 × 30.5 cm
Courtesy of the artist
Copyright Jeff Koons

In *Rabbit*, Koons has converted the image of an inflatable toy rabbit into an art object. A cheap, blow-up carnival toy has been transformed by changing its scale (*Rabbit* stands just over a metre high) and by using an expensive material (stainless steel).

This is a twist on the Postmodern technique of rebelling against traditional techniques and media. Koons has broken away from the idea of the precious object. He has taken the cheap toy and transformed it into an artwork, making a light, short-lived and familiar object into a weighty and more permanent art object.

New York–based Jeff Koons is one of the most innovative and provocative figures of **contemporary** art. Koons makes art from what has previously not been considered as art. He has coated some of his sculptures with gold plate, chrome or stainless steel to turn **kitsch** objects into precious, high art objects. He is commenting on the 'fake luxury' of the American consumer culture of the 1980s. Koons's works are symbols of the deterioration of modern culture, our Postmodern society of the 1980s and 1990s. He comments not just on popular imagery and mass production, as did the Pop Artists of the 1950s and 1960s, but also the throwaway nature of it. His work also questions the whole concept of what art is.

String of Puppies 1988
Life-size painted wood
Courtesy of the artist. Copyright Jeff Koons

Koons's work has often met with international media coverage and great public attention as well as controversy. In one instance, Koons was taken to court (in 1990) over his life-size wooden sculpture of a man and woman holding eight German shepherd puppies, called *String of Puppies*. It was ruled that Koons violated copyright law when he appropriated a photograph from a greeting card. Italian artisans produced the sculpture on Koons's request. Koons had already sold three copies at $125 000 each at the time of the court case.

The appropriation of images from past art or popular culture is a central strategy of Postmodernism. By doing this, artists are commenting on our society, which is overloaded with images. Postmodern artists think an image has a different meaning according to how and where it is viewed (its context). An artwork will have a different meaning depending on whether it is in an art gallery, in an advertisement for chocolate, or in a health insurance commercial on television.

Koons in his work questions the nature and influence of popular culture and its relationship to such issues as class, race, sex and identity.

Puppy 1995
Height 12.4 metres, flowering sculpture
Museum of Contemporary Art, Sydney. Photograph: Brendan Read
Courtesy of the artist. Copyright Jeff Koons

Puppy, a four-storey-high flowering sculpture of a West Highland terrier, was installed by Koons in December 1995 on the forecourt of the Museum of Contemporary Art, Sydney, and remained there as part of the Sydney Festival in January 1996. The giant stainless steel frame, an engineering feat achieved through computer-aided design, supported 60 tonnes of soil and more than 50 000 flowering plants, including petunias, marigolds, impatiens and chrysanthemums. These are non-traditional art materials and were not put together by the artist.

Koons's first *Puppy* was installed in front of a castle in Arolsen, Germany, in 1992. The Sydney *Puppy* is a unique demountable structure that was exhibited around the world before returning to Sydney for the Olympic Games in 2000.

'I've always thought of *Puppy* as a very spiritual piece', says Koons, 'and I've never found anybody who hasn't responded to it in a favourable way. It's very beautiful and very baroque because after the piece is planted … it's out of control. And this is another God-like quality, because what it's going to look like is really out of my hands and in the hands of nature'.[13]

STUDYING ART

Critical study
Postmodern frame
1. In what way is Koons's *Bunny* a criticism of our culture?
2. *Puppy* is not a one-off masterpiece. It has been built before and will be reconstructed and exhibited again. How has our understanding and acceptance of art changed from the period when the *Mona Lisa* was painted to modern times? How is this change a product of our present society?
3. Humour is often an important consideration in Postmodern art. Can you see any instances of humour in Koons's work? Does he use satire or parody?
4. Given that Koons has said he wants to make art from what has previously not been considered as art, suggest three words to descibe Koons's subject matter.
5. Discuss examples of artworks that you have seen in advertisements in magazines or on television. How does this appropriation of artworks change their meaning? How do the artworks add to the meaning of the advertisement?

Historical study
6. Art critic and historian Robert Hughes has said of the social context of Jeff Koons's art: 'Nature is dead, culture is all, everything is mediated to the point where nothing can be seen in its true quality, representation determines all meaning … (producing) art given over to information and not experience'.[14]

What do you think this quote means? Do you think Hughes is being complimentary to the work of Jeff Koons?

What frame do you think Hughes is writing in — subjective, structural, cultural, or postmodern?

MAKING ART

1. Take a photocopy of an artwork from the past, or scan it into a graphics program, and turn it into an advertisement for a product today. Research what the function and meaning of the artwork may have been in its historical context and consider how they will be altered by your appropriation.
2. Design a piece of sculpture that you think would be a humorous criticism of our society, and put it in your Visual Arts Process Diary. In your design, show your ideas, research and consideration of parody or appropriation. Mention scale and materials to be used.

Bronwyn Oliver

(b. 1959, Australian)

Frame: structural
Form: sculpture
Conceptual framework: Many of Oliver's sculptures are designed to be placed outside, allowing them to relate to the environment and letting a wide audience experience them by walking around them.

Vocabulary

monumentality: grand scale, solidity and impressiveness
organic: based on nature, on living things
patina: green coating that occurs on aged metal
translucent: allowing some light to pass through

CRITICAL STUDY

Unicorn is delicate in form as well as materials, subtly hinting at a sea creature, perhaps a type of mollusc. It seems to have associations with many forms, both natural and manufactured. There is a suggestion of a life force.

Unicorn has an almost mathematical, abstract structure built of repeating units. It suggests **organic** growth. The basic shape is of a narrowing spiral. The paper is **translucent**, like a thin shell. It creates a feeling of the ephemeral, of passing time, a short lifespan. Sculpture usually has a sense of the timeless **monumentality** of bronze or stone. This work does not. It appears to be fragile. The combination of materials — cane, wire, hair and thin paper — adds to the delicate nature of this sculpture. The subtle textures of the different materials are an important feature of *Unicorn*. A soft shadow appears below the sculpture, the framework of wire and cane creating stronger lines of shadow.

In *Entwine*, Oliver creates a geometrical type of open structure formed from intricate patterns of wire. It suggests the skeleton of some living form, a network of patterns that twist to form a voluptuous curving volume. It is elegant and has a sense of refinement, precision and simplicity.

Unicorn 1984
Paper, tissue, wire, hair, cane
700 × 70 × 270 cm
Gift of the artist under the terms of the NSW Travelling Scholarship 1986
The Art Gallery of New South Wales
© Bronwyn Oliver

Bronwyn Oliver is an artist based in New South Wales. In 1993 she was awarded the Moët & Chandon Fellowship for her sculpture *Eddie*, a delicate copper wire work. She has exhibited regularly in Australia since 1986 and in Europe since 1988.

In *Unicorn*, Oliver has rejected the traditions of the art-and-craft nature of the materials she has used, making this work Postmodern.

Oliver's sculptures have structure and order, and show awareness of how to build logically using the sculptural medium in order to create beauty. Oliver is also very concerned with space and the effects of light on her work. Shadows projected on the walls from the patterns of her linear structures add another dimension to her work. Some of her copper wire work has a **patina**, suggesting they are relics of past cultures.

Although her sculptures remind us of structures in nature, Oliver denies that nature is the source of her inspiration. 'My ideas do not begin with natural forms. My ideas develop from the materials which I use and are not even remotely concerned with natural observation. I am interested in structure and in what materials will do.'[15] Her sculptures are very labour-intensive, particularly those welded from copper wire.

She has stated that she is 'trying to create life. Not in the sense of beings, or animals, or plants, or machines, but "life" in the sense of a kind of force, a presence, an energy … that a human being can respond to on the level of soul or spirit'.[16]

It is this sense of mystery, together with the delicate nature of Bronwyn Oliver's work, that makes her sculptures so intriguing.

STUDYING ART

Critical study
Subjective frame
1. Write two sentences about one of Oliver's works using some of the words below:

wrapping	precision
emerging	binding
framework	expanding
organic	swelling

Postmodern frame
2. Oliver takes objects out of their normal contexts. They appear to be objects washed up on a beach or part of a museum exhibit. By exhibiting them as art pieces, what questions are being asked? How is she changing their normal meaning and function or retelling their history?

MAKING ART

1. Create a sculpture inspired by structures found in nature, such as sea creatures or insects. Keep the work light and intricate by your choice of medium. Use wire or cane for your framework and experiment with various papers such as tissue or rice paper.
2. Create a sculpture using shapes found in mathematics, such as cones ▼, hyperbolas ⊂ ∪, and spirals ◎ ✎, as your basic structure. Consider a way of including movement in this work.
3. Draw or scan one of Oliver's sculptures and create a fantasy or surreal landscape around it.

Entwine 2001
Copper, Height 125 × 130 × 110 cm
Courtesy of the artist and Roslyn Oxley9 Gallery, Sydney

John Davis

(1936–2003, Australian)

Frame: postmodern
Form: sculpture
Conceptual framework: Davis not only responds to the environment but also uses materials from it in his artmaking. His works have a close relationship to his life experiences.

Vocabulary

site-specific: designed for a particular place

transitory: temporary, impermanent; often associated with Postmodern work

Discussion

Cultural frame

Discuss how Davis and other artists have responded to the issue of the destruction of our environment. (Hint: Look at the work of Mandy Martin, page 120.)

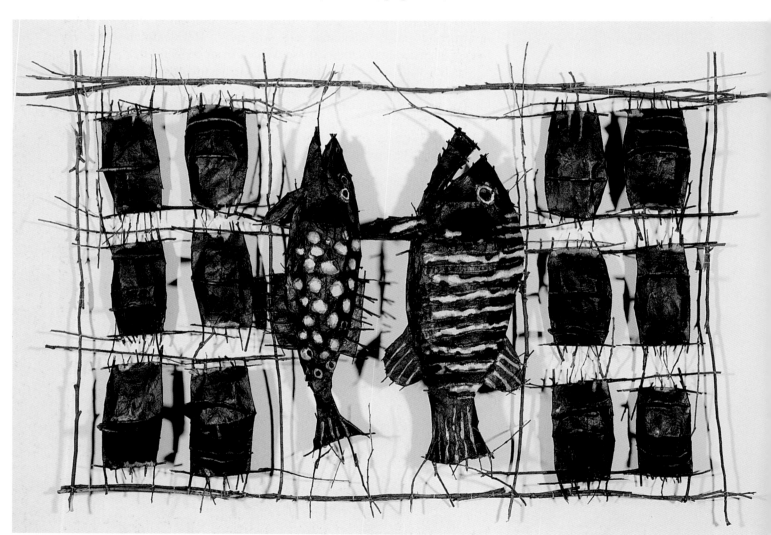

Fish and Pebbles 1989
Eucalyptus twigs, paper, calico, Bondcrete, bituminous paint, 90 × 137 × 16 cm
Photograph: Michael Szczepanski
Photograph courtesy of the artist
© John Davis, licensed by VISCOPY, Australia, 2004

At first we notice the fragile nature of this piece. It gives an impression of being **transitory**. This is created partly by Davis's choice of media but also by the concept of trapped, supposedly dead fish. The work suggests the catching of fish because of the net-like structure. The use of bitumen, which has a similar colour to an oil slick, also hints at wider issues, such as the pollution of waterways.

Fish and Pebbles can also be interpreted as a cultural statement. We are reminded of the haphazard nature of our bush by the uneven twigs bending at random. The work also reminds us of Aboriginal basketry, tent making and canoes in the way the twigs are bound together with careful attention to detail.

John Davis was born in Victoria. He began his career as a woodcarver and art and craft teacher. He later became a lecturer in sculpture at the Victorian College of the Arts. His work has included **site-specific** sculpture, performance pieces and the exploration of environmental issues expressed in found objects. *Fish and Pebbles* could be interpreted as a continuation of the ideas and methods he expressed in *Tree Piece*, constructed for the Mildura Sculpturescape in 1973. This work consisted of latex, canvas and string wrapped around tree trunks in an open site.

Davis's work relates to his experiences as a boy in the Mallee country of north-western Victoria and the Murray River, as well as his present concerns regarding the destruction of our environment.

Davis has stated: 'Fish seem to embody many of our responses to nature in the way we respond warmly to dolphins and whales yet destroy them in huge oil spills and through drift-net fishing'.[17]

His work is a political statement about a social problem.

STUDYING ART

Critical study
Subjective frame
1. What personal experiences or places does *Fish and Pebbles* remind you of?
2. What mood is created by the choice of colours and shapes?

Structural frame
3. Describe Davis's use of space and repetition.
4. How have the fish been used as symbols?

Postmodern frame
5. How is this artwork a statement about the assumption that artworks should be timeless and precious?
6. How is this Postmodern work a development from the assemblages of Duchamp (see page 90).

FURTHER RESEARCH

Historical study
Cultural frame
Find artworks from the past and from different cultures that have sea life as their subject matter. How has the subject been represented in each work? For example, is it represented as a religious symbol or as food? Is it decorative, realistic or simplified? What does each artwork tell us about the time and place in which it was created?

MAKING ART

Postmodern frame
Using found objects and charcoal drawings, create an installation about pollution. Document the process using a digital camera.

Merran Esson

(b. 1950, Australian)

Frame: subjective; cultural; structural
Form: ceramics
Conceptual framework: Esson's pots are her response to the natural world of sea life.

Vocabulary

glaze: a liquid painted on before the last firing to make a ceramic object waterproof. It can add colour, a dull shine (matt finish) or a glossy finish.

CRITICAL STUDY

These fanciful pots suggest sea life by their incised line decorations. Their supports and handles are similar to octopus tendrils and other sea creatures. They are made from thick, rough, hand-pinched coils.

Esson colours her pots rich turquoise and deep purple to match the underwater theme. The textured surface makes us think of ancient pots and metal vessels corroded by the sea.

Starfish
From series *Beneath the surface*, 1993
Height 40 cm
Ceramics, coloured slips, dry glazes, metallic leaf

Merran Esson has experimented with traditional clay vessel forms. At times she joins two together, placing them on stands which defy their weight, or she creates non-functional jug shapes. Her vessels are whimsical in mood, sculptural in form, and exciting to look at. Her forms at times also remind us of the amoeba-like simple life forms found in Miró's paintings (see page 52). Esson works extensively with contrast. She may combine smooth wheel-thrown shapes with free-form, hand-built additions, or intricate metallic inlay work with bold matt **glazes**. In her earlier work she used geometrical inlays of coloured clay to create contrast and pattern.

Esson's pots are unique because she creatively uses coloured clay with oxides and stains and unusual glazing techniques. She has a strong sense of sculptural balance and a playful imagination.

Jelly Fish Lugs
From series *Beneath the surface*, 1993
67 × 40 cm
Ceramics, coloured slips, dry glazes, metallic leaf

STUDYING ART

Critical study
Subjective frame
1. What is your reaction to Esson's pots? How do they make you feel?
2. In what ways do these pots remind you of sea life?

Historical study
Structural frame
3. Why do you think Esson was commissioned to create a series of pots to be sold at the Art Gallery of New South Wales shop to coincide with the Surrealism Exhibition?

Cultural frame
4. Artisans of the ancient civilisation of Crete also used images of sea life to decorate their pots. Draw an example of a Cretan pot and explain why the decoration reflects the Cretans' culture or way of life.

MAKING ART

Cultural frame
1. Investigate sea life which is unique to Australia, then use it to make a cultural statement. Consider environmental issues, a travel poster, or a functional design. You may use any media.

Postmodern frame
2. Create a bowl shape in clay, and decorate the inside with sea creatures (for example, mermaids, shells, lobsters). These could be added in relief.

Murray McKeich

(b. 1961 New Zealand, working in Melbourne)

Frame: postmodern
Form: digital imagery
Conceptual framework: McKeich relates to our technological world and the idea of the cyborg. He creates artworks that disturb the viewer.

Vocabulary

hybrid: made from many sources; composed of different things

mutation: the process of changing form, creating a new type of organism

photomontage: artwork composed of sections of photographs arranged and pasted down

tactile: relating to the sense of touch; inviting the viewer to touch

CRITICAL STUDY

In *Untitled*, McKeich has assembled parts into a fantastic **hybrid** 'monster' that could be called grotesque. If we disregard the suggestion that it is either an alien creature or a genetic experiment gone wrong, we can appreciate the artist's vivid imagination and the interesting surface textures and forms that he has created. We are intrigued, because the 'creature' seems to be still emerging or evolving. His work has the power to unsettle and disgust but, at the same time, it appeals to our imagination.

Artist's practice

McKeich transforms found objects into monsters that are strange and disturbing, yet compellingly beautiful. An underlying theme is the convergence of humans with machines. His monsters have human-like forms, yet flesh and machine parts seem to be melded together by a machine process.

McKeich has an imaginative approach that brings unusual things together, and seeks to create the marvellous — an approach that reminds us of the Surrealist art movement. He creates a kind of beauty by merging incongruous things. His work is about change, transformation and **mutation**.

McKeich scans photographs, other images and objects, then intensifies the surfaces of certain things such as glistening entrails. He achieves this effect by using filters to manipulate light and texture. In the process of building up the textural components of his **photomontages**, McKeich uses the techniques of layering and masking. But his works go beyond simple photomontages, as he uses a complex process of assemblage and transformation. The results are his discomforting, yet fascinating, **tactile** works.

McKeich's art reflects the potential for invention and innovation created by new technologies. It also reflects our acceptance of the ugly, disturbing images often associated with violence, which bombard us in video clips and movies.

STUDYING ART

Subjective frame

1. How do you react to McKeich's images? Do they invoke fear, curiosity, repulsion or some other reaction?
2. What is your opinion of his work?

Cultural frame

3. How does McKeich's work relate to our present world and your own experiences? Perhaps you are reminded of a video clip or movie.

FURTHER RESEARCH

Compare the work of Patricia Piccinini with that of McKeich: www.patriciapiccinini.net

MAKING ART

Create your own 'monster' by scanning different parts of animals into the computer. Use software such as Photoshop to distort and combine your images.

Dread 1999
Digitally
manipulated
photomedia
17.6 × 29.5 cm
at 300 dpi
8-bit greyscale

FOCUS WORK
CRITICAL STUDY

Frame: postmodern
Form: sculpture
Conceptual framework: Goodwin is making a comment on the art world.

Richard Goodwin
(b. 1953, Australian)

SUBJECTIVE FRAME

1. What is your first impression of this work? What do you see?
2. Why do you think Goodwin included a rider on this horse? How does it widen the meaning of the piece?
3. What do you feel about this artwork? What memories, dreams or experiences does this bring to mind?
4. What is the mood of this work? Does it suggest any of the following emotions?

   fear, hope, excitement, longing, pride, anger, power, violence, freedom

   Write one sentence explaining the mood of this installation.
5. Do you see the rider on the horse as a warrior, a victim, or is there another possibility?

STRUCTURAL FRAME

6. This work has also been exhibited as an installation with a drawing on the wall behind it depicting a silhouette of a horse behind a piece of machinery. An installation is an arrangement within a space. It is usually displayed in this way for only a short time. Do you think the meaning of an artwork can change subtly according to how or where it is displayed?
7. The horse is suspended from the ceiling. What does this suggest to you?
8. Describe Goodwin's use of texture.
9. Where and how has line been used in this work?
10. Why do you think Goodwin has kept this work basically white? How is its meaning changed by not being in realistic colours?
11. Horses have been used as a symbol for many things, such as power (in ancient battles) and love (the love of a child for its animal). What do you think this horse is symbolising?
12. How has the artist's decision on the size of the sculpture added to its meaning or impact?

CULTURAL FRAME

13. When was *Soho Horse with Rider* exhibited? Is this subject of special importance to this country or its history?
14. Can you think of an Australian poem or film about a horse and rider?
15. Do you think this sculpture is about only Australian culture or do you think it is making a universal comment? (Does it refer to other countries also?)
16. Are horses symbolic of anything to people now? Adolescents living in the city are often 'horse-mad'. Why?

POSTMODERN FRAME

17. What would you expect a sculpture of a horse to be made from?
18. What do you think could be the significance of Goodwin using recycled cotton clothing?
19. A horse is usually considered an object of beauty. Goodwin has altered its normal appearance. Is it still beautiful?
20. What is missing from this work that you would expect to see?
21. Do you see any humour in this work?

ACTIVITY

Write a short critical review of *Soho Horse with Rider* for a newspaper.

ESSAY

Now that you have analysed and formed your own opinions on *Soho Horse with Rider*, write a one-page essay on the following topic:

Evaluate *Soho Horse with Rider* by Richard Goodwin, mentioning the influence of his choice of media on its meaning.

Before you begin your essay, read 'Writing about art' at the end of this book (see page 201).

To help you in your answer, read the following quote by Graeme Sturgeon:

> Rather than use one of the traditional approaches, modelling in clay or carving in wood or stone, Goodwin builds up his forms by wrapping a steel armature with discarded articles of clothing which, not unimportantly from his point of view, carry strong suggestions of a previous existence and of human mortality.[18]

Soho Horse with Rider 1984
Life-size sculpture, recycled cloth, acrylic, steel
Collection: Hugh Jamieson
Photograph courtesy of the artist

OBJECTS

DISCUSSION

1. You have been asked to curate an exhibition of one of the artists in this chapter. Work in groups and discuss the following: What key work would you choose for the cover of your catalogue? What would the opening line of your catalogue be? What catchy title would you use to advertise the exhibition? What colour would you paint the walls in the gallery? What food would you serve on opening night?

2. Take on the role of an art critic and write a review, within the *subjective frame*, for a newspaper on one of the artworks opposite.

3. Imagine you are an art historian. Choose two works from this chapter that you believe are significant to the history of art, perhaps because they influenced many artists after them or they created a new approach to art. State your reasons and write an article for an art journal within either a *structural* or *cultural frame*.

Greek pottery

(Black-figure ware, sixth century BC)

Frame: cultural
Form: ceramics
Conceptual framework: The functional objects are designed for the needs and interests of the period.

Vocabulary

kiln: large 'oven' capable of creating high temperatures, used to fire clay

leather hard: semi-dry, but still capable of being worked on

narrative: a story

slip: liquid clay of fine texture

thrown: made on a potter's wheel

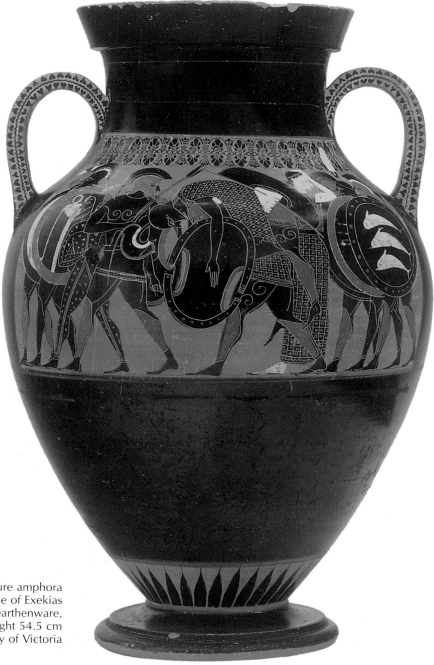

Greek (Attic) black-figure amphora
After the style of Exekias
Sixth century BC, earthenware,
height 54.5 cm
National Gallery of Victoria

This pot has been carefully designed to fulfil its function as a storage jar (for wine, oil or honey). This type of vessel is called an amphora, which means 'to carry on both sides', owing to the two handles which made it easy to carry when full. The opening or neck of the pot is large enough to allow a large spoon or ladle to be inserted.

This pot can also be considered as an art object because of its pleasing proportions and the sensitive relationship between its decoration and its shape. The geometrical band of decoration at the base emphasises the tapering of the pot. Its small base gives it a feeling of lightness and elegance. The band of decoration around the widest section consists of finely drawn black figures against a red background. One side of the pot depicts a battlefield, the other a wedding celebration.

In the sixth century BC, Athens became the principal ceramic centre of Greece and the largest exporter of its six basic shapes of ceramic ware. Each shape was developed to suit a particular purpose. For example the three-handled hydra was easy to carry and pour, and the kylix was a drinking cup.

The amphora had either a wide foot or base, as in the example here, or it had a pointed base so that it could be sunk into the ground. The pots were **thrown** in sections, then joined at the **leather hard** stage.

Athenian pots were known for their decorations, which included **narratives** of their heroes and gods as well as contemporary scenes of races, battles and celebrations. In black-figure ware, the figures were mostly men; women's faces and bodies were shown in white.

To create the black-figure ware, the figures in the design were painted with **slip**, and details were incised (scratched in). Other colours were sometimes added. The slip was originally the same colour as the pot, but turned black after undergoing a three-part firing process. The first firing (oxidising) turned both pot and slip red. The second firing (reducing), when the oxygen to the **kiln** was shut off, turned both pot and slip black; but during the third firing the coarser material of the pot re-absorbed the oxygen while the smoother, silica-laden slip did not and remained black.

Black-figure ware was at its finest around 500 BC. The work of Exekias was particularly beautiful. The black-figure style was gradually replaced by the red-figure style. This style allowed a greater sense of realism. The background was painted black while the figures were left red, with details painted in black line.

STUDYING ART

Critical study

Structural frame
1. Describe the method used by the Greeks to make their pots.
2. List the stages in the decoration of the pots during the black-figure stage.
3. How has movement been shown in the decoration of the pot?

Cultural frame
4. What can you learn about the civilisation of the ancient Greeks around the sixth century BC by looking at their pots? Consider the functions of the pots, the types of subjects used in the decorations, and the way the people are dressed and portrayed.

Postmodern frame
5. Do we have the same need for pots like this today? Why or why not? For what reasons do we value this pot now, and why are they different from the reasons it was valued when it was created?

FURTHER RESEARCH

Historical study
1. Draw and label the six types of shapes designed by Greek potters to suit various purposes.
2. Discuss the development of the depiction of figures from black-figure ware to red-figure ware. Consider how the painter has indicated space or depth. Is there more awareness of anatomy? How are they standing? Is there more movement?

   (To collect this research, what frame would you be working in?)

MAKING ART

Cultural frame
Design a functional object. Decorate it with images to reveal our culture to future generations.

Write an evaluation of your design. Consider your success in communicating the attitudes, concerns and beliefs of our society. Consider also the function of the object and the relationship of decoration to form. Present this as a desktop published document. Include an image of your object and labels that give your evaluation of it.

Richard Sapper

(b. 1932, German)

Frame: structural
Form: designed objects
Conceptual framework: The designer has produced an efficient object to be used by the consumer (buyer), yet it is also elegant and pleasing to the viewer.

Vocabulary

aesthetically: relating to one's sense of beauty

innovative: new, different, ahead of its time

minimalism: style that doesn't have unnecessary detail or adornment, but instead has refined simplicity

rationalism: the principle of taking a sensible, reasoned approach

CRITICAL STUDY

Tizio Table Lamp 1972
ABS plastic and aluminium
Height when extended 118.1 cm
Manufactured by Artemide, Milan, Italy
Philadelphia Museum of Art, gift of
Artemide Inc.

The *Tizio* lamp has become an icon of **innovative** design representing the 1980s and 1990s. Sapper has followed his principle that the technological function of an object should determine its appearance. The *Tizio* lamp has formal elegance and technical precision. It has achieved worldwide acceptance as a standard item in fashionable modern interiors.

The lamp has a certain simplicity or **minimalism** in design. It is skeletal, and has been called almost insect-like. It is a cleverly engineered object with concealed workings, which creates a sense of magic. The lamp's arms are designed to act as counterweights. The slightest touch will re-position it without causing it to overbalance. It is made of ABS plastic and aluminium, and is rendered in matte black. The red switch and red highlights at key joints add interest but do not dominate. Its technical advantages are that it is lightweight, adaptable and uses a low voltage halogen bulb, which provides a concentrated light source.

This lamp has become a symbol of contemporary lifestyle. It is a quality design, efficient, adaptable and **aesthetically** pleasing.

The *Tizio* lamp won the Compasso d'Oro prize in 1979 and is still one of the company's best-selling designs.

Another consumer product that has become a design classic is Sapper's *Bollitore* kettle, which he designed for the Alessi company in 1982. It is made from stainless steel with a copper base for good heat conduction on all types of stoves. The position of the sturdy handle and the innovative spring mechanism for opening the spout make the kettle easy and safe to use. Sapper also introduced a sense of fun to the product by adding a brass whistle with two pitch pipes that play melodic notes when the kettle boils.

HISTORICAL STUDY

Richard Sapper was born in Germany but has spent much time in Italy. His designs combine the sculptural elegance of Italian design with the **rationalism** and emphasis on function that are characteristic of German design.

Sapper was trained in engineering and economics, working with Daimler Benz (1956) in Germany before moving to Italy in 1958. Sapper worked with Gio Ponti until 1977, mainly in consumer electronics. From 1970 to 1976, he was consultant to Fiat and Pirelli. In 1980, he became an industrial design consultant to IBM. He has designed domestic products for Alessi, Kartell and Artemide. Sapper is responsible for many twentieth-century design classics. His own view of his work is that 'As designers we see our responsibility as being to create things which improve life and the future for everyone'.[1]

Bollitore Kettle, 1982
Stainless steel body, copper base
Height 19 cm, diameter 16.5 cm,
capacity 2 litres
Manufactured by Alessi, Italy

STUDYING ART

Critical study
1. Good design should be pleasing to the eye. What other concerns must a designer consider?
2. Mention at least two reasons why the *Tizio* lamp is so successful as a designed object.
3. Explain how Sapper's understanding of engineering would have helped him to make the *Bollitore* kettle a practical and successful designed product.

Historical study
4. What aspects of Italian and German design can be seen in the *Tizio* lamp?
5. List some of the types of designed products with which Sapper has been involved.

MAKING ART

Richard Sapper believes that homes and workplaces need designs that make life easier and more beautiful. Choose an everyday domestic or office product and think about redesigning or improving its form and features. Make pencil sketches that illustrate your ideas. Try to include a special 'fun' feature that will increase its appeal for consumers.

Philippe Starck

(b. 1949, French)

Frames: structural; subjective; postmodern

Form: designed objects

Conceptual framework: Designers consider society's needs and attempt to alter or develop the buyer's sense of style.

CRITICAL STUDY

This office chair is a sculptural form that resembles the roots of a living plant, yet is streamlined and reflects contemporary technology.

The *Costes Chair* reminds us of the traditional armchair, but it has been reinterpreted to suit the modern love of simplicity in design and the needs of mass production. It is extremely simple with its tubular frame, oval shell and three perfectly balanced legs.

Juicy Salif is a controversial design for a lemon squeezer. Some argue its exciting sculptural design is innovative among other boring household utensils. Others see it as a piece of flamboyant nonsense. Once again, Starck has created a new interpretation of the commonplace, designing a distinctive object that stands alone in its form yet is functional. Starck has designed an object that is exciting to possess — not just one that is needed for a purpose.

HISTORICAL STUDY

Philippe Starck began as an interior designer in the early 1970s. In 1979 he founded the Starck Products company. In 1984 he did the interior design for the Café Costes in Paris, which included the now famous *Costes Chair*. His business expanded to include architecture and industrial design. In 1988 he began a collaboration with Alberto Alessi.

Starck's output has been prolific, and he has worked in a wide field of design. His interiors are highly original, and include the Royalton Hotel in New York which he completed in 1988. Here he created new designs for lights and furniture, and reworked the space, creating an intimate social meeting place. Starck has also worked in the field of industrial products: in 1994 he designed the television named *Jim Nature*, made from high-density wood and plastic, for the Saba Company in France. This product raised the issues of recycling and the need for a more natural approach to technology design.

Philippe Starck is known as one of the world's best contemporary designers.

STUDYING ART

Critical study

Subjective frame

1. Create a short piece of critical writing, giving your opinion of one of Starck's designed objects.

Artmaking practice

2. How does the practice of a designer differ from that of an artist?
3. A number of 'copies' or similar designs to Starck's *Costes Chair* have entered the market. What does this say about the 'success' of this design?

MAKING ART

Design a garlic press. In your design, consider the sculptural appearance of the object.

Costes Chair
1982
Black
lacquered or
varnished
wood, leather
cushion,
tubular metal
Courtesy
Studio Starck

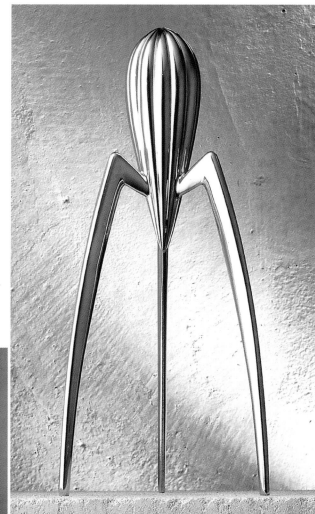

Juicy Salif Lemon Press 1990
Alessi, Milan
Courtesy Philippe Starck

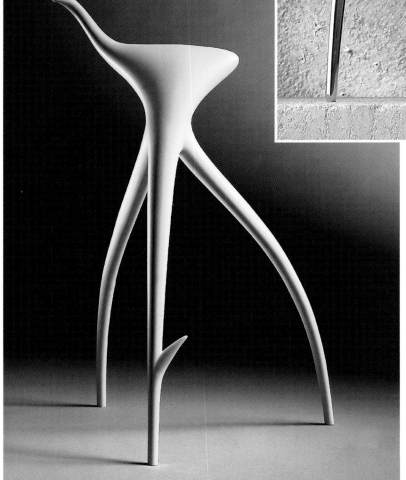

WW Stool 1990
Lacquered aluminium
Manufacturer: Vitra AG, Basel,
Switzerland
Design Museum, London
Courtesy Philippe Starck

Paul Cézanne

(1839–1906, French)

Frame: structural
Form: oil painting
Conceptual framework: Cézanne reacted to his world in an objective, analytical way. He wished his artworks to have a feeling of permanence and worth.

Vocabulary

abstraction: art that is non-representational, achieving effects through colour, line, form and so on (see Malevich, page 160)

composition: the placement of figures and objects; the organisation of an artwork

IMPRESSIONISTS

a group of French artists intent on showing the passing effects of light and atmosphere on everyday scenes and landscapes. They used short brushstrokes of pure colour (see Monet, page 110).

POST-IMPRESSIONISTS

included Cézanne, Gauguin, Van Gogh and Seurat. They went on to create a unique style of their own.

CUBISTS

a group of artists working from 1907 to 1925 who reacted against the established way of looking at things. They worked from multiple viewpoints, analysing and dissecting parts of items and rearranging them (see Picasso, page 14).

Apples and Oranges c.1895–1900
Oil on canvas, 73 × 92 cm
Musée d'Orsay, Paris

Cézanne's pieces of fruit are rich in colour and solid in form. They seem to have weight. The folds of the tablecloth create a rhythm in the painting, which helps to hold the fruit together. There is a feeling of calm and timelessness in this work.

In the **composition** of this painting, Cézanne has used colour to bring out the structure or volume of his objects: cool colours (blues and greens) are used in the shadows and warm colours (pale lemon, orange) are used for highlights.

The fruit, the tablecloth and the area behind seem to be close to the viewer. There is little sense of depth.

Cézanne began as an **Impressionist**, but he became disillusioned with the way light seemed to dissolve the forms. Cézanne didn't want to paint a fleeting glimpse of an image like the Impressionists, but wanted to create an art which had a feeling of permanence, a sense of structure. He developed his own individual style. He did, however, adopt from the Impressionists their love of unmixed, pure colour and thick, short brushstrokes. He added a sense of solidity to his objects by the careful placement of colours rather than the use of tone (the adding of black or brown to colours) favoured by earlier artists. He worked with the principle that cool colours recede whereas warm colours come forward in a painting.

Cézanne's brushstrokes became more block-like as his style developed. He added defining lines. He is generally termed a **Post-Impressionist**. The Post-Impressionists began working in the Impressionist style then went their individual ways, each creating a unique style. Each artist was a great influence on future artists. Van Gogh, the next artist discussed in this book, is also termed a Post-Impressionist.

With his use of coloured patches in a shallow space, Cézanne led the way in a new approach to depicting reality, seen particularly in the later work of the **Cubists**. Art was heading towards **abstraction**.

STUDYING ART

Critical study
Structural frame
1. How has Cézanne depicted the objects in his painting? Has he softly blended his colours, used great detail or adjoined strokes of colour?
2. What was new about Cézanne's method of creating tone?
3. What purpose does the drapery (tablecloth) fulfil in the composition of the painting? Can you see any other colours in it other than white?

Historical study
Cultural frame
4. How does Cézanne's work differ from that of the Impressionists?
5. In what ways did Cézanne's style change or develop over the years?
6. How was the work of Cézanne a great influence on future modern artists? Make a flow map or diagram to show the major art styles after Post-Impressionism.

Structural frame
7. Locate other examples of paintings by Cézanne. Was fruit a popular choice of subject for Cézanne? What else did he paint?

FURTHER RESEARCH

Fruit has been a popular subject for still life paintings since ancient Roman times. Find two examples from different times or cultures and dicuss how they have been painted and why (their purpose).

MAKING ART

Structural frame
1. Paint a bowl of fruit, emphasising the solidity and roundness of the fruit. Try placing a lamp on one side so that you get definite shadows. Like Cézanne, avoid using black or brown.
2. Create an interesting design for a juice container. For inspiration, look carefully at the shape, texture and inner structure of fruit.

Postmodern frame
3. Appropriate (borrow) the image of the bowl of fruit in Cézanne's painting. Change its surroundings to create a comment on gluttony or world starvation. Use any media you wish — charcoal, ink, pastels, paint, collage, graphics software, digital media. You may include words to help communicate your meaning.

Vincent Van Gogh

(1853–90, Dutch)

Frame: subjective
Form: oil painting
Conceptual framework: There is a strong relationship between what Van Gogh painted and his life experiences and moods.

CRITICAL STUDY

This is Van Gogh's own chair, and his pipe and tobacco. It is painted with bright, bold colours, yellow against blue. A single chair as a subject seems to suggest loneliness.

The paint has been applied thickly, creating texture. The short, choppy brushstrokes and the dashes of colour he learnt from the Impressionists have been exaggerated. The chair has strongly drawn blue outlines, which relate to the walls. This creates unity in the painting. Colour and texture are the most important elements in this work.

The angle of the chair and the slight tilt of the floor draw the viewer into the painting. The dominance of diagonal lines and the close-up focus add to the emotional impact.

This simple room interior gives us clues about Van Gogh's life. He obviously lived a fairly hard life with few luxuries. Look at the paintings of rooms by Margaret Olley (page 84) and Chardin (page 102) to compare their way of life.

The Chair and the Pipe 1888
Oil on canvas, 50 × 63 cm
Reproduced by courtesy of the Trustees, The National Gallery, London

HISTORICAL STUDY

Van Gogh decided to be an artist at the age of twenty-seven. He had earlier put the enthusiasm, intensity and dedication that we see in his paintings into other careers, including art dealer and preacher. None of these suited his personality.

Van Gogh's first drawings and paintings were of fields and labourers in the Netherlands. In 1886 he moved to Paris and began to choose lighter colours and more cheerful themes. On his move to Arles in the sunny south of France, his works became luminous and energetic. In his studio in 'The Yellow House' he considered himself an independent artist, and experimented with the many theories he had heard in Paris.

The chair in *The Chair and the Pipe* had been depicted earlier by Van Gogh in *Bedroom at Arles*, a painting which was to decorate his house in anticipation of the arrival of his friend and fellow artist Gauguin. Van Gogh hoped to set up an artists' colony in Arles. In *Bedroom at Arles* the room is shown empty with an air of expectancy. Here everything is in pairs, two pictures, two pillows and two chairs. He had hoped his loneliness would end but the friendship did not last. With its single chair, *The Chair and the Pipe* was painted when Van Gogh realised that Gauguin was likely to abandon him.

While in Arles, Van Gogh painted landscapes, still lifes and penetrating self-portraits. His life was a constant struggle against poverty, loneliness, alcoholism and insanity. His experiences and emotions are expressed in his art. Van Gogh suffered a series of violent mental episodes and shot himself in the chest at the age of thirty-seven. He is generally termed a Post-Impressionist because his work was influenced by the Impressionists' love of light and obvious brushstrokes. Van Gogh, like the other Post-Impressionists, went on to create a unique style of his own.

STUDYING ART

Critical study

Subjective frame
1. What do you like most about this artwork?
2. How does it make you feel? Would you like to be in this room?
3. Why do you think Van Gogh included the pipe?
4. What qualities in *The Chair and the Pipe* do you think are unique to Van Gogh?

Structural frame
5. Describe Van Gogh's paint application.
6. How has Van Gogh made a painting of a simple chair interesting?
7. What do you feel is the most important part of the picture? How has the artist made that part stand out from the rest of the painting?

Historical study

8. Name three other well-known Post-Impressionists.
9. During the ten years that Van Gogh struggled for self-expression, he wrote constantly to his brother, Theo, who provided spiritual and financial support. In a letter to Theo in 1882, Vincent wrote:

'I want to reach so far that people will say of my work: he feels deeply, he feels tenderly — notwithstanding my so-called roughness, perhaps even because of this . . . It is true that I am often in the greatest misery, but still there is within me a calm pure harmony and music.'[2]

Considering this evidence, from what frame of art do you think Van Gogh approaches his paintings — *subjective*, *structural* or *cultural*? What was Van Gogh's view on life and his art?

Structural frame

10. From a letter from Van Gogh to Theo, 10 September 1889:

'[A]rrange your brushstrokes in the direction of the objects — certainly it is more harmonious and pleasant to look at, and you add whatever you have of serenity and cheerfulness.'[3]

In a letter to Theo in October 1888 Van Gogh wrote:

'This time it's just simply my bedroom, only here colour is to do everything . . . is to be suggestive here of rest or of sleep in general . . . looking at the picture ought to rest the brain or rather the imagination.'[4]

What do these two quotes tell you about Van Gogh's working methods? What was he aiming to do in the painting of his bedroom? What methods was he using to achieve it?

FURTHER RESEARCH

Postmodern frame
Several artists, such as Brett Whiteley, Martin Sharp and Gordon Bennett, have appropriated images from Van Gogh's paintings and transformed them into a new artwork. Locate one of these artworks and explain how the reference to Van Gogh has added meaning to the work.

MAKING ART

Subjective frame
1. Do a painting of an object in your bedroom, using colour and brushstrokes to show your mood and personality.

Postmodern frame
2. Combine various images from Van Gogh's paintings to create your interpretation of his life experiences.

Max Dupain

(1911–92, Australian)

Frame: structural
Form: black and white photography
Conceptual framework: Dupain wished to use photography as a means of recording his world in such a way that viewers would see its beauty and sense of order.

Vocabulary

idiosyncratic: unique to a particular person; distinctive, unusual

Eggs c. 1930–35
Black and white photograph, 28.8 × 27.4 cm
Photograph courtesy of Jill White Photography

This photograph is a statement about the beauty of simplicity. The mood is calm. It implies a respect for everyday objects. We appreciate the purity of form of these objects.

The ovoid forms stand in contrast to the textured diagonal planks of wood. The strong light causes crisp shadows. These shadows emphasise the form and the relationships between the eggs and the wood. The high viewpoint is different from our normal perception of the subject. Dupain has taken eggs on a table and made them into art through his careful control of the image. The eggs have become an arrangement of abstract forms. The date of this photograph places this image within the era of Modernism in Australia.

By 1932–33 Dupain had begun to respond to modern European photography. He began to photograph industrial subjects such as wheat silos around the Pyrmont docks. His photography focused on geometry and starkness. The composition was often from an unusual viewpoint. Strong shadows were very important.

Dupain's work is expressive of Australian art in the 1930s and 1940s. At this time there was a growing acceptance of the simplification that came with Modernism. The sharp focus evident in his photographs helped him to create pure form and abstraction. He used shadows as a design element.

In the late 1930s Dupain experimented with Surrealism. He created puzzling imagery by means of multiple exposures and darkroom developing techniques.

Dupain's style is characterised by low- or high-angled viewpoints and close-ups, which communicates a feeling towards the subject.

Edmund Capon, director of the Art Gallery of New South Wales, was quoted as saying shortly after Dupain's death: 'To be a creative photographer, you have to have an **idiosyncratic** eye — to see the mundane subject through a different viewpoint, and that is what (Max) was able to do. He created a new view of things and opened that view up to the outside world and made them more aware of photography'.[5]

STUDYING ART

Critical study
Structural frame
1. Dupain restricted his work to black and white photography. Do you feel *Eggs* would have been as successful in colour? Back up your opinion by referring to particular aspects of the photograph.

Historical study
Subjective frame
2. Consider the statement by Capon as to what is needed to be a creative photographer. Do you agree with this statement regarding Max Dupain? You might like to look at other examples of Dupain's work before you form your opinion.

FURTHER RESEARCH

Structural and cultural frames
Investigate the work of photographer Olive Cotton, for example, *Tea Cup Ballet* (1935), and Margaret Preston's painting *Implement Blue*. (Both images can be seen in the Art Gallery of New South Wales. Go to www.artgallery.nsw.gov.au, click on 'Collection', then 'Simple search'. Read and accept the conditions, then enter the artist's name and title of the work to view them online.)
1. What similarities do you see in these artworks and the work of Dupain?
2. What can we learn from these images about the lifestyle and attitudes of Australia in the 1930s?

MAKING ART

Cultural frame
1. Arrange a group of mundane objects which would reflect Australia in the 1990s. Take a series of photographs using Dupain's techniques of strong light across the objects and unusual viewpoints.

Postmodern frame
2. Appropriate (borrow) Dupain's arrangement of objects, but alter their surfaces to make them a social comment on the twenty-first century. (If possible, transform them into colour.) You might like to consider humour in your work.

Margaret Olley

(b. 1923, Australian)

Frame: structural
Form: painting
Conceptual framework: Olley paints her personal world, creating a feeling of joy, lusciousness and vitality for her audience to enjoy.

composition: the placement of figures and objects; the organisation of an artwork

still life: arrangement of lifeless things such as ornaments, fruit, flowers and musical instruments

Pomegranates 1966
Oil on board, 75 × 100 cm
Private collection, courtesy of the artist

CRITICAL STUDY

This **still life** is naturalistic and rich in colour. It expresses Margaret Olley's joy in living things and pride in her possessions. Her brushstrokes are heavily laden with paint, free and expressive. Fruit balances precariously amongst the folds of fabric. The fruit is bursting open, reminding us of its short life. There is a feeling of abundance or lusciousness. This is mainly created by the thick, glossy paint and vibrant colours.

Form has been carefully created by Olley's use of light and colour. Her objects have been given a sense of weight. The use of blue unifies the work. A whitish blue has been added to the highlights while a grey-blue is used in the shadows. This gives life and vitality to her basically red/ green colour scheme. The definite light source adds to the sense of volume of the objects. The spaces in between the objects are as important as the objects themselves to the **composition**.

Her subject matter is a still life, and it suggests her personal domestic surroundings.

HISTORICAL STUDY

Margaret Olley was born in Lismore, New South Wales, and educated in Brisbane. In 1943 she moved to Sydney and studied at East Sydney Technical College (then Sydney's best art school). She graduated with first class honours. She later studied in Paris for a time. Her usual subject matter is immediate environment, including room interiors, still lifes and self-portraits.

Olley has been highly regarded by her contemporary artists. Many painted her, including Russell Drysdale, Donald Friend and William Dobell, who won the Archibald Prize in 1948 with her portrait (see page 23). Jeffrey Smart also included her in one of his paintings exhibited at the Australian Galleries in 1995.

Olley was influenced by the colours of Matisse (see page 13), the forms of Cézanne (see page 78) and the simple solidity of everyday objects of Chardin (see page 102), amongst others.

It is as if she is bringing together all the traditions of the still life in art history. Many of the objects in her works have symbolic meanings similar to the work of the northern Renaissance painters such as Van Eyck. In Olley's paintings, sun-coloured fruits, marigolds and sunflowers represent fertility. Cherries are symbolic of optimism. Apprehension is represented by apples and dandelions.

Olley paints to a self-imposed schedule, working from early in the morning. 'I'm using my environment, it's always changing, evolving — nothing ever stays the same', she explains. 'Smell is a very important element. If you can capture smell that is really achieving something.'[6]

Artist and art critic James Gleeson has said: 'I can think of no other Australian painter of the present time who orchestrates his or her themes with such undiluted richness as Margaret Olley ... a painter who ... expresses her joy in the beauty of living things.'[7]

STUDYING ART

Critical study
Subjective frame
1. What do you feel when you look at Olley's pomegranates? Describe them.

Structural frame
2. Which of the following is important in Olley's paintings? movement, direction, form, line, tone, texture, dramatic emotion, colour
3. List the objects you see and describe their surface texture.
4. How does the surface of the background add to the effect of this painting?
5. Where is the light coming from and what effect does it give to the work?

Historical study
Subjective frame
6. Look at the portrait of Margaret Olley by William Dobell on page 23. Do you think the mood of the still life by Olley matches the mood or personality of her portrait by Dobell? How?

FURTHER RESEARCH

Cultural frame
Find two examples of still life paintings other than the examples in this book. Explain how they reflect the culture or time in which they were painted. How are they similar to or different from the work of Olley?

MAKING ART

Subjective frame
1. Arrange a still life with objects from your home. Interpret it as a drawing, painting or pastel work.
2. Scan into your computer photographs of fruit from magazines. Manipulate these using Photoshop or another graphics program.

Janet Fish

(b. 1938, American)

Frames: structural; cultural
Form: oil painting
Conceptual framework: To Fish, the art object is more important than reflecting her world.

POP ART

> an art movement of the 1950s and 1960s originating in London and New York. It used images of popular culture and consumer society and often borrowed techniques from commercial art.

SUPER-REALISM

> style of art influenced by photography, and characterised by sharp focus and precise realism

CRITICAL STUDY

A row of bottles has been painted without emotion. Realism and the play of light on transparent, reflecting surfaces seems to be important. There is no apparent meaning attached to the objects.

Structurally the artwork is ordered and in sharp focus. The pattern created by the strong light falling on liquids, shaped glass and relief lettering is of major importance in the painting. The activity within the objects and the play of light is more interesting than the edges or form of the objects. Fish has shown us the beauty present in everyday objects. These objects are part of our present culture. The way they are set in such a shallow space is suggestive of mass media advertising.

HISTORICAL STUDY

During the late 1960s, after **Pop Art**, a highly realistic style of painting developed called **Super-Realism** or Photo-Realism. Its main influence was photography. The snapshot instantaneity, stop-action stillness, and sharp focus possible with a photograph were painstakingly transferred into paint. There was a reappearance of the still life as subject matter. This allowed for experimentation with the formal elements of art, a working out of theories. As Fish has said, 'I always pick things for formal reasons rather than for content'.[8]

Unlike most of the Photo-Realists, Fish does not actually work from a photograph. But her work is in the same realistic style and shows an awareness of sharp focus and reflections, both characteristic of Super-Realism.

Gordon's Gin Bottles is part of Fish's earlier body of work, in which she concentrated on crowded rows of glasses or bottles, for example *6 Vinegar Bottles* and *Kraft Salad Dressing*. Her work in the 1980s still showed an interest in liquids and reflections on glass. These days, Fish includes a wider variety of objects within a single still life arrangement. Colour and light continue to dominate.

STUDYING ART

Critical study
Structural frame

1. Look at the dimensions of this painting. How does the view of these bottles at such a large scale affect your interest in or impression of the work? What areas appear more important?
2. Which do you think is more important to Fish — the abstract effects of light on her shapes or the depiction of three-dimensional form (weight and volume)?

Historical study
Cultural frame

3. Can you see any influence from Pop Art in *Gordon's Gin Bottles*?
4. We are confronted by the images, not led into the space as in the work of Cézanne. How does this reflect the historical time and culture of each artwork?

ESSAY

Art practice

Both Andy Warhol (page 96) and Janet Fish have created artworks showing glass bottles. The methods used in these works were similar, but Andy Warhol moved away from handpainting his artworks. Research other examples by Warhol and explain how the art practice in them varied.

MAKING ART

1. Take a series of photographs of glass objects, concentrating on sharp focus, reflections and transparent effects.
2. Do a detailed drawing of a section of a glass, bottle or glass jug partly filled with a bubbly drink such as cola. Try to choose a glass item which has a pattern cut into it or a textured surface.

Gordon's Gin Bottles 1972
Oil on canvas, 183 × 112.4 cm
© Janet Fish, licensed by VISCOPY, Australia, 2004

Yasumasa Morimura

(b. 1951, Japanese)

Frame: postmodern
Form: digital manipulation
Conceptual framework: The idea of the originality of an artwork has been challenged. The audience requires art knowledge to appreciate many of Morimura's works.

Vocabulary

appropriation: the act of putting a familiar image in a new context to change its meaning

mediated: not direct or immediate; conveyed through a second or third medium, such as television

pastiche: art that borrows from different styles and combines them into a new artwork

Discussion

Is this artwork more relevant to you — to your life and the present — than the original by Cézanne? (see page 78)

Criticism and the Lover A 1990
Coloured photograph, transparent medium, 180 × 225 cm
© the artist. Collection Iwaki City Art Museum
Photograph courtesy of the artist

At first glance we see Cézanne's still life *Apples and Oranges* (1895) (see page 78). But on closer inspection we see that the apples and oranges have 'grown faces'. Morimura has interpreted Cézanne's artwork with humour. The apples and oranges have been transformed by the use of a computerised image scanner.

There is a hint that modern technology may replace the skill of the artist. This artwork seems to be asking if our attitudes towards art masterpieces are still valid in this time of mass media and modern technology.

Morimura has been placing images of himself in paintings and exhibiting internationally since 1988. In his coloured photograph *Daughter of Art History Theatre A* (1989) he inserted his image in the French Impressionist Manet's painting *The Bar at the Folies Bergère* (1981). With this work we have to re-interpret not only an Eastern face in a Western painting, but also a change in sex.

Morimura's work displays many of the devices and attitudes of the Postmodern style. Characteristics of Postmodernism include:
- crossing of conventional boundaries, mixing of styles and drawing upon several art traditions
- **appropriation** and **pastiche**
- belief that nothing is original, that it has all been done before
- ideas — social, political, gender-based, racial, philosophical, and artistic — often old ideas in new contexts, producing new results
- the use of contemporary culture as subject matter
- a reaction against the narrowness that Modernism had developed into, particularly abstract and minimalist art
- satire, humour, parody.

Postmodernism was a reaction against some of the ideals of Modernism, particularly the concept of purity, of striving for something new and original.

The Postmodernists realised that in our present **mediated** world of mass production and advertising, the original image may not exist. We see the *Mona Lisa* in advertisements, on travel posters, even on tea towels. Postmodernism blurs the division between so-called 'high art' and popular culture. Popular culture became valid subject matter. Artists appropriated images from past styles or other cultures and placed them in a new context, thus giving them new meaning.

Morimura does not confine his interest to Modernist painters; for example, he has appropriated the paintings of Rembrandt, a seventeenth-century Dutch artist. It is interesting that a Japanese artist chooses Western masterpieces to appropriate. He uses artists like Monet, Manet and Gauguin, whose imagery was influenced by Japanese art.

Postmodernists have also incorporated new forms of art derived from modern technology (such as computer imagery), as in the work of Morimura.

STUDYING ART

Critical study

Subjective frame
1. Describe the expression on the faces in *Criticism and the Lover A*.
2. What do you think Morimura was trying to say in this artwork?

Cultural frame
3. Is this work a comment about place, time, class, race or gender?

Structural frame
4. Can you think of an advertisement or video clip where a computer image scanner has also been used to blend unusual images together in this way?

Postmodern frame
5. Look up the definition of the words 'irony' and 'parody' in a dictionary. Would you apply either word to this artwork?
6. How does Morimura make you reassess Cézanne's original artwork *Apples and Oranges*?

Historical study
7. Which characteristics of Postmodernism do you think best apply to this work by Morimura?

FURTHER RESEARCH

Investigate the influence of Japanese art on Monet and Gauguin.

MAKING ART

Postmodern frame
Incorporate photocopies or computer-scanned images of your own face into a past artwork of your choice to create a humorous Postmodern artwork.

Marcel Duchamp

(1887–1968, French)

Frames: structural; cultural
Form: ready-made sculptures
Conceptual framework: Duchamp was largely responsible for widening what is acceptable as art. He established that artists' ideas and perception were important — not just their skill.

Vocabulary

ready-made: a selected object in its unaltered state which is exhibited as a work of art

DADA   **a modern art movement that was anti-art and tried to shock its audience (from a French word meaning 'hobby horse')**

CRITICAL STUDY

Two commonplace items have been joined, given a title, and exhibited by a practising artist (a painter). They have been transformed into a work of art.

Duchamp invented a new form of art. Such common objects (sometimes altered) presented as a work of art have become known as **ready-mades**. In *Bicycle Wheel*, the stool reminds us of the tradition of displaying sculptures on an elaborate base or pedestal. Overall it is an 'anti-art establishment' statement and raises questions such as: where is the traditional skill of the sculptor as carver, modeller or metal caster? How is it a beautiful, 'precious', original art object?

Bicycle Wheel also appears as a comment on mechanisation, the wheel being the invention which eventually led to the mechanical age.

Duchamp originally hung *Hat Rack* (opposite page) from the ceiling in his New York apartment. Like *Bicycle Wheel*, it no longer fulfils its original function. Without its function, we look at the form itself and the shadow it creates. 'Asked why he occasionally hung works from the ceiling, Duchamp replied that it was to escape the conformity which dictated that works of art should be hung on a wall or presented on an easel.'[9] This quote from the artist helps us understand the main intention of his artmaking: to be different; to create artworks that break traditions and shock the viewer.

Bicycle Wheel New York 1951
(third version after lost original of 1913)
Assemblage: metal wheel, 63.8 cm diameter, mounted on painted wood stool, 60.2 cm high: overall 128.3 × 63.8 × 42 cm
The Museum of Modern Art, New York
The Sidney and Harriet Janis Collection
Photograph © 1996 The Museum of Modern Art, New York
© Marcel Duchamp, licensed by VISCOPY, Australia, 2004

Duchamp was born in France. His early art training was in Paris, where he began painting in a Post-Impressionist style. When Duchamp exhibited a bicycle wheel on a stool and called it 'art', it shocked the public. These pre-made objects, turned into art by their title and exhibition in an art space, became known as ready-mades. Duchamp's ready-mades included a bottle rack, a urinal (upside down) and a hat rack suspended from the ceiling. His titles often reveal his humour; for example, a snow shovel has been titled *In Advance Of a Broken Arm*.

Hat Rack 1917 reconstructed 1964
Wooden hat rack
no. 2 from an edition of 8
23.5 × 44.0 cm
signed on bottom of base, fibre-tipped pen, 'Marcel Duchamp'
Purchased 1973
NGA 1973.481
National Gallery of Australia, Canberra
© Marcel Duchamp, licensed by VISCOPY, Australia, 2004

Duchamp worked in New York from 1915, along with Spaniard Francis Picabia and the New York photographer Man Ray. Their ideas and style of working were very similar to the **Dada** movement that would be established in 1916 in Zurich, Switzerland. Dada was a reaction to the outrage and grief of World War I which had begun in 1914. Within the protest against war was a protest against the mechanisation of the world, since victory in war goes to the side which invents the swiftest, most powerful machines. Dada was more a cultural revolt by artists than an art movement as such, and it spread throughout Europe. Dada produced fascinating and illogical artworks which were anti-art in approach. Some were nonsensical; others carried a social or political message of outrage. Its mood was explained by Hans Richter: 'We destroyed, we insulted, we despised — and we laughed'.[10]

In 1919 Duchamp returned to Paris and associated with the Dada group there. The fantasy style of Surrealism was greatly influenced by Dada, with its concept of the random selection of objects and the element of chance. Surrealism was also influenced by Dada's method of combining objects and images in unusual ways.

Duchamp settled permanently in New York in 1942, and became a United States citizen in 1955.

STUDYING ART

Historical study
Structural frame
Art historian Norbert Lynton has written that although Dada art is diverse, the unifying feature is 'the intention of challenging established notions of what art should be'.[11] What methods did the Dadaists use in their attempts to challenge the idea of what art was at the time?

ESSAY

Conceptual framework
How did the work of Duchamp change the role of the artist and question the traditional idea of what an artwork is?

FURTHER RESEARCH

Find an example of poetry written at this time (1915–1920), which involved the random choice of words, resulting in a poem more reliant on the rhythm of sounds than on meaning. How was the attitude of the writer similar to the Dada artists?

MAKING ART

Cultural frame
Create a sculpture using a ready-made object. Transform an existing object to make a statement about your society.

Rosalie Gascoigne

(1917–99, New Zealand, worked in Australia)

Frames: postmodern; structural; cultural

Forms: sculpture; installations

Conceptual framework: Gascoigne reacted directly with her world, collecting objects to create sensitive artworks that suggest various meanings to the viewer.

Vocabulary

assemblage: a collection of 'found' materials arranged to make a two- or three-dimensional composition

icon: a well-known, respected image (original meaning: a sacred image)

recontextualise: to change the way objects/materials are normally seen

CRITICAL STUDY

With the sculpture *Tiepolo Parrots*, Rosalie Gascoigne took familiar, discarded objects and made us look at them in a new light. These remnants of country living and of outback Australia are given new meaning. She did not choose perfect, new objects as symbols. She used old, weathered pieces of timber and parts of packing cases with their labels attached. This creates a wonderful arrangement of contrasting textures. We are drawn to the tones and colours of the wood, to the shadows of the dents.

The materials themselves seem to suggest a history; there is evidence of old nail holes, for example. Wooden packing cases are no longer used much when transporting items such as fruit, vegetables and bottles. Plastic crates are now more often used. Gascoigne's selection of old wooden cases thus suggests the past. She also used the 1930s parrot logo for Arnott's biscuits as a further social comment. The parrot is a symbol of the bush and the logo is an **icon** of domestic Australian culture.

Steel Magnolias is a low-relief sculpture that hangs on a wall. It is constructed of old, weathered pieces of corrugated iron attached to a backing of wood. The pieces of iron have been collected then carefully arranged according to their texture, colour and length. We appreciate it almost as a painting in subtle greys and beiges. The interesting textures are created by the peeling paint and nail holes rather than by the artist's brushwork.

Tiepolo Parrots 1976
Wood, cardboard, coloured inks, metal, 61.2 × 56.4 × 23 cm
Reproduced by permission of the National Gallery of Australia, Canberra
© Rosalie Gascoigne, licensed by VISCOPY, Australia, 2004

Gascoigne arrived in Australia in 1943. Her sculptures reflect the landscape and culture of country life in Australia. She assembled remnants (discarded fragments or pieces) of outback Australia helping us to see meaning in them. She collected wasted objects, making them new again by her arrangements and her works force us to think about re-using the useless. We no longer see these objects just as functional items; for example, sheets of corrugated iron are not merely building material, but are beautiful objects in terms of their shape, texture and colour (particularly with the process of rusting). *Tiepolo Parrots* is part of a series of **assemblages** based on beeboxes found at an abandoned apiary near Canberra.

In Gascoigne's later work there is a strong link to the landscape rather than to containers or objects. She used weathered wood, road signs and natural materials, and though the materials seem randomly selected, they were placed in a carefully proportioned order. 'My environment is what has conditioned me and what I respond to daily. It's what I've got. My art must come out of that ... I combine things until they've got a presence — they're not a proper nothing, they are something, something else.'[12]

STUDYING ART

Cultural frame

1. Gascoigne's work refers to a way of life that is based in the country rather than in the city. What evidence do you see of this in her work?

Postmodern frame

2. How did Gascoigne **recontextualise** objects (change how and where they are normally seen) to give them new meaning?

Historical study

Structural frame

3. How did Gascoigne develop this form of art — the ready-made — from how it was originally used by Duchamp (see page 90)?

4. Artists practice: From Gascoigne's statements, what do you learn about her working methods and attitude towards her work?

Steel Magnolias 1994
104.5 × 98.5 cm
Collection of Amanda and Andrew Love, Sydney
Courtesy of the artist and Roslyn Oxley9 Gallery, Sydney

Ken Unsworth

(b. 1931, Australian)

Frames: subjective; postmodern
Forms: sculpture; installations
Conceptual framework: There is a strong relationship between the artist and his artworks. He involves his audience through the use of sound and movement or by requiring the audience to do something

Vocabulary

installation: an arrangement created for a particular site or gallery, creating an environment in itself

CRITICAL STUDY

There is a feeling of disquiet in *Table Piece*. It does not confront us but suggests to us the relationship of nature to manufactured objects, and the idea of gravity and balance. There is a feeling that an event or ritual has taken place. Something has definitely occurred. It seems to be an artwork of personal reflections, particularly if we compare it to the brash, popular imagery of Maria Kozic (see page 100).

Table Piece is an **installation**, which is a series of objects designed within a space. We are looking into a window of Unsworth's ideas and emotions. An image of a natural landform is on the wall and the two tiny figures in it suggest to us the power and majesty of nature. This is echoed in the large river stones or boulders resting precariously on the chairs. The stones are defying gravity, as are the chairs in the way they are suspended yet piercing the table. The fact that there are three chairs and three stones suggests an ancient ritual or religious event. The number three has throughout history had symbolic and spiritual significance (three represents the trinity in Christianity).

We are left to interpret the work ourselves from the range of ideas and emotions presented. A story seems to be told within this installation. Our understanding of it relies on our individual experiences and imagination.

This work is Postmodern in the way it expands our ideas about what art is and how it can be experienced. No rational answers are given.

Discussion

In *Sundry Appearances*, a more recent example of his work, Unsworth has continued with the ideas of anti-gravity and the tension between the manufactured and the natural object. Do you think he is commenting on any other issues?

HISTORICAL STUDY

Unsworth has worked in a variety of forms, including sculpture, which he began to exhibit from 1967. His sculptures of 1973–78 included outdoor earthworks. His performance work began in 1975, but by 1980 included only static human participation. His 1975 performance work *Five Secular Settings for Sculpture as Ritual and Burial Place* dealt with suspension, balance and the mass of the body as an element in space. A highly charged emotional atmosphere accompanied these performances. They were very theatrical, with controlled lighting, timing and atmosphere. In one performance, *Body as Object* (1975), the body was suspended by the neck from large beams of wood, suggesting sacrifice or crucifixion.

From 1976 Unsworth worked with environmental installations, usually motorised elements and sound. His installations are frequently rooms with limited access, which we view through a window, or standing at an entrance. We, the spectators, are allowed to see only fragments of Unsworth's emotions and life experiences. He does not explain his work, but we experience it like a poem; that is, pieces and suggestions are given in which we may find meaning. In his installation *Adieu* (1987), a curtain flapped at a window, creating a sense of mystery.

STUDYING ART

Critical study

Subjective frame

1. We do not normally think of the objects 'chair' and 'stone' together. Why do you think Unsworth has put them together in the one work and what effect does this have?
2. *Table Piece* is objects only, but is the presence of humans hinted at in any way?

Structural frame

3. Unsworth is using the traditional sculptural idea of volume (three-dimensional form) in space. What other sculptural ideas has he used?

Postmodern frame — Conceptual framework

4. How does Unsworth extend the traditional media of art and the concept of an artwork being a precious, timeless object to be kept in a gallery?

FURTHER RESEARCH

Historical study

1. Research other artworks by Unsworth in which he has used river stones, for example *Untitled*, 1975. How does the use of these natural objects have relevance to past cultures and ceremonies or rituals?
2. Investigate the work of early performance artists in Australia. Consider the work of Mike Parr, Kevin Mortensen, Stelarc and Jill Orr (see page 18).

MAKING ART

Structural frame
Design a sculpture/installation which is a statement about balance and gravity.

Table Piece 1985
Mixed media, 89 × 189.5 × 114.7 cm. Exhibited in the Bicentennial Perspecta, The Art Gallery of New South Wales. Courtesy Boutwell Draper Gallery

Sundry Appearances 1995
Piano, wood, 136 × 148 × 62 cm
Courtesy Boutwell Draper Gallery

Andy Warhol

(1928–87, American)

Frames: cultural; structural
Form: painting
Conceptual framework: Warhol challenged the art object and the role of the artist. His artworks were designed to appeal to a wide audience.

Vocabulary

POP ART

an art movement of the 1950s and 1960s originating in London and New York. It used images of popular culture and consumer society and often borrowed techniques from commercial art.

Discussion

Pop Art was originally viewed with distaste and ridiculed by the critics. Norbert Lynton wrote: 'Pop Art seems on the whole to leave aside the basic questions and values of art'.[13] Alan Solomon believed that 'the new artists have brought their own sensibilities and their deepest feelings to bear on a range of distasteful, stupid, vulgar, assertive and ugly manifestations of the worst kind of our society'.[14] Do you agree with these quotes? The surprising thing was that most of these early Pop Art exhibitions were sell-outs. Why do you think this was so?

CRITICAL STUDY

This artwork consists of multiple images of an everyday supermarket food item. By their repetition we are reminded of their mass-produced origin. This is not a traditional still life of fruit but a reflection of our modern consumer world. The bottles act more as symbols than as individual objects.

Even the way the bottles have been reproduced against a pristine white background makes them impersonal. There is no hint of the artist's personal involvement or emotional response to the object. Its reality has been taken away by its duplication and in the process the representation of these objects becomes an artwork. We respond to them in art terms, being aware of the repetition of line, shape and pattern, the careful placement of the objects creating a sense of order or unity and a gentle rhythm. These bottles have gained a new meaning.

Green Coca-Cola Bottles 1962
Oil on canvas, 209.6 × 144.8 cm
Collection of Whitney Museum of American Art
Purchase, with funds from the Friends of the Whitney Museum of American Art
© 1997 Andy Warhol Foundation for the Visual Arts, New York
Photo by Geoffrey Clements
Photograph © 1996: Whitney Museum of American Art
© Andy Warhol, licensed by VISCOPY, Australia, 2004

Andy Warhol has been called the king of **Pop Art**. He was obsessed with stars and celebrities, and constantly sought publicity himself. Often criticised for being a shrewd businessman and a workaholic, he achieved the fame and celebrity status he sought, and his artworks have become some of the most notable images of this century.

In 1949 Warhol went to New York and became a successful commercial artist and illustrator. By the early 1960s he had begun to paint comic strip characters and images derived from advertising, such as Campbell's soup cans and Coca-Cola bottles. He also painted celebrities at this time. The soup cans were painted by projecting a photograph onto the canvas and tracing it. By 1963 he had substituted a silkscreen process for hand painting. By using photographic techniques and the silkscreen method, Warhol commented on the mass media world of America at the time. His other subjects included multiple images of Elvis Presley and Marilyn Monroe, symbols of the mass media age.

Warhol saw himself as a machine for creating pictures. He called his studio 'The Factory', and employed assistants there. This was against the Modernist idea that an art object must be original and unique. His artworks were an upmarket version of commercial advertising, such as the posters that decorate bus shelters; anything personal or intimate was eliminated. Even his portraits were not based on drawings but on polaroid camera shots. In the mid 1960s he made films. In the 1970s he began to paint again, this time monumental portraits of Mao Tse-tung.

Warhol's artworks stand as a record of the 1960s in America, from the grieving Jackie Kennedy to Dick Tracey, from the American dollar bill to images of film stars. Food, death, sex and fame were his subjects.

STUDYING ART

Critical study
Structural frame — Art practice
1. Describe the methods used by Warhol to create his art.
2. How do you think his early training as a graphic artist influenced his work?
3. What did his use of repetition achieve?

Historical study
Structural and subjective frames
4. An art critic wrote in 1973 that 'Warhol correctly foresaw the end of painting and became its executioner'.[15] What is this critic talking about? Is this an emotional statement or simply a statement of fact?

Cultural frame
5. By looking at Warhol's work and that of other Pop Artists, what do you think was their main subject matter? How did it represent America in the 1960s? The following quote by Pop Artist Richard Hamilton may help you.

'The surprising thing is that it took until the mid-fifties for artists to realise that the visual world had been altered by the mass media and changed dramatically enough to make it worth looking at again in terms of painting.'[16]

Postmodern frame
6. Do you see any social comment in Warhol's works? Consider how consumerism and mass production have increased since the time of Pop Art.

FURTHER RESEARCH

Research the work of the British Pop Artists. How was their work slightly different from American Pop Art? Why do you think this is so?

MAKING ART

Cultural frame
1. Choose symbols for Australia in the 1990s. Create a drawing or painting of one.
2. Create a video representing the culture of present times.

Claes Oldenburg

(b. 1929, Swedish, working in America)

propaganda: biased information that aims to further one's cause or damage another cause or group

tactile: relating to the sense of touch; inviting the viewer to touch

Discussion

An art critic at the time made this statement about Pop Art: 'As hideous, vulgar, repulsive and cheap as some of them may appear, these commercial artefacts constitute a new potent means of visual communication.'[17] Do you think this criticism is still relevant today?

CRITICAL STUDY

A commercial foodstuff, french fries, has been presented with a humorous twist in *Shoestring Potatoes Spilling From a Bag*. This giant-sized hanging sculpture was made from painted canvas and filled with kapok.

What is the symbolism in having the bag upside down with the chips falling out? Are they not edible? They are no longer hot. Are they there as a display item only? The bag itself appears as a symbol of its commercial, fast-food, mass-produced nature. The meaning would not be the same if the chips were presented on a plate.

Oldenburg's original interpretation of this mundane food item stands for the popular culture of America.

With *Floor Cone*, Oldenburg has taken an ice-cream cone — a familiar object from everyday life — but encouraged us to look at it in a new way. What is normally an inviting food object has become unappetising and possibly unhygienic. Oldenburg has created a large-scale, soft sculpture using synthetic polymer paint (acrylic) on canvas filled with foam rubber and cardboard boxes. This work relies on contrast. What is normally hard is now soft; what is normally small and upright (in your hand to avoid drips) is huge and lies along the floor.

Scale plays another important part in the transformation of this everyday object. The contrast in size between this sculpture and the real object gives this new object power as an artwork since it changes our perceptions.

HISTORICAL STUDY

Claes Oldenburg belonged to the Pop Art movement. In the mid 1950s, this developed simultaneously in the two biggest, busiest and most commercial capital cities in the Western world — London and New York. American Pop Art represented mass-produced urban culture, and accepted products of modern life as valid art forms.

Until this time, art had been for a select few: those with art understanding and knowledge. It had been unique, precious and enduring. The Pop Artists intended their art to be for the masses, to be young, witty, gimmicky and glamorous. It reflected the popular images of 'big business', and Pop Art subjects came from mass production and the media: comics, advertising, billboards, movie stars. Oldenburg chose common, mass-produced items of American society, which he transformed with his sense of humour. For example, he created a giant garden trowel which was exhibited in a park, and a clothes peg (*Clothespin*). The peg stood nearly as high as the multi-storey buildings behind it. Oldenburg was making fun of our dependence upon prized household goods.

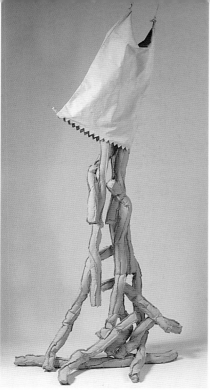

Floor Cone (Giant Ice-Cream Cone) 1962
Synthetic polymer paint on canvas filled with foam rubber and cardboard boxes
136.5 × 345.4 × 142 cm
The Museum of Modern Art, New York. Gift of Philip Johnson
Photograph © 1996 The Museum of Modern Art, New York

Shoestring Potatoes Spilling from a Bag 1966
Canvas stiffened with glue, filled with kapok, painted with acrylic
274.3 × 132.1 × 101.6 cm
dimensions variable
© Claes Oldenburg and Coosje van Bruggen

Oldenburg employs two main devices to transform his objects. He changes the scale or size so that his slice of hazelnut cake seems to take up a whole room. He also changes the medium so that what is normally hard, such as a toilet or typewriter, is remade in soft, floppy vinyl or canvas.

Oldenburg has created art from the symbols of popular culture.

STUDYING ART

Critical study
Subjective frame
1. Would you like to eat the ice-cream as portrayed in *Floor Cone*? Give reasons.
2. What words come to mind when you look at Oldenburg's version of an ice-cream?

Structural frame
3. What visual and **tactile** qualities have been changed from reality in Oldenburg's sculptures?
   What flavour do you think *Floor Cone* represents? How has Oldenburg symbolised this?

Cultural frame
4. What do you associate with eating ice-creams? Why and when do you eat chips (french fries)?
   Do you think these were the ideas behind or reasons for Oldenburg's choice of subject?

Historical study
Cultural frame
5. Art historian Robert Hughes has written: 'How you feel about Pop Art depends, to some extent, on how old you are'.[18] What he is referring to is that if you were born before 1960 and grew up with the optimism of mass media at a time when television, comics and advertisements in glossy magazines were new, you would react differently to someone born after 1960. Keeping in mind the changes that have occurred in popular culture since the 1960s, can you see why the public was excited by Pop Art?
   Hughes goes on to say that Pop Art was **propaganda** for its own culture. Look at Oldenburg's work and that of Warhol (see page 96) to find evidence to support this statement.
6. Who were Australia's leading artists at this time?

MAKING ART

Cultural frame
Design a piece of sculpture based on the idea of food being a cultural statement. Consider food's place in rituals and ceremonies (parties, weddings, religious rituals and festivals) or as a symbol of a country or race.

Maria Kozic

(b. 1957, Australian)

Frame: postmodern
Form: acrylic painting
Conceptual framework: Kozic makes the audience consider the purpose of an artwork.

Vocabulary

appropriate: put a familiar image in a new context to change its meaning

parody: a humorous exaggerated imitation

CRITICAL STUDY

Kozic has **appropriated** the image of Warhol's famous work *Campbell's Soup* (1965), and shattered the image. In doing so she also destroys the myth that art is precious and unique. Nothing is sacred.

Masterpieces (Warhol) 1986
Synthetic polymer paint on wood
182 × 122 cm
Collection of Museum of
Contemporary Art, Sydney
Reproduced courtesy of the artist and
Anna Schwartz Gallery, Melbourne

Masterpieces (Warhol) is a carefully painted version of Warhol's original silkscreen. By changing the media and altering the image, Kozic has made us look again and consider the image's social significance at the time it was created (in 1965), and its significance to our culture now. We are also made to consider the meaning and purpose of art.

In *I, Woman (Babet)* we see one of six dolls. Each has a Hollywood starlet's name, such as Tiffany, Melody or, in this case, Babet. Each doll stares wide-eyed across to her pocket-sized mirror image (the same except for closed eyes). This image of Babet appears to be more a portrait of a doll, complete with its wrapping of cellophane, than of a real person. The full lips, wide eyes and small nose are the typical features of dolls, and perhaps the ideals of starlets.

But this doll is not quite perfect — one eyebrow is smudged, a piece of hair falls down over the face, and there is a bruise on her cheek. Is this the result of hasty, cheap manufacturing in our fast consumer world? Is it cellophane wrapping or a plastic body bag?

HISTORICAL STUDY

Kozic makes us look again. Her *Nine Carnivorous Cats* (1980) are painted cut-outs, each side a different species. In another work — *Brady Bunch* — the image changes as you walk from one side to another, due to its concertina surface.

Kozic's images are generally taken from our present popular culture, for example television, comic romances, film posters and billboards. The form of her work also relates to mass media, as she often works in series. Her billboard project, which travelled around Australia in 1990, was a **parody** of the power of such advertising and a statement about the role of women.

It consisted of an image of herself with power drill and a collection of small male dolls. One doll was held in her hand, another strapped to her waist. It was completed with the caption 'Maria Kozic is a Bitch'.

Maria Kozic comments on our popular culture and mocks many of the respected great artists, including Picasso, Lichtenstein and, as we see here, Warhol.

I, Woman (Babet) 1994
Detail from diptych
Acrylic on cotton, 198 × 198 cm
Private collection, Melbourne
Reproduced courtesy of the artist and Anna Schwartz Gallery, Melbourne

FOCUS WORK
HISTORICAL STUDY

Frames: structural; cultural
Form: painting
Conceptual framework: Chardin and Fragonard reflect different attitudes towards their world.

Jean-Siméon Chardin
(1699–1779, French)

JEAN-SIMÉON CHARDIN
The Officer's Mess or **The Remains of a Lunch** c. 1763
Oil on canvas, 38 × 46 cm
Louvre, Paris

Chardin was a French painter of the **Rococo** period. His main subject was the still life.

ACTIVITY

Looking at these two artworks, what evidence can you find about life in eighteenth-century France? (This could be a class discussion.)

ESSAY

Discuss the significance of Chardin as a still life painter.

You will need to consider the following quotes by art historians. Consider also how Chardin's art differs, firstly, from other art of the time (for example, Fragonard's *The Swing*) and, secondly, from works of artists who painted still lifes after Chardin, and whose work you have seen in this chapter.

'Jean Chardin was one of the supreme artists of the eighteenth century and probably the greatest master of still life painting in the history of painting... His work was not of a social recorder... He ignored the public ostentation of his time, as well as the private misery ... idealizing the sober life of the Parisian petite bourgeoisie as embodied in his own household ... [His work] took place in the midst of an efflorescence of luxury, art — pink bodies, swirling fronds of gold ornament ... the Rococo style ... He deeply affected Cézanne and Matisse.'[19] (Robert Hughes)

'French artist Chardin showed what magical transformations could be effected in still lifes which are no longer cluttered inventories of luxuries but solemn, harmonious arrangements of everyday objects ... Chardin's colour is rich yet muted, the texture of his paint revealing in the humblest ingredients, nourishment for the spirit ... A painting in praise of the miracle of natural light falling on a group of familiar objects.'[20] (David Piper)

JEAN-HONORÉ FRAGONARD 1732–1806 (Rococo)
The Swing 1766
Oil on canvas, 83 × 66 cm
Reproduced by permission of the Trustees of the Wallace Collection, London

PLACES AND SPACES

DISCUSSION

1. Select one artwork from the selection opposite. Debate whether this artwork should be purchased by a major art gallery.
2. Imagine the artworks on the opposite page were exhibited together in a gallery under the title 'Places and Spaces'. Write a review of the exhibition for a newspaper.
3. As a group, select one artwork from this chapter that you would carry to safety if a fire broke out and you could save only one. Discuss what qualities make this artwork so valuable.
4. Look carefully at the artworks in this chapter and see if you can see any common subjects or themes.

Claude Lorrain

(1600–82, French)

Frame: structural
Form: oil painting
Conceptual framework: What at first appears to be just a realistic painting of a scene is actually instructing the audience on a mythological tale about Greek goddesses and gods.

Vocabulary

background:	area of a painting that depicts the far distance
Classicism:	style that refers back to Greek and Roman art, and has a sense of order and harmony
composition:	the placement of figures and objects; the organisation of an artwork
foreground:	part of a painting that depicts the area nearest the observer
melancholy:	gloomy state of mind; sadness
mythological:	belonging to a traditional myth or legend, usually to do with gods and goddesses
narrative:	a story

Landscape wth Ascanius Shooting the Stag of Sylvia 1682
Oil on canvas, 120 × 150 cm. Presented by Mrs W. F. R. Weldon in 1926
Ashmolean Museum, Oxford

The **composition** of this artwork is arranged to lead the eye to the horizon. It is a very careful, ordered approach to painting a landscape. Because Claude Lorrain (known as Claude) has concentrated on the organisation of this painting, we can say he has been working within the *structural frame*. The distant hills give a feeling of deep space. The three overlapping sections of **foreground**, midground and **background** create an extensive space which seems to dwarf the figures. There are columns in the foreground leading the eye to a circular building, to trees in the midground and then back to the distant hill in the background. If we look carefully, we see that this seemingly quiet, peaceful landscape holds the threat of violence: an arrow has been drawn and will soon be shot. Even the trees bend in the wind, suggesting a change is about to take place; they also act as a frame to focus our attention on the centre of the picture. The figures have a purpose in this landscape, for they tell the story of Ascanius shooting a stag. The silver-blue and green colours create a feeling of sadness.

Claude was a French artist who spent most of his life in Rome. Here he was inspired by the ancient architectural ruins and statues which he included in his beautifully ordered landscapes. He and Poussin are the two main artists of the style we call **Classicism**. In the seventeenth century, landscape was not considered worthy of being a subject in itself. Thus Claude has included in his work ancient ruins and figures from **mythological** or biblical **narratives**. Even though he did many sketches of real-life scenes on which to base his paintings, he carefully arranged the areas in his paintings to create what he thought was a perfect landscape — one of order and beauty like the most admired art of Rome.

Claude is also famous for the glowing light in his landscapes. The light gives a feeling of peace and sometimes a certain **melancholy**, as in *Landscape with Ascanius Shooting the Stag of Sylvia*. This painting was the last picture painted by Claude. The subject is taken from Virgil's epic poem *Aeneid*, in which Aeneas's son Ascanius kills a pet stag, thus provoking a war.

STUDYING ART

Critical study
Structural frame
1. How has Claude created a feeling of depth (being able to see into the distance) in this painting?

Cultural frame
2. Could this painting be an Australian landscape? Explain your reason.
3. What evidence do you see that this painting was created in another time?

Historical study
4. Why is this painting a Classical landscape rather than just a scene that Lorrain observed and painted?

ESSAY

Artist's practice
Look at the work of Mandy Martin on page 120. Do you think she could have been influenced at all by Claude Lorrain's landscape painting? Write a 500-word essay discussing each artist's art practice, including their:
- attitude towards the landscape
- use of light
- use of tone
- .painting techniques.

MAKING ART

Structural frame
Trace the main shapes and outlines in this painting. Look at the line along the top of the columns of the building in the front left corner. See how the line slopes downwards. Draw along the line, extending it until you reach the horizon. Do any other lines or shapes lead your eye to this spot — the focal point of the painting? Draw them in. Using the same basic composition of foreground, midground and background and the same focal point, change the buildings and landscape to create a contemporary Australian landscape drawing.

Joseph Mallord William Turner

(1775–1851, English)

Frame: subjective
Form: painting
Conceptual framework: Turner's artworks express his romantic response to the world, particularly the forces of nature and the effects of the weather on his subject.

Discussion

In 1836 John Ruskin wrote of Turner: 'He can... by the roll of his brush, and, with a few dashes of mingled colour... express the most complicated subject'.[1]

What evidence do you see in this painting to support Ruskin's opinion?

The Burning of the Houses of Lords and Commons, 16 October, 1834 1835
Oil on fabric, 92.7 × 123.2 cm. © The Cleveland Museum of Art, 1996
Bequest of John L. Severance, 1942.647

CRITICAL STUDY

The overall impression of this work is one of an awe-inspiring version of the forces of nature as a fire rages out of control. A glow of colour is caught in the billowing smoke and reflected in the water. The solid forms of bridge and buildings almost seem to melt into the hazy atmosphere. We can only just make out the crowds of people watching along the banks. The fire and the light itself appear to be the central theme.

In this painting Turner was working within the *subjective frame*, his approach being one based on his felt experiences and imagination. Turner used layers of thinned paint, then swirling, expressive brushstrokes on top. Layered washes of varnish were applied and plenty of linseed oil was used to keep the surface wet as he worked. This allowed him to create textures and areas of luminous light.

HISTORICAL STUDY

Turner was admitted to the Royal Academy of Art at the age of fourteen, and first exhibited there the following year. Most of his early works were watercolours. He went on many sketching trips in search of new dramatic landscapes to paint around England and Italy. There he was influenced by the work of Claude Lorrain. He was also influenced by the effects of light in Venice, where the light shimmers and is constantly reflected in the water.

In trying to depict the forces of nature, Turner arrived at his own unique kind of semi-abstraction. He constructed paintings out of light and colour. Turner was an innovative painter. He challenged tradition with his new technique and lack of solid, real forms and detail.

At the time, Turner's style was heavily criticised by the critics. In 1812, Sir George Beaumont stated, in regard to Turner's work, that 'much harm ... has been done by endeavouring to make painting in oil appear like watercolours ... in attempting to give lightness and clearness, the force of oil painting has been lost'.[2] But Turner also had his supporters. In 1816 Hazlitt called Turner the 'ablest landscape painter now living ... the painter of the elements'.[3]

Turner's main subject was the power and beauty of nature — snow storms, mist, frosty mornings, bright orange sunsets, windstorms, sleet and steam, recording nature's every mood. He is known as a Romantic painter owing to his personal poetical expressions of nature and the notion in his work of humanity pitted against the elements. Turner accompanied the exhibition of *Buttermere Lake with part of Cromack Water, Cumberland: A Shower* with lines of poetry. He agreed with the accepted opinion of the time that paintings should be morally and spiritually uplifting.

Turner's lighting, brilliant colour and atmospheric quality were a great influence on the Impressionists who followed. Turner produced over 20 000 artworks in his lifetime.

STUDYING ART

Subjective frame
1. How would you feel if you were one of the figures in the boat?
2. Write three lines of poetry to accompany this work.

Structural frame
3. Compare and contrast this work by Turner and the work by Claude Lorrain (see page 106). What are the differences in subject matter, composition, colour and paint application?

Historical study
4. List two influences on Turner's work.

ESSAY

Art practice
Discuss the methods and interests of Turner and Monet (page 110) in depicting the landscape.

FURTHER RESEARCH

John Constable and Turner were the most significant Romantic painters in England. They were both landscape painters but approached their work in different ways. Research these differences and explain why each artist is termed a 'Romantic' artist.

MAKING ART

Subjective frame
Create a painting or video inspired by a poem about nature. Record the poem in your Visual Arts Process Diary, and include with it the images and feelings it suggests to you.

Claude Monet

(1840–1926, French)

Frame: subjective; structural
Form: oil painting
Conceptual framework: Although Monet painted his own garden often, his main concern was to paint artworks that depicted the effects of light and weather on forms. Monet had a great effect on the art world.

Vocabulary

plein-air: painted out of doors, directly from nature
spontaneous: quickly done, unplanned, instinctive, unconstrained

IMPRESSIONISM   a modern art movement concerned with depicting light on the surface of objects

White Water Lilies 1899
Oil on canvas, 89 × 93 cm
Pushkin Museum, Moscow

Monet uses a new **spontaneous** approach. The flickering effects of the sun seem to be more important than realistic detail. There are patches of light and shadow, and the surface of the pond shimmers. There are clusters of pastel-coloured lilies that form horizontal bands. These are cut through with the vertical reflections of the weeping willows. Forms are dissolved in the light, so there are no clear outlines to the shapes.

Pure, unmixed colour has been thickly applied with obvious brush-strokes to create a brilliant, sparkling effect. As in Turner's work (see page 108), Monet shows similar interest in atmospheric effects.

The bridge forms an unbroken curve from one side of the canvas to the other.

HISTORICAL STUDY

Claude Monet was an important member of the **Impressionist** movement. Impressionism was the beginning of modern art. It developed at a time of social and technological change. The invention of the camera, for example, replaced one of the functions of art. No longer was the exact, detailed likeness of a subject the most important thing to achieve. Artists were now freer in the way they depicted their subject. Impressionists were concerned with depicting light on the surface of objects.

White Water Lilies depicts a very personal place for Monet. He created a superb garden, including this water garden, at his house in Giverny, France. Today, it is still possible to visit and admire his house and garden, which inspired his paintings for twenty years. This particular work is one of eighteen views of the Japanese-style, delicately arched wooden footbridge that Monet painted during 1899.

Monet's water lily paintings were very original for their time. In later works he enlarged smaller areas of the pond onto huge canvases so that he could experiment with his real interest — light and weather. He sometimes painted the same scenes over and over again at different times of the day. He did this to capture the effects of the changing sunlight. It was thus important to paint outside, directly from nature (**plein-air**).

Other Impressionist artists included Manet, Renoir, Sisley, Pissarro and Degas.

STUDYING ART

Critical study
Structural frame
1. How would Monet have had to paint to capture the changing effects of the weather and the time of day?
2. Describe Monet's method of applying paint.

Historical study
Structural frame
3. How does Monet achieve his brilliant, sparkling colour effect?

Cultural frame
4. Monet was painting at a time when the camera had just been invented. What effect do you think this may have had on Monet's subject and technique?
5. How long did it take for Impressionism to influence Australian artists? Look up the work of Streeton and Jane Sutherland.

MAKING ART

Subjective frame
1. Create a garden from your imagination and paint it in a similar way to Monet.

Structural frame
2. Observe, and record in paint, a corner of your garden at home at different times of the day to see how the light, colours and shadows change.
3. Scan a landscape image and manipulate it digitally to suggest different seasons or weather conditions.

Maurice de Vlaminck

(1876–1958, French)

FAUVISM

a modern French art movement that began around 1905, and which was interested in bold colour and decorative line

EXPRESSIONISM

a trend in modern European art in which the work emphasises emotion and the projection of inner feelings

Discussion

'If you are a painter, you have only to look inside of yourself.'[4] (Maurice de Vlaminck) What does *Houses at Chatou* reveal to you of Vlaminck's character and attitude to nature?

Houses at Chatou c.1905
Oil on canvas, 81.9 × 100.3 cm. Gift of Mr & Mrs M. E. Culberg, 1951.19
Reproduction, The Art Institute of Chicago
© Maurice de Vlaminck, licensed by VISCOPY, Australia, 2004

In *Houses at Chatou* we see a dramatic, emotional approach to landscape. Because Vlaminck is working from emotional experiences, we can say that he has executed his work from the *subjective frame*.

The colours are bright, intense and unnatural. Reds, oranges, blues and greens contrast with each other. There is a feeling of energy.

All detail has gone and the shapes are vividly outlined. His technique is painterly, with bold, powerful, obvious brushstrokes. Note that there is no attempt at depth, the red and blue roofs seeming to come forward.

Vlaminck is normally called a **Fauve** artist because of his interest in strong, pure colour and the avoidance of all shadow. His emotional, spontaneous style also links him with **Expressionism**. He was greatly influenced by the emotional brushstrokes and intensity of colour in Van Gogh's art (see page 80). He was also influenced by the striking, flat colour of the Fauve artist Matisse (see page 12). His friendship with André Derain, also a Fauve artist, resulted in a period of painting in which he concentrated on experiments with colour.

In 1905, Vlaminck and others displayed their work at the Salon d'Automne exhibition, during which a critic labelled the artists 'fauves' (meaning 'wild beast' in French). The Impressionists had begun to break the old traditions of realistic painting and Vlaminck took it further. The Modernists were not interested in trying to give the illusion of real space and depth in a painting. The Modernists, particularly the Fauves, were more concerned with the surface of the painting and elements such as the emotional impact of colour, and strong, decorative line. Vlaminck's style consisted of violent, spontaneous colour, with slashes of red, blue and green contrasting dramatically with strong, dark colours. He was to work in this style of still life and landscape painting for the next four years.

STUDYING ART

Critical study

Subjective frame

1. Vlaminck has been referred to as the fiercest of the Fauves. What can you see in this painting that suggests a wild or fierce approach or feeling? What feelings do you experience when you look at it?
2. What is your judgement of this painting?

Structural frame

3. Like Monet (see page 110), Vlaminck painted 'en plein-air'. What does this mean?
4. How has the colour been applied in this painting?

5. Describe how line has been used in this painting.

Historical study

6. How do the colours used and the method of paint application differ from Monet's *White Water Lilies* (see page 110)? How has this changed the mood?
7. List two characteristics of Fauvism.
8. In what way is Vlaminck's style similar to Expressionism?

ESSAY

Subjective frame — Critical writing
Imagine you have just seen an exhibition of the work of Vlaminck and John Olsen. Write a critical review for a newspaper, giving your opinion and analysis of the works.

MAKING ART

Subjective frame
Paint an area of the school playground (include buildings and trees if there are any) in the bold, colourful, expressive manner of Vlaminck.

Wassily Kandinsky

(1866–1944, Russian)

Frame: subjective
Form: painting
Conceptual framework: Kandinsky worked out his theories of art with his artworks.

Vocabulary

abstract: not representing anything from real life; non-representational

Bauhaus: an innovative art school, particularly in its methods of teaching design, which originated in 1919 in Germany

exalted: higher, more powerful

expressive: showing emotion or personal feeling

semi-abstract: not quite abstract; containing some reference to the real world

spontaneity: quality of being quickly done, unplanned, instinctive, unconstrained

Discussion

Art historian Robert Hughes has written of Kandinsky:

'Kandinsky's life work was based on the belief that art, like religion, must disclose a new order of experience ... *exalted* states and ... the spirit.'[5] 'Abstraction did not, in the end, become the universal system Kandinsky believed it would.'[6]

Kandinsky's abstract paintings were an attempt to create an art which appealed to the mind and the emotions (the spirit). Did Kandinsky achieve what he wanted to do? In what way was he successful?

Murnau with Church II
1910
Oil on canvas,
96.5 × 105.5 cm
Stedelijk Van Abbe
Museum, Eindhoven

Kandinsky's thick, diagonal brushstrokes in *Murnau with Church II* create linear patterns and rhythms more than they describe landforms. There is a suggestion of a church tower, houses and hills, but they seem to be more a symbol from Kandinsky's imagination than a present experience. The effect is dream-like. It is **semi-abstract**.

Kandinsky, a Russian-born artist, painted one of the first **abstract** paintings around 1911. At the same time, a group of Russian artists (called Suprematists), led by Kasimir Malevich (see page 160), created abstract works using geometric shapes. However, Kandinsky's abstraction evolved from a more emotional, personal approach developed from his studies of landscape. Robert Hughes has written of Kandinsky that 'while he did not invent abstract art on his own ... he certainly did more to promote the notion of ideal abstraction, in those distant years before World War I, than any other European artist'.[7]

From 1910 Kandinsky exhibited with the Blue Rider (Der Blaue Reiter) group of the German Expressionists, whose main concern was personal expression, or emotive response. His works after *Murnau with Church II* became increasingly abstract in his attempt to express a spiritual ideal and emotional states through colour, shape and line. Kandinsky wrote two books on his theories of art: *Concerning the Spiritual in Art* and *Point and Line to Plane*. In these writings he questioned the nature and purpose of art, suggesting it should be detached from the real, material world and instead value the spiritual means of communication. He believed the role of art was to reveal the inner life of humanity. Kandinsky believed that painting could develop the same energies as music, and that form and colour could affect the emotions in the same manner as music. 'Music expresses itself by sounds, painting by colours', wrote Kandinsky.[8]

Kandinsky's first abstract paintings were generally called 'improvisations'. These works have a wonderful sense of freedom and **spontaneity** with their **expressive** free line work and rich colour (see also page 200). In his second period of abstraction in the 1920s, while he taught at the **Bauhaus**, Kandinsky's works were more geometric, with a constant emphasis on circular shapes. These he called 'constructions'.

STUDYING ART

Critical study
Subjective frame
1. What objects and colours can you see in *Murnau with Church II?*
2. What feelings do you experience when you look at this landscape?

Historical study
Subjective frame
3. In describing one of his first abstract pictures, Kandinsky wrote how he worked 'in a state of strong inner tension ... so intensively do I feel the necessity of some of the forms that I remember having given loud-voiced directions to myself; as for instance: "But the corners must be heavy" ... The observer must learn to look at the picture as a graphic representation [symbol] of a mood and not as a representation of objects'.[9]

What can you find from this quote to help you understand Kandinsky's working methods and attitude towards painting?

MAKING ART

Subjective frame
Close your eyes and think of your favourite place. Remember your feelings as well as what it looks like. Does it suggest one of the following moods: tranquil, energetic, lively, expectant?

Quickly paint your impression of your favourite place, using ink and brush.

Fred Williams

(1927–82, Australian)

Frames: structural; cultural
Form: painting
Conceptual framework: The artworks are a creative representation of the Australian landscape.

Vocabulary

calligraphic: containing marks that suggest a type of handwriting

foreground: part of a painting that depicts the area nearest the observer

monotony: sameness, uniformity

palette knife: a very thin, bendable metal blade used for mixing or applying paint

Discussion

Art critic Patrick McCaughey has said that Williams 'had striven to show the basic, enduring and underlying forms and textures of the Australian landscape'.[10] Do you agree?

CRITICAL STUDY

Even without the title *Upwey Landscape II*, Fred Williams's painting is obviously a landscape. It suggests rather than describes a landscape, with its horizon line and swirls of paint to represent vegetation. The colours also help establish it as an Australian landscape. Although *Landscape '74* (see opposite) has no horizon line and the colours are unnatural, it does hint at land and trees. It is as if Williams has developed his own symbols or visual language for vegetation.

His paintings do not represent a particular view or place but rather his interpretation of a region. Look at the way the dabs of paint and lines representing trees are repeated, creating a rhythm, yet each 'tree' is different. His 'quick flicks' of paint representing trees have, in fact, been carefully placed. On close inspection, tiny flecks of blue, green, pink, mauve and yellow can be seen. These appear at first glance to have been squeezed out of a tube, but have actually been carefully shaped with a **palette knife** and sometimes contain scratch marks that add to the interesting surface texture.

Have you ever gone on a long car trip and been struck by the **monotony** of the Australian countryside and the feeling of vast, unending *space*? Williams has managed to capture this feeling. He has depicted Australia's wide expanses that allow us to see the dramatic meeting of sky and land. Williams has also made us aware of its subtle, delicate details, showing us the quiet beauty of our land.

Upwey Landscape II 1965
Oil on canvas, 183.2 × 147.6 cm
Reproduced by permission of the National Gallery of Australia, Canberra

HISTORICAL STUDY

Fred Williams updated the tradition of Australian landscape art, with its sense of space and light captured by the Heidelberg artists (including Tom Roberts and Arthur Streeton). In *Upwey Landscape II*, Williams used the same ochres, russets and dull brick-reds associated with the Heidelberg artists' interpretation of the bush.

Landscape '74 1974
Oil on canvas,
200.5 × 373 cm
Reproduced by
permission of the
National Gallery of
Australia, Canberra

Williams began to concentrate on using the landscape as his subject in the late 1950s. He had been influenced by the work of the Post-Impressionist Cézanne (see page 78) and the Cubist painter Georges Braque. By the process of selecting, simplifying and combining, Williams developed a style of landscape painting that was original. He became known internationally as representing the uniqueness of Australia.

Williams was not concerned with the traditional representation of distance, with **foreground**, midground and background (far distance), as in the work of Claude Lorrain (see page 106). There is no clump of trees or rocks to lead your eye into the landscape as in traditional European painting. Instead, Williams emphasised the immense flatness and openness of Australia through his composition. Art historian Sasha Grishin has written that, like Streeton and Roberts, Williams 'introduced us to a new way of seeing our environment. His **calligraphic** shorthand for trees and vegetation, his sense of colour and his resolution of that dramatic meeting point of the sky and earth on the horizon have struck most of us as a new vision of our country'.[11]

STUDYING ART

Critical study
Structural frame
1. How has Williams indicated the feeling of space in the Australian landscape?
2. Describe the different kinds of textures he has used in painting trees.
3. What are the main art elements (line, direction, size, colour, tone, texture) used by Williams?
4. How has Williams created and used symbols in his work?

Cultural frame
5. What evidence of people can you see in Williams's landscapes? How does this add to the meaning of the work?
6. Would *Upwey Landscape II* make a good cover for a book on Australia? Why?

Historical study
7. In what ways is Williams's work similar to the Heidelberg artists (look at Arthur Streeton on page 137 and Tom Roberts on page 148)?
8. How has Williams's work developed away from the Heidelberg artists to create his own unique style?

FURTHER RESEARCH

1. Find an example of Williams's etching and describe how the different medium alters the effect.
2. Write a critique in which you compare Fred Williams's interpretation of the Australian landscape with that of another artist of your choice from this chapter. Approach this critical study from a *subjective*, *structural* or *cultural* frame. This could be presented using PowerPoint.

MAKING ART

Cultural frame
1. Create your own interpretation of what you feel is typically Australian, be it outback, bush, beach or rainforest. You may include collage if you wish.

Structural frame
2. In your Visual Arts Process Diary mark a rectangular area 18 cm × 14 cm. In this rectangle recreate a section of one of Williams's paintings in order to explore and understand his style of paint application. Write a few key phrases around the rectangle describing his method.

John Olsen

(b. 1928, Australian)

Frames: subjective; structural; cultural

Form: acrylic painting

Conceptual framework: Olsen interprets his world through his feelings. The audience is drawn into his works by his expressive line, detailed focus areas, and sense of vitality.

Vocabulary

expressive: showing emotion or personal feeling
linear: containing lines as an important feature of a work
non-figurative: not containing likenesses of objects, places or people
spontaneous: quickly done, unplanned, instinctive, unconstrained
vibrancy: quality of being lively, thrilling, energetic

CRITICAL STUDY

Look at the title of the work opposite. What is another name for a sea port? The arrow on the left-hand side seems to draw you into the painting, as if Olsen is taking you on a journey of his experiences and feelings concerning Sydney Harbour. We could thus call this painting **expressive** in style, as the artist's approach is through the emotions.

Olsen has painted this landscape from an aerial viewpoint, as if he was looking down from an aeroplane. This has allowed him to imagine a wider view of the harbour. But he has recorded more than just the water and land. Olsen has included objects and symbols to give you a feeling of the **vibrancy** of Sydney's foreshores.

Olsen tries to get on canvas the whole feeling of a place or occasion. To do this, his application of paint must be rapid. In *Bush Walk* he applied brilliant washes of colour then added his linework and thicker colour in a **spontaneous** way. Our eye is led along the tracks around the canvas and even beyond it. At times we are drawn into detailed areas yet also given places of emptiness to rest.

Olsen paints in a very **linear** way, giving his lines the freedom to twist and turn, to form symbols and create a sense of movement. In *Entrance to the Seaport of Desire* we see the ships coming in and out, the dawn, the sun, cranes, men working and the traffic all weaving backwards and forwards.

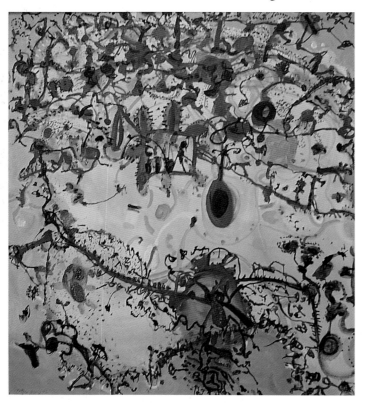

Bush Walk 1972
Synthetic polymer paint on composition board
122.1 × 107.1 cm
Collection: Bendigo Art Gallery
© John Olsen, licensed by VISCOPY, Australia, 2004

HISTORICAL STUDY

John Olsen's works are a visual diary of his experiences and travels. He records his personal reactions, from his excitement of returning to Sydney Harbour in the 1960s, to the despair of the drought in outback Queensland in 1993. In *Entrance to the Seaport of Desire*, we follow the lines on his canvas as if he is telling us a story, a personal history of our land and its culture. The work was painted while Olsen was living at Watsons Bay. He reveals the beautiful as well as the vulgar or ugly side of the harbour. He thus works mainly within the *subjective* and *cultural* frames.

STUDYING ART

Subjective frame

1. What words could you use to describe the mood of *Entrance to the Seaport of Desire*? For example lively, flowing, static, spontaneous, joyful, dull.
2. How has Olsen created the feeling of life or energy?

Structural frame

3. Draw five symbols you can see in the artwork and write the meaning of each one. Are they universal symbols (ones we can all read) or personal symbols?
4. Look at the size of this artwork and the watery paint and ink Olsen has used. Do you think he painted this on an easel propped against a wall or on the floor? How would this method have helped to create his effects?
5. Which area is the most complicated? Explain or draw what you see.
6. Which of the art elements (line, direction, colour, tone, texture) has Olsen used as his building blocks to create this work?
7. Describe how Olsen has used line and colour. Does he want to communicate something in particular by their use?

MAKING ART

1. Imagine a helicopter journey from your home to the local shopping centre. Record this journey using ink and brush in a similar way to Olsen's paintings. Include signs, symbols and objects.
2. Think of yourself on top of a mountain. Using watery paint, create a creek that curves its way from the mountain to the sea. Now, using another medium (pastel, ink, poster paint), draw symbols along the way to represent rocks, water currents, roots, trees, tracks, insects, and so on.

Olsen has created a unique vision of the Australian landscape. He paints the poetry and mystery of the land — the flow of water, the hidden movement of birds and animals, and flowers blooming. Olsen's works suggest all the sensations; not just the sight of the landscape but the sounds, smells, changes and physical interactions. He paints his present responses as well as his memories and moods. He basically approaches his paintings from an aerial view, creating a type of map. He also looks beneath and around things, giving us a total experience.

Olsen is recognised as one of the first of the **non-figurative** painters in Sydney. He developed a free, almost abstract approach which is generally termed linear abstraction.

Entrance to the Seaport of Desire 1964
Synthetic polymer paint on canvas, 167.6 × 213.4 cm
Gift of Mrs M. A. McGrath 1968, The Art Gallery of New South Wales
© John Olsen, licensed by VISCOPY, Australia, 2004

FURTHER RESEARCH

Critical study

Structural frame

1. Find a painting by Olsen of the outback, such as his painting of Lake Eyre or the Simpson Desert. Compare and contrast this work with *Entrance to the Seaport of Desire*.
2. Art historian and critic Bernard Smith has written: 'Like most abstract expressionists, John Olsen seeks to discover form and image in the actual process of painting'.[12] Within what frame does this statement belong — *subjective* or *structural*?

Historical study

3. Olsen has often been inspired by poetry. Find the poem 'Pied Beauty' by Gerard Manley Hopkins and Kenneth Slessor's 'Five Bells'. Now find Olsen's paintings by these names. What relationships can you see between the poems and the paintings?

Mandy Martin

(b. 1952, Australian)

Frames: subjective; cultural; postmodern
Form: painting
Conceptual framework: Martin represents her experiences of places but also relates these artworks to artworks from the past, giving them a sense of timeless beauty that reaches out to the audience.

Vocabulary

appropriate:	put a familiar image in a new context to change its meaning
commission:	authorise to be done
context:	the circumstances, surroundings or situation of an artwork
text:	words of a document
tonal contrast:	light against dark

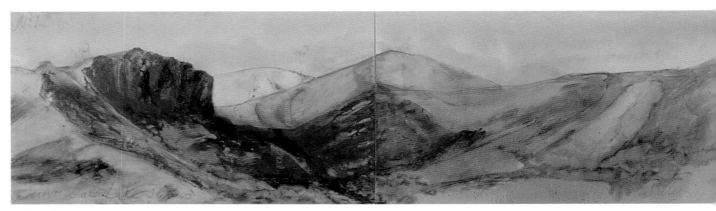

Lake Julius 1994
Oil with ochres and pigment on linen, diptych, 152 × 550 cm
Courtesy of the artist and Roslyn Oxley9 Gallery, Sydney

CRITICAL STUDY

Mandy Martin has reacted to a particular place, Lake Julius, at a particular time. She has written on the work 'Sunrise, Lake Julius' and in the bottom right-hand corner, 'July', yet this painting hints at more than just a record of what has been seen. It includes many of Martin's personal feelings and ideas about its present, past and even future.

Look at the measurements of this painting — it is on a large scale. This creates a sense of majesty or power of the land, drawing the onlooker into it. This feeling of space is heightened by the thick texture in the foreground. This is in contrast to the thin washes of paint which reveal sensitive drawing and notations beneath. It is almost as if the land is being surveyed for future development. In this way Martin refers to a landscape's history. Her main concerns are the European cultural and industrial colonisation of Australia.

The yellow glow of the sky in *Lake Julius* not only documents it as a sunrise but gives it an almost ethereal or spiritual effect. Look at *Folly*, opposite, and note the same interest in atmospheric effects provided by the shafts of light in a glowing sky.

In *Folly* a sense of drama has been created by the changing sky and the strong diagonal lines. The harsh texture of the rock in the foreground against the smooth water gives a feeling of deep space. There is a strong **tonal contrast** of black against pale orange. This painting is a comment on the impact of people and industry on the landscape, and suggests tragedy. It is also a haunting, disturbing image of power and beauty. It depicts the struggle between people and their environment. Martin does not try to give us the answer or to show us the winner, but makes us aware of the delicate balance. On another level, *Folly* is also a reference to the role of landscape as a subject throughout art history.

Mandy Martin is an Australian artist whose main theme is landscape. Her works, such as *Folly* and the etching *Beyond Eden*, indicate her concerns about people's intervention in the landscape. (For this reason her work is also relevant to chapter 6.) Martin's landscapes in the 1980s were of mining sites and the effects of industrialisation. She painted factories and barren landscapes, hinting at our destruction of the environment. Martin's paintings and etchings are concerned with social values and concerns. They should therefore be looked at as belonging to the *cultural frame* of art. Her work is also very much linked to her personal, emotional experiences of places, and so belongs within the *subjective frame* of art as well. Her use of **text** and her reference to historical artworks and values — the use of the past in order to comment on the future (changing an artwork's **context**) — also places her as part of the *postmodern frame*.

The inclusion of writing and surveyors' notations can also be seen in Martin's 1991 Strzelecki Desert series. She has **appropriated** text from the writings of Ludwig Becker (artist and writer on the Burke and Wills expedition), and combined them with oil refinery plant diagrams and her own sketch book jottings.

Martin painted *Red Ochre Cove*, which is said to be the largest painting in Australia. It was **commissioned** in 1987 for the Main Committee room of the new Parliament House in Canberra.

STUDYING ART

Critical study
Subjective frame
1. Think of a movie or video that you have seen where the landscape was treated with the same feeling of strength, beauty and grandeur as in Martin's paintings. Name it, and state how the feeling was created and whether the movie was set in the past, present or future.

Cultural frame
2. How do Mandy Martin's landscapes reflect the past, present and future? Do you think they are typically Australian or do they represent a universal vision (that is, relate to issues in many countries)?
3. What four questions would you ask Mandy Martin if you were able to interview her?

Historical study
Cultural frame
4. The yellow glow of the sky in *Lake Julius* relates it back to the Romantic, awe-inspiring visions of European artists such as Turner (see page 108). The same atmospheric effects in the sky can be observed in *Folly*. There are shafts of light from a glowing sky in Martin's work, a rainbow in Turner's. How has Martin gone beyond painting a Romantic landscape and made her work a comment on our present society?

Folly 1988
Oil on linen, 280 × 455 cm
Courtesy of the artist and Roslyn Oxley9 Gallery, Sydney

MAKING ART

Subjective and cultural frames
Create your own comment on our exploitation or destruction of the environment. Focus on your own local environment or on a global issue.

Michael Nelson Tjakamarra

(b. 1949, Australian)

Frames: cultural; structural
Form: acrylic painting on canvas
Conceptual framework: In Aboriginal art there is a very close relationship between the land, the artwork and the beliefs of the artist's language group. Often the art contains hidden meanings that cannot be conveyed to a wider audience.

CRITICAL STUDY

In this painting can be seen a simplified image of a snake and geometrical patterns such as dots, wavy lines and concentric circles or roundels. They appear to be signs or symbols, telling a story and leading the eye from left to right across the painting. The central interconnected roundels divide the painting in two. The colours are mainly those we find in soil and rocks, with the addition of blue.

HISTORICAL STUDY

The works of Aboriginal artists are mostly about *places*, about sites created by ancestral beings in the Dreamtime. Since many of the stories of the Dreamtime are sacred and belong to the artist or a group of people, without their assistance and permission it is not possible to understand the meaning of the stories or appreciate how important the land is to Aboriginal people. These paintings also provide us with a map-like image of the enormous *space* in which Aboriginal people exist and travel.

Aboriginal art is a means of communicating information about religious beliefs. Indigenous people believe the power or spirit of Dreamtime beings still exists within the land. The making of artworks is part of the ritual associated with appealing to these ancestral beings.

Each site or place included in the Dreamings or stories is a special place to Aboriginal people. The paintings can be interpreted as a type of map of the landforms created during the Dreamtime. The group of people owning particular Dreamtime stories therefore also owns the land represented in the artworks. Aboriginal paintings have been used even in a court of law as a title deed or land map of ownership in land rights claims.

Michael Nelson Tjakamarra was born at Vaughan Springs, Northern Territory. He now lives in Papunya, Northern Territory — the centre of the Western Desert Art movement. In 1984 he won the National Aboriginal Art Award.

Five stories are represented in *Five Dreamings*. The central roundels depict the Watunuma or Flying Ant Dreaming at a place called Yuwintji, located to the west of Vaughan Springs. The large and smaller circle to the right above the central line represents the Possum Dreaming at two sacred sites north of Vaughan Springs: Tjangakulangu and Mawitji respectively. Yilkiri, a site near Mount Singleton, is also shown. This represents where a willy-willy turned into Wanampi, Rainbow Serpent, seen here in the form of a snake. Below the Rainbow Serpent's body can be seen the tracks of a rock wallaby journeying between two sacred sites. Three other circles can be seen in the bottom left corner. These represent Miruwarri, a Rain Dreaming site to the west of Mount Doreen.

The Aboriginal people at present are trying to find a balance between keeping information secret to keep alive their laws, beliefs and social structure, yet sharing information in the hope of achieving understanding and the recognition of their rights. Aboriginal paintings thus fulfil an important role — making sure their culture is passed on to future generations. Their art is a rich visual language of signs and symbols.

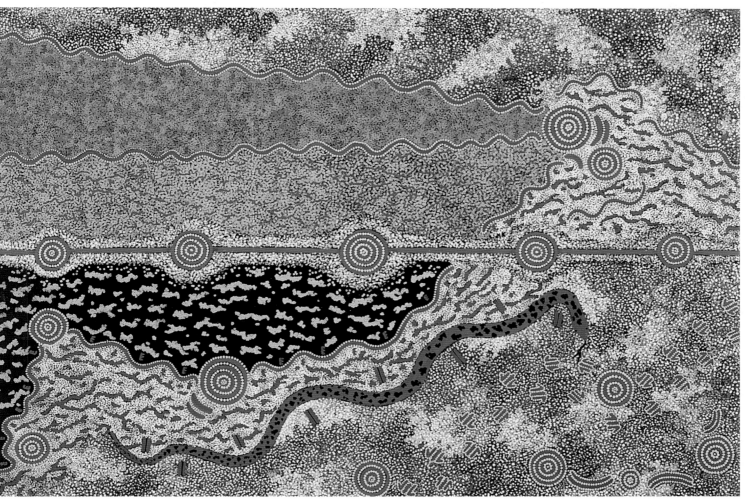

Five Dreamings 1984 (collaboration with Marjorie Napaljarri)
Synthetic polymer on canvas
122 × 182 cm
Gabrielle Pizzi Collection, Melbourne. © Aboriginal Artists Agency, Sydney

STUDYING ART

Critical study
Subjective frame
1. What evidence do you see in this painting to suggest a journey?

Structural frame
2. How has the land been depicted? We do not see the traditional Western idea of foreground, middle ground and background. What is the viewpoint? How many different colours and patterns can you see? Draw them.
3. Shading and tone to create solidity do not seem to exist in Aboriginal art. What art elements are used instead?
4. Draw three of the symbols in the painting. Other than the meanings of the symbols you have been given here, do they suggest any other meanings or associations to you?

Historical study
Cultural frame
5. Why are the Dreamtime stories important to Aboriginal people?
6. In what way are Aboriginal paintings like maps?

FURTHER RESEARCH

What impact did Geoff Bardon, a teacher at the Papunya settlement in the early 1970s, have on Aboriginal art?

MAKING ART

Structural frame
Create a plan or aerial view of your school and its surroundings. Use symbols and patterns to represent different objects, materials and vegetation.

Robert Dickerson

(b. 1924, Australian)

Frames: cultural; subjective
Form: oil painting
Conceptual framework: There is a strong relationship between artist and artwork and between artwork and audience.

Vocabulary

manifesto: public statement of theories or policy
monotony: sameness, uniformity
scale: relative size, proportion
urban: to do with towns or cities

Discussion

'Dickerson paints not people but the gulfs between them.'[13] (Robert Hughes) What evidence do you see in *Woolloomooloo Landscape* to support this statement?

Woolloomooloo Landscape 1973
Oil on board,
122 × 152 cm.

CRITICAL STUDY

Robert Dickerson has titled this painting a 'landscape'. Does it suggest a landscape to you? Are there trees? Is it painted in the subtle greens, greys and ochres we associate with an Australian landscape?

What we see is a row of buildings. They do not appear as welcoming homes, but as a repeated formula reflecting the **monotony** and conformity of **urban** living. There is a figure placed just off centre demanding our attention. The figure is alone, standing in contrast to the buildings behind. Dickerson has expressed the emotional effects of inner-city life.

Dickerson has created an empty space between the figure and the row of terraces — the large, dark-blue area, which is cold and uninviting. The figure seems small in comparison with the **scale** of the buildings. The figure has her head down, and appears to be a victim of this urban life.

Despite the interest in abstraction in the 1950s in Australia, Dickerson at this time was essentially a figurative painter and as such was asked to exhibit with six other young artists in Melbourne. The other artists were Arthur Boyd, David Boyd, John Brack, Charles Blackman, John Perceval and Clifton Pugh. They were to become known as the Antipodeans. A statement written for the opening of this exhibition in 1959 was called the Antipodean **manifesto**. It stated the artists' interest in the free expression of figures and their opposition to abstraction. They wished to draw inspiration from their own lives and the lives of those around them by imagining society's feelings and attitudes. They worked primarily within the *cultural* and *subjective frames* of art.

STUDYING ART

Subjective frame
1. What are your personal reactions to these paintings? Do they reflect your views of city life now?
2. What three words would you use to describe *Woolloomooloo Landscape*?
3. How do you think the meaning of *Woolloomooloo Landscape* would be different if no figure had been included?

Structural frame
4. Briefly explain how the composition of the artwork shows us Dickerson's attitude towards inner-city living.
5. In half a page, discuss how Dickerson has used colour, tone and simplified shapes to create a mood.

Cultural frame
6. What aspects of Sydney's culture — its social values — does Dickerson explore in *Woolloomooloo Landscape*?
7. Can you think of a video clip which deals with city slums or feelings of sadness and loneliness as a result of social pressures? Can you see any similarities to Dickerson's painting? How is the video clip used to reinforce the words or music? Would they suit Dickerson's painting?

Man Asleep on the Steps 1954
Synthetic polymer paint on composition board
76.2 cm × 101.6 cm
Purchased 1954, National Gallery of Victoria

FURTHER RESEARCH

Historical study
Art historian Bernard Smith has written: 'Dickerson's emphasis upon the isolation of the individual is a feature of the figurative painting of the post-war years.'[14]
Look at the work of Dickerson's contemporaries John Brack (see page 150) and Charles Blackman (see page 16) to find any evidence to support this statement.

MAKING ART

Cultural and subjective frames
1. Paint or draw in charcoal a back alley in a city street. Cut out a figure from a magazine or newspaper and place it within your artwork to suggest loneliness. You will need to carefully consider scale and the position of your figure. Blend your figure into your artwork by adding charcoal or paint.
2. Take a series of photographs to show your views of urban life.

Jeffrey Smart

(b. 1921, Australian)

Frame: structural; subjective
Form: oil painting
Conceptual framework: Smart paints traditional oil paintings that comment on our contemporary urban world.

Vocabulary

composition: the placement of figures and objects; the organisation of an artwork
dramatic: exciting
urban: to do with towns or cities

Discussion

Cultural frame

1. *Underground Car Park* was painted in Italy, but does it remind you of an underground carpark you have visited? What does this painting tell you about city life?

Structural frame

2. Do you think *Parking Lot near Bologna* would have been as interesting without the shadows? What part do they play in the painting?

Parking Lot Near Bologna 1992
Oil on canvas, 30 × 87 cm

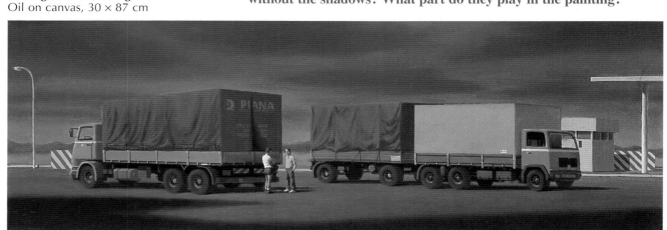

CRITICAL STUDY

The **urban** environment has provided inspiration for artists in various ways. Look carefully at *Parking Lot Near Bologna* and *Underground Car Park*. Do you think Smart is trying to show the joy of city life or the isolation and loneliness of it?

Smart works within the *structural frame*. He is certainly concerned with the **composition** of his paintings. See how he has changed the letter H in his pencil study (opposite) to the letter E because it leads the eye into the painting, towards the arrow, then back to the red van. The arrow is an obvious way of directing you towards the light, but what else has Smart done in this work?

Underground Car Park 1993
Oil on canvas, 76 × 110 cm

You might not think a car park would be an interesting subject for a painting, but Smart has made it intriguing and **dramatic**. In *Parking Lot near Bologna* we see further evidence of Smart's concern with balancing his shapes and areas of colour. Look at the way the colour red has been repeated, and the position of the people — not quite in the centre yet leading the eye from one truck to the next.

HISTORICAL STUDY

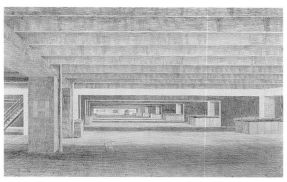

Study for **Underground Car Park**
Pencil on paper, 52 × 80 cm

Jeffrey Smart was part of the modern movement of Australian art in the 1940s. In 1963 he left for Italy, where he still lives, but he continues to have exhibitions in Australia. Smart's paintings are definitely about the modern world: freeways, towers, high rise buildings, road signs and factories. He depicts cities as strange, inhuman places. Even though he includes people, they seem dwarfed by the buildings. They act as a contrast to the landscape rather than belonging to it. Smart's dark skies and deep shadows combined with his precise painting technique create a haunting effect. Smart shows us the beauty of the modern constructed environment: its strong, simple shapes, lines and patterns (stripes in particular). He uses the signs and symbols of urban life to balance the geometric shapes of trucks, walls and bridges. Unlike Olsen's works (see page 118), Smart's paintings are a universal statement about all cities rather than a reaction to a particular place.

Smart will often take his ideas for a painting from several different places that he has visited and will painstakingly rearrange the images to suit his idea for the composition. This sometimes means turning arrows around so that traffic is pointed in the wrong direction.

Even though his paintings appear too perfect to be real, and almost unfriendly, they do include parts of real places and, at times, his friends. Smart opens our eyes to the wonder and timelessness of our cities.

STUDYING ART

Critical study
Cultural frame
1. What is missing in *Underground Car Park* and *Parking Lot Near Bologna*?
2. Look at the dates of these artworks by Smart. Do the symbols used represent this time?
3. Is the subject of *Parking Lot Near Bologna* two men chatting? Or are they there to show the size of the trucks and emphasise the loneliness of being on this highway, a symbol of modern life?

Historical study
Cultural frame
4. What is the meaning of Smart's work in our present time and culture?
5. Art historian Robert Hughes finds Smart's work 'lacking in emotion ... [having] deadpan mysteriousness ... their flavour often verges on the surreal'.[15] Do you agree? Explain your view in a paragraph.

Structural frame
6. List or draw the symbols you see in *Parking Lot Near Bologna*. What do they represent?
7. What are the main colours?
8. In comparison with Olsen's work (see page 118), Smart creates his work over a long period of time. What evidence do you see of this?
9. Choose three of the following words to describe Smart's application of paint and write them in a sentence:
   precise, expressive, gestural, tonal, methodical.

FURTHER RESEARCH

Cultural frame
Smart has said that he was influenced by the timelessness and colours of Della Francesca. Can you see this influence in his works?

MAKING ART

Structural frame
Collect images of city buildings and road signs and billboards from magazines and create a collage of a city. Like Smart, consider scale and the placement of your shapes carefully before you glue them down. You may wish to scan in your images and manipulate them using a computer program.

Grace Cossington Smith

(1892–1984, Australian)

Frame: structural
Form: oil painting
Conceptual framework: Cossington Smith painted the world around her in an objective way, concentrating on colour.

Vocabulary

cool colours:	blue, green, purple
form:	shape or solidity, volume
Modernism:	a twentieth-century art movement that broke away from the traditions of realism, eventually reaching abstraction
mundane:	ordinary, everyday
vibrant:	rich, thrilling

Interior with Wardrobe Mirror 1955
Oil on canvas on paperboard
91.4 × 73.7 cm
The Art Gallery of New South Wales
© AGNSW

Cultural frame

How does the view in *Interior with Wardrobe* differ from your bedroom? What is missing? What does it tell you of Cossington Smith's lifestyle in 1955? Compare this with Brett Whiteley's room (see page 132).

CRITICAL STUDY

Grace Cossington Smith has painted a view from her everyday life — her bedroom and belongings — yet it is far from boring. We are attracted by the impression of sunlight, the reflection in the mirror and the wonderful patterns of **vibrant** colour. Notice the **cool colours** that have been added to the shadows, giving them a sense of energy. Her technique involved carefully placing short, square brushstrokes of brilliant colour side by side, building **form** in colour. Some of the brushstrokes overlap, while others allow the background colours to show through.

HISTORICAL STUDY

Cossington Smith was one of the earliest Australian artists to be influenced by the European Post-Impressionist movement. She was particularly influenced by the work of Cézanne (see page 78) and Van Gogh (see page 80). With colleagues and friends Roland Wakelin and Roy de Maistre (who later painted Australia's first abstract painting), she led the break away from Australian Impressionism.

Cossington Smith's works were quite daring for the time, particularly as they were done by an unassuming female. She was a contemporary of Margaret Preston (see page 42). Cossington Smith's main interest was colour — bright shimmering colour filled with reflected sunlight. Even her shadows glow with patches of pure colour.

Cossington Smith made a great contribution to Australian art. She supported **Modernism** and developed her own individual technique. She is mainly known for her inspiring transformation of the **mundane**, particularly room interiors.

STUDYING ART

Critical study

Structural frame

1. Look at the yellow wall in the background of the painting. How has the paint been applied? List all the colours you can see in that wall.
2. Are all the little squares of thick paint the one size and are they all in the one direction?
3. Draw the main areas or objects in this painting. Now describe the composition and the main direction of the lines.
4. List all the objects you see in this room.
5. What is your opinion of this painting?

FURTHER RESEARCH

1. Find a landscape painting by Grace Cossington Smith. Does she paint landscapes in the same way as she painted *Interior with Wardrobe*?
2. In half a page, compare Cossington Smith's painting technique with that used by Donald Friend to paint his interior (see page 130).

Cultural frame

3. Investigate other room interiors by Cossington Smith. Describe her surroundings and the type of life she lived in suburban Australia at the time. Import the images, and use a computer graphics program to create a brochure suitable for an exhibition of her work.

MAKING ART

Structural frame

1. Draw three different viewpoints or corners of your bedroom in your Visual Arts Process Diary. Choose one and develop it into a painting, with an emphasis on sunlight and vibrant colour similar to the paintings of Grace Cossington Smith.
2. Scan in a room interior photograph from a magazine and add texture and different effects using software such as Photoshop.

Donald Friend

(1915–89, Australian)

Frame: subjective
Forms: painting; drawing
Conceptual framework: Friend reacts to his world with feeling, creating a mood for the audience to interpret. He created his artworks for his own benefit, not just for the art world.

CRITICAL STUDY

Donald Friend's superb, sensitive linework and love of rich colour can be observed in *Upstairs Front Room*. This interior has a feeling of intimacy. We are asked to share the artist's delight in the pattern of the wooden floor, the wrought iron of the balcony and the geometrical pattern on the rug. It is a vital, welcoming space with the door opening inwards, letting the air and sunlight fill the room. It appears a casual record of an experience.

The composition is quite balanced, with order being created by the chair in front of the open doors.

This interior is portrayed in a personal, frank and honest manner. Friend's expressive use of line helps to give an individuality to the mundane (ordinary), everyday objects.

Lake Farm, Landscape Study
(Donald Friend diary, 1982–1988)
National Library of Australia

HISTORICAL STUDY

Donald Friend, an Australian artist, began keeping a diary when he was only fourteen years old. He continued this habit until he was close to death and could no longer paint or write. His diaries, most of which are kept in the Australian National Library, are a lively, witty record of his experiences, relationships, travels, correspondence and, in particular, his ideas, working drawings and evaluations of his artworks. Note the expressive drawing in his diary entry *Lake Farm, Landscape Study*. He has taken obvious delight in the different patterns and textures of the vegetation. Friend's particular skill with pen and ink and his quick and astute observational skills led him to become an official war artist.

Friend longed for the exotic throughout his life and his artworks reflect this search. Art critic Robert Hughes has written of Friend that 'his work is animated by a real passion'.[16] Friend's sumptuous use of colour adds to the impression that *Upstairs Front Room* was a special, loved place. In fact the work was created on his return to Australia from his beloved Bali, due to problems of old age and illness.

Friend's love of drawing and great talent lasted until he could no longer hold a pen or brush. After a stroke left him unable to draw with his left hand, he taught himself to paint with his right hand.

Upstairs Front Room
(Donald Friend diary, 1982–1988)
Pen and coloured wash
National Library of Australia

STUDYING ART

Critical study

Subjective frame

1. How does the view of the balcony in *Upstairs Front Room* make you feel? What time of the day and what day of the week do you think it might be?

2. Look at the linework on the doors. How old do you think these doors might be? From just this small section of the house, can you guess what type of house it is?

3. If you were asked to add something to this painting, what would it be?

4. What is your opinion of this work?

Artist's practice

5. By reading the *Historical study*, what have you learnt about Donald Friend's art practice — his working methods, approach to artmaking, subjects and choices of subject matter?

Historical study

6. Why do you think Friend's diaries are kept in the National Library of Australia? In what way could they be important to the history of our nation?

MAKING ART

Subjective frame

1. Choose a favourite corner in your house. Paint your reactions to the patterns, colours and lines that you see.

2. For one week, keep a diary of your experiences, the places you visit, the food you eat. Include, like Friend, both written thoughts and drawings.

Brett Whiteley

(1939–92, Australian)

Frame: subjective
Forms: printmaking; drawing
Conceptual framework: Whiteley reacted to his personal spaces, such as his home and studio, and to the natural world.

Vocabulary

etching: a form of printmaking using a metal plate

silk-screen (print): print made by forcing ink or paint through unmasked areas of silk

CRITICAL STUDY

Looking at these examples of Brett Whiteley's work, what impresses us first is his free-flowing, expressive lines, which create movement and energy. Whiteley created original responses to his environment. We are very much aware that *The Cat* is a personal expression of his home at Lavender Bay in Sydney (see also page 193). This is evident not only from the view beyond the window, but by its contents. We see examples of his still lifes and his figure work, in the form of nude drawings on paper, ceramics and sculpture. These objects are held together by his skilful organisation of space in this interior scene.

The Most Beautiful Mountain is a personal response to the patterns and textures of a particular place. It is a provocative work, breaking traditional boundaries of representation. It stimulates our imagination with its distorted shapes and empty spaces. At first glance it appears unfinished — we are enticed to fill in the gaps ourselves. Our eye is led from the more defined palm tree in the bottom left corner to the layered textures and washes of ink in the mountain.

Brett Whiteley's attitude to his work was mainly within the subjective frame. (See also page 196.)

The Cat 1980
Photo-silkscreen, 83.5 × 81.5 cm
Private collection
© Wendy Whiteley

HISTORICAL STUDY

In 1960, at the age of twenty-one, Brett Whiteley won a scholarship to study painting in Europe. London's Tate Gallery bought his *Untitled Red*, making him the youngest contemporary artist to have his work purchased by the gallery.

Whiteley had the ability to focus on the essence of things and translate it to the viewer in an exciting, expressionist way. His works were inventive yet began with his acute observation. He was essentially a draughtsman (someone who draws skillfully), so his works translated well into the printing media of **silk-screen** and **etching**. His skill as a painter, particularly his handling of colour (his favourite was ultramarine blue), must also be acknowledged.

The Most Beautiful Mountain 1969
Pen and ink wash, 56.5 × 51 cm
Private collection
© Wendy Whiteley

In 1977 Whiteley became the winner of three major Australian art prizes — the Archibald, Wynne and Sulman. This was not only a tribute to his talent but also a recognition of the wide range of his art.

Brett Whiteley did more than record what he saw. He interpreted his subjects for us in an original, lively, sensuous way. He had a unique way of handling line, colour and space, and saw a link between the landscape and the female nude, so his hills often appeared with the contours of hips. The curve, as we see in these works, was very important in his work. Whiteley did not hide his influences, which included Van Gogh, Chinese and Japanese art, and Francis Bacon.

Whiteley's last project was a fifty-panel sweep of Australia from Bondi to Uluru, from the coast through the city, suburbs, and on to the red centre. Although incomplete, it stands as Whiteley's personal expression of Australia: the land, its birds and animals as well as the political, historical and cultural aspects of our country.

Jennifer Turpin and Michaelie Crawford

(b. 1958, Australian; b. 1964, Australian)

Frame: postmodern
Form: site-specific artworks
Conceptual framework: The artworks use natural elements. They relate both to the built environment and nature. Because of their large scale and the fact that they are generally constructed in public spaces, they involve and engage a wide audience.

Vocabulary

installation: an arrangement created for a particular site or gallery

kinetic: relating to motion; moving

site-specific: designed for a particular place

POSTMODERN

influenced by an experimental, contemporary art movement associated with post-industrial societies. It usually breaks the boundaries of art, challenges the idea of originality, and often draws on several art traditions.

CRITICAL STUDY

In the **installation** *Water Works III*, Jennifer Turpin comments on the ever changing nature of water, including its transparent quality. The work also comments on the space in which it is exhibited, in this case the entrance to a public art gallery. As such it is also a reflection on the nature of art and its display.

Water Works III involves water peacefully dribbling down string as it might dribble down a vine in a rainforest. We should listen to as well as watch the water in its gentle, tranquil movement. The work suggests nature, in contrast to the manufactured world of the gallery.

Tied to Tide uses the energy created by water and wind, and also involves sound. Suspended red ladders bob up and down according to the water movement and the tides. They seem to move magically, like dancing acrobats. This work relates to the water as well as the boardwalk. The ladders are similar to the structures of cranes and boats in the area. It is the wind and the water that cause the individual differences in the positions of the ladders. They are capable of a 360-degree swing in a high wind. As the tide goes up, the ladders dip down. Passers-by can't help but stop, watch and be amused.

JENNIFER TURPIN
Water Works III 1991
Art Gallery of New South Wales
North and South vestibules 6 metres high
Water, nylon lines, copper pipes and tanks
© Jennifer Turpin, licensed by VISCOPY, Australia, 2004

HISTORICAL STUDY

Jennifer Turpin and Michaelie Crawford are each artists in their own right but have formed a collaborative team due to their similar interests. When working on her own, Turpin created installations using water, arranging each installation so it was a complete environment. Installations cannot usually be sold; they are displayed for only a limited time. After that, all that remains is documentation of the work in the form of drawings, photographs or video. This idea that an artwork need not be lasting and unique is a **Postmodern** concept.

JENNIFER TURPIN AND MICHAELIE CRAWFORD
Tied to Tide 1999
A floating, **kinetic**, tidal, wave and wind-activated artwork
Pyrmont Point Park, Sydney
8 units, each 10 metres long
Hardwood timber, stainless steel, fibreglass, aluminium
© Jennifer Turpin, licensed by VISCOPY, Australia, 2004

In collaboration Turpin and Crawford have been working mainly on commissions, creating challenging, large-scale public works. The concept of working in collaboration is a growing trend in contemporary art practice, as it allows artists to involve a range of technologies and expertise and widen the possibilities of artworks. With public art commissions, the artists have to consider certain restrictions. The obvious ones are the budget and how much time they are given, but they must also consider safety and vandalism. Another collaborative work of theirs is *Tank* (1977) in the tunnel linking Museum Railway Station, Sydney, with the old Mark Foys building. This work uses old display cases filled with constantly moving and reflecting water. One wall involves old maps and legal documents relevant to water ownership in the area. Public art commissions often include a request to consider a historical or cultural comment.

Turpin and Crawford's work can be classified as Postmodern because it challenges the traditional role and value of visual art, and uses unconventional media. It is **site-specific**; that is, designed for a particular place.

STUDYING ART

Critical study

Subjective frame
1. What is the mood created by *Water Works III*?
2. What is your personal opinion of *Tied to Tide*?

Structural frame
3. What methods and materials has Turpin used in *Water Works III*? What other things has she had to consider?
4. Give your definition of an installation.
5. How has Turpin's choice of venue (that is, where *Water Works III* is exhibited) added to the work's meaning?

Postmodern frame
6. What is different and challenging about Turpin and Crawford's work?
7. How does their work widen our ideas on art?

Historical study

8. The choice of site has also been very important to the form and meaning of such artists as Robert Smithson and Christo. Discuss the form of site-specific art. Include Turpin and Crawford in your answer.

MAKING ART

Work in groups to create an installation, using either earth or water as your main element. In your Visual Arts Process Diary document your ideas, sketches and the process of creating your installation. Take photographs or a video of your installation. Write an evaluation of your work.

Arthur Streeton

(1867–1943, Australian)

Frame: Cultural
Form: painting
Conceptual framework: In representing the harshness of the Australian bush, Streeton instils a sense of national identity or pride in the audience.

SUBJECTIVE FRAME

1. What was your first impression of this painting?
2. Given that the words 'fire's on' were yelled as a warning to miners that explosives had been lit, what do you think is happening in this painting?
3. How does this painting make you feel about the early pioneers of Australia?

STRUCTURAL FRAME

4. How would you describe the sense of space in this painting? Look at the distance from the spectator's vantage point to the top of the receding hill. Would it have been a long walk to the top of the hill?
5. Streeton has carefully considered scale in this work. How has he done this and what effect is created?
6. List the colours you can see in this painting as descriptively as you can, for example warm brown, creamy yellows.
7. Describe some of the different textures in this painting, for example the surface of the rocks and the grass.
8. Look carefully at the painting and note the strong contrasts of colour and light and dark, particularly at the bottom of the painting. What does this help to achieve?

CULTURAL FRAME

9. Would you have picked this place as being in Australia? Why?

10. What is more dominant in this painting — the people in the mine or the landscape? What might this tell you about the relationship of people to the land in Australia at this time?
11. What does this painting tell us about life in Australia in the 1890s?

POSTMODERN FRAME

12. How is this different from a present-day mining site? Is anything missing?
13. Can we interpret any power or gender issues in this work by looking at it from the perspective of the present?

CLASS DISCUSSION

Discuss how this painting could help you explain Australian history and geography if you were an exchange student giving a talk at a school overseas.

ESSAY

Now that you have looked carefully at *Fire's On (Lapstone Tunnel)* and formed your own opinion of the work, write a one-page essay on the following topic. (Note: Read 'Writing about art' (see page 201) to help you in your essay writing.) Word process your essay and import images.

How has Streeton depicted the harshness and power of the Australian bush?

Fire's On 1891
Oil on canvas, 183.8 × 122.5 cm
The Art Gallery of New South Wales

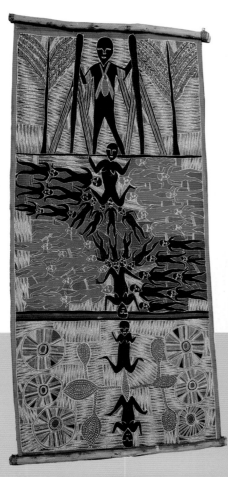

EVENTS

DISCUSSION

1. Look at the artworks shown on the page opposite. Which artwork stirs your emotions most? Why?
2. If you had to organise an exhibition on the use of symbolism in art, which two artworks out of those opposite would you include and why?
3. Important moments in life, such as birth and death, are given a timeless quality in art. Events involving violence or conflict are also popular in art. Consider how the methods and depictions of violence have changed over the years. What do we learn of the social backgrounds of these artists?

Edvard Munch

(1863–1944, Norwegian)

Frame: subjective
Form: printmaking
Conceptual framework: A close relationship exists between the artist and his artworks. The audience is emotionally drawn to the theme of death and the distress of the innocent child.

Vocabulary

aquatint: an etching process in which tiny specks of resin are sprinkled on a metal print plate to protect the metal while in the acid

burin: sharp pointed needle used in etching

etching: lines drawn through a wax coating on a metal plate. When the plate is put in acid, the lines are eaten away and ink is then rubbed into the lines. These lines are transferred under pressure onto dampened paper.

lithograph: a print created by using wax crayon on stone. The principle is that water is repelled by wax.

printmaking: general art term for the process of creating multiples of an image, each one being unique

woodcut: print created from block of wood on which unwanted parts are cut away from the surface and the remaining areas printed

EXPRESSIONISM

a trend in modern European art in which the work emphasises emotion and the projection of inner feelings

The Dead Mother and her Child 1901
Zinc etching with aquatint, 31.1 × 48.1 cm
Munch Museum, Oslo. Photo © Munch Museum (Svein Andersen/Sidsel de Jong)

This etching is a highly emotional, personal statement of the event of death. We look at this image of grief and are moved by the young child. It also makes us think of the wider questions of the meaning of life.

The child has been drawn turning away from the figure, rejecting death. Her plea is directed towards us, the viewer.

Munch has simplified his shapes, using harsh, multiple outlines to increase the emotional impact. He has used the **burin** to scratch into the zinc plate as he would use a pencil on paper. Munch has drawn quick, sketchy lines, outlining the forms and building up areas of tone. The light, all-over shade on the girl's dress, for example, has been added with **aquatint**.

Munch's paintings and prints are a reflection of his unsettled family background, and are an expression of his own personal experience. His mother died of tuberculosis when he was five. His sister, who was a year older than him, died of the same disease when he was fourteen. His younger sister became mentally ill and was at times confined to a mental institution. His father also suffered from bouts of depression and rages bordering on insanity. It is no wonder that Munch suffered from insecurities and became obsessed with the states of loneliness, sickness and death. Munch's art was a means of expressing and exploring emotional and psychological themes and events — of love and death, desire, loneliness, anxiety and despair. He did this in painting as well as **printmaking**.

Munch's interest in printmaking developed at the same time as the French Impressionists were making **etchings**, Gauguin was making bold **woodcuts**, and Henri de Toulouse-Lautrec was creating his **lithographs**. This new importance attached to printmaking was due to a revived interest in crafts and in the growing importance of industrial design. Commercial posters and new graphic images for the printed page gained in prominence. During his lifetime Munch created more than 800 images. He worked with equal mastery in all three major graphic techniques — etching, lithography and woodcut. His lithographs and woodcuts were often an extension of an image he had already expressed in an oil painting, such as the famous *The Scream*, but his etchings were independent originals.

The main aspect of his work is the mood. Its emotional quality greatly influenced the development of German **Expressionism**, a modern art movement.

STUDYING ART

Critical study
Subjective frame
1. List three words to explain the emotions expressed by the girl in *The Dead Mother and her Child*.
2. How has Munch made you feel sympathy for the girl?

Structural frame
3. How does the position of the girl and the bed (the composition) add to the emotional impact of the work?
4. Which two of the art elements listed below are the most significant in this work?
   line, direction, shape, size, tone, texture, colour
   Describe the way they have been used.

FURTHER RESEARCH

Historical study
Discuss the methods Munch used to express emotional states or events. Research the work of the Expressionists James Ensor and Emil Nolde in order to discover their methods of expressing emotion. This could be a group presentation using PowerPoint.

MAKING ART

Subjective frame
Think of an unhappy event in your life. Write down in your Visual Arts Process Diary the thoughts and feelings you felt at the time, and how you feel now, thinking back on it. Draw some of the images that come to your mind. Using black line and ink wash, create an artwork to communicate your feelings about this event.

Davida Allen

(b. 1951, Australian)

Frame: subjective; structural
Form: painting
Conceptual framework: Allen's artworks are very personal to her. The forceful colours, bold application of paint and distortion confront the viewer.

Vocabulary

Archibald Prize:	New South Wales portrait competition
controversial:	causing argument
expressive:	showing emotion or personal feeling
impasto:	thick, obvious paint
naive:	childlike, simple
spontaneous:	quickly done, unplanned, instinctive, unconstrained
universal:	relevant to all

Discussion

Graeme Sullivan has written of Davida Allen that she explores an 'intimate world of private thoughts, feelings and anxieties'.[1] Do you feel Allen's work is more powerful because of its personal nature?

CRITICAL STUDY

In *With Knowledge of my Fourth Pregnancy* Allen is boldly stating a woman's experience. It is full of emotion, with its strong diagonals, strong colours and thickly applied paint. Her brushstrokes are vigorous and full of energy. The figures have been simplified so that they are symbols for her experiences and emotions. The figures are confined by the edge of the canvas, but they extend right to the edge, creating tension. Her images are done in a childlike, **naive** way. They are free, **expressive** and **spontaneous**.

The Death of My Father shows the moment when her father's soul leaves his body. The child floating through the air suggests a symbol of new life. (Allen had just found out she was pregnant at the time of her father's death.) The father reaches out but there is no hand. Tension has been created between the figures. Crows, a common symbol for death, appear to be attacking.

HISTORICAL STUDY

Davida Allen lives in Queensland with her husband and four daughters. Her paintings are like a visual diary.

Allen expresses individual as well as social issues. She explores her intimate private thoughts, feelings and anxieties. She is also representing such **universal** themes as sex, birth, motherhood, religion and death. Her art is concerned with family relationships from the point of view of a wife and mother who is also an artist. It challenges the traditional female role. She is honest, yet passionate, about the constricting elements of her life. Her emphasis is on the family, its conflicts and frustrations, as well as her own search for her role or identity within it.

Allen's work can be roughly broken up into three stages: the first stage, from 1973–79, is imaginative and personal; in the second stage, 1980–83, the female is threatened, and there is conflict in the family; in the third stage, from 1983 to the present, there is freedom to enjoy relationships with children as they become more independent, and there is a hint of humour. In 1986, her **controversial** portrait of her father-in-law, Dr John Shera, in shorts watering the garden, won the **Archibald Prize**.

Allen is generally termed a Neo-Expressionist due to her use of **impasto** and strong brushmarks and the forceful emotion in her paintings. She works mainly within the *subjective frame*.

With Knowledge of my Fourth Pregnancy 1981
Oil on canvas, 200 × 165.5 cm
Art Gallery of South Australia, Adelaide
A. M. Ragless Bequest Fund 1981, courtesy of the artist

The Death of my Father 1981–82
Oil on canvas, 165.3 × 271.9 cm
National Gallery of Victoria

Théodore Géricault

(1791–1824, French)

Frame: subjective
Form: oil painting
Conceptual framework: The audience is emotionally drawn to the tragedy of the shipwreck.

ROMANTICISM

nineteenth-century art movement that emphasised emotion and tended towards dramatic or exotic themes

Discussion

Cultural frame

The Raft of the Medusa enjoyed a great deal of success at the time it was first displayed. Why do you think it was so liked by the public? Does it have the same appeal to you? What changes have occurred in society since 1819 which might explain why we react differently to the dramatic, sensational nature of the painting? Are paintings the only way you see dramatic images today?

The Raft of the Medusa 1819
Oil on canvas, 491 × 716 cm
Louvre, Paris

In this artwork by Géricault, a moving, emotional *event* has been dramatically captured. A shipwreck has occurred, and the stranded, dying survivors point and lean towards possible hope on the horizon. Many emotions and states have been expressed, including despair, rage, hunger and death. The overall mood is one of awe and terror.

Virtually all the lines are diagonal — the men straining forward, the bodies of the dead and dying, the planks of the raft and the lines to the mast. This adds drama as well as movement. They all lean towards the focal point, the man standing upright, signalling to the rescue ship. Colour has been used as an important vehicle for the expression of emotion. The dramatic lighting heightens the emotional impact, and expresses the changing forces of nature, its power and grandeur. The composition is basically contained within a triangle created by the raft and its mast.

Romanticism flourished in France during the reign of the Bourbon monarchy — the Restoration of 1814–30. Romanticism in painting was characterised by the artist's own attitude, feelings and mood towards a subject. As a Romantic artist, Géricault explored the continuing battles between humanity and nature. The event so impressively captured by Géricault was the shipwreck of the French frigate 'La Medusa', which had been carrying soldiers to the west coast of Africa. The shipwreck was considered a national tragedy.

Géricault set to the task of recording this event with enthusiasm and a search for truth as he saw it. He interviewed the survivors, read reports and drew sections of bodies in various states of decay. But Géricault did not just achieve reality; he created a highly emotional scene in his portrayal of heroism and tragedy.

Géricault chose to paint the most dramatic moment of the shipwreck drama, when those on the raft had just sighted a rescue ship. This makeshift raft had held more than 150 people. Only fifteen of the passengers were finally rescued. The survivors described horrific events such as drowning, mutiny and even cannibalism. Stylistically, *The Raft of the Medusa* is painted in a realistic way, with emphasis on the expression of emotion.

STUDYING ART

Critical study

Subjective frame
1. What is your opinion of the relationship of humans to nature in this painting? (Are humans in control of nature?)

Structural frame
2. Describe how Géricault has used the art elements of tone, colour and direction to emphasise the drama and emotion of this event.

Cultural frame
3. Compare this painting's purpose with the role of photojournalism today. Collect images from newspapers and magazines which depict present-day disasters. Have any methods similar to Géricault's been used to attract our attention and involve us emotionally?
4. Art practice: What was Géricault's inspiration? How did he decide on his images and composition? What technique did he use?

Historical study

5. In what ways does this artwork belong to the Romantic style of painting?

FURTHER RESEARCH

Compare this artwork with the historical event depicted by Eugéne Delacroix in his painting *Liberty Leading the People*. What is the artist's intention in each work?

MAKING ART

Subjective and structural frames
Use strong tonal contrast and diagonal direction to record an act of nature to give it a Romantic feel or sense of importance. Your subject could range from a single leaf falling from a branch, water flowing around a rock, or storm clouds, to a natural disaster such as a bushfire or an earthquake. Your artwork could be a painting, drawing, digitally generated image or photograph.

Pablo Picasso

(1881–1973, Spanish)

Frame: subjective; cultural; structural

Forms: mural; oil painting

Conceptual framework: This is a personal statement from Picasso of an event in his country. He was trying to create an emotional response in the audience.

Vocabulary

minotaur: mythical creature that was half-bull, half-man

CRITICAL STUDY

Guernica is a powerful, imaginative expression of the brutality of war. Picasso has created writhing, distorted figures and animals to show us the horror and suffering caused by war. He has emphasised hand and facial gestures. The figures claw the air and scream in despair.

This work on canvas is painted in sombre black, grey and white. Its sheer size has great impact on the viewer.

Picasso often used the bull/**minotaur** as a personal symbol (from his own experience of bullfights). His use of the bull here may symbolise approaching death. The hand clutching a sword may represent defiant opposition. The horse rears in pain and fright. It screams in agony, possibly symbolising the terror of the Spanish people.

Human suffering has been powerfully expressed by the soldier lying broken at the bottom of the painting and the mother attempting to escape with her dead child.

Colour has been kept to a minimum. The painting could be called monochromatic (one-colour) since a hint of blue is the only colour used. There is no joy of colour in this depiction of war. By working on a large scale, Picasso increases the work's emotional impact. A large triangle behind the smaller shapes holds the composition together.

Guernica is a social comment by Picasso and expresses his shock, horror and protest at the bombing of a defenceless Spanish town, Guernica, during the Spanish Revolution.

Guernica 1937
Mural, oil on canvas, 349 × 777 cm, Museo Nacional Centro de Arte Reina Sofia, Madrid.
© Pablo Picasso, licensed by VISCOPY, Australia, 2004

This painting by Pablo Picasso records the event of the aerial attack on the Spanish town of Guernica at 4.40 pm 26 April 1937. General Franco, to further his bid for power, allowed Hitler to bomb Guernica as a demonstration of military power. The town was undefended, populated only by civilians, and was well behind the battlefront. The bombardment lasted for three hours. One out of every seven people in the town was killed.

Although *Guernica* originated from the reaction to a particular incident, it has taken on universal significance as a powerful visual statement of protest against the senseless brutality of war.

Picasso himself was reluctant to explain the symbolic meaning of the images in the painting. 'It isn't up to the painter to define the symbols', he said, though he did confirm that it expressed his horror at the misery caused by the Spanish Civil War.

The mural was completed within a month, a reflection of Picasso's strong commitment to the subject and to the Spanish Republican Government. It was hung on their behalf at the Paris World Fair in June 1937. It was later given to the Museo del Prado in Madrid.

Discussion

'Neither Picasso's left-wing friends, nor his critics on the right, were happy about 'Guernica' but with the passing of decades the painting has embedded itself firmly in modern consciousness. The bombing of that Basque town is now remembered more often because of the painting than as history.'[2]

What do you feel are the merits and pitfalls of painting as a medium for recording political history?

STUDYING ART

Subjective frame
1. What aspects of this work affect you emotionally?
2. Can you relate this at all to your own experiences or imagination?
3. Write two sentences describing your reaction to *Guernica*, using at least three of the following words:
   emotional, symbolic, simplified, reaching, jagged, expressive, imagery, distorted, monochromatic

Structural frame
4. List five ways in which Picasso has shown chaotic destruction and agony.
5. Near the old-fashioned lamp and above the horse's head is an eye-like shape with an electric light bulb at the centre. What do you think it symbolises?

Cultural frame
6. Why do you think Picasso has included a horse in this painting?
   What symbols would you use to express war today?

Historical study
Cultural frame
7. In what ways is *Guernica* a modern interpretation of war? Compare it with an ancient example of art depicting war. You might like to look at Greek or Assyrian art as your example. What changes in society do you see between the ancient example and *Guernica* by Picasso?

MAKING ART

1. Look through papers and magazines to collect images of war or violence. Create a collage (cut out images, carefully arrange them, then stick them down or scan them and arrange them digitally) to show your views on war or violence in today's society. You may include photocopies, your own drawings, and words.
2. Choose a current song with lyrics suggesting violence or aggression and make a video exploring this theme.
3. Create an animation based on horses. Use past artworks that include animals as backdrops; for example, works by Franz Marcs or by Rubens. Also look at Richard Goodwin's *Solo Horse with Rider*, page 69.

Tom Roberts

(1856–1931, born in England, worked in Australia)

Frame: cultural
Form: oil painting
Conceptual framework: This work expresses Roberts's reaction to the Australian outback and his desire to share a sense of national identity with the audience.

A Break Away! 1891
Oil on canvas, 137.2 × 168.1 cm
Art Gallery of South Australia, Adelaide
Elder Bequest Fund 1899

Discussion

James Smith, an art critic for the *Argus* at the time, wrote of Roberts's painting that it was 'slap-dash brush work ... a pain to the eye'. Do you agree with this critic? Is it considered slap-dash brush-work now? What has happened to change our opinion? From what frame was Smith writing (*subjective*, *structural* or *postmodern*)?

CRITICAL STUDY

In *A Break Away!* we are witness to an Australian pastoral event — a stampede. It is a moment of action as the sheep panic at the smell of water. A horseman bravely tries to turn them around. There is a clash between the violent movement of the horse and rider and the stillness of the bush. It is an heroic moment — the strong, powerful Australian male battling against the odds. The painting is also about the drought-stricken land. Light seems to drench the whole painting and be caught in the dust created by the stampeding sheep.

HISTORICAL STUDY

Tom Roberts spent six weeks on the road with drovers in the Riverina district of New South Wales, making sketches for this work. He then returned to the Brocklesby shearing shed near Corowa in New South Wales where he had painted *Shearing the Rams* the previous year (see page x). *A Break Away!* continues Roberts's portrayal of subjects that expressed national identity. The late 1800s was a time of nationalism in Australia. Until the Depression of the 1890s, wool was Australia's major industry.

Roberts has shown Australia as a hot, barren country where life is harsh. (There had been a succession of droughts in the 1880s.) But he also shows us its beauty — the clear blue skies, delicate foliage and glaring sun. The country life is shown as good, honest, hard work.

Although Roberts composed and painted *A Break Away!* in a shearing shed away from the scene, he had, in the Impressionist manner, made preliminary oil sketches in the open air in order to capture the harsh light and colours of the bush. Roberts was a member of the Heidelberg School of art (look at the work of Arthur Streeton on page 137).

STUDYING ART

Critical study

Subjective frame
1. How do you feel about the land in *A Break Away!*? Choose three words from the list below and write a description of your reaction to it.
   harsh, lush, dry, welcoming, sparse, dusty, rich, peaceful, eventful, shady, drought, heat
2. Do you see any evidence in this painting of people struggling to control and live in this land?

Structural frame
3. The rider leaning to the side causes a strong diagonal in the painting. How has Roberts balanced this?
4. How has Roberts created the feeling of urgency?

Cultural frame
5. What can you learn about farming methods from Roberts's recording of this historical event?

Historical study
6. Look at the paintings by Tom Roberts (see also page x) and Arthur Streeton (see page 137) in this book. Write down three characteristics of the Heidelberg School of painting. What do these works communicate about the time and place in which they were created?

FURTHER RESEARCH

Cultural frame
1. Read some of the literature and poems written around this time, such as that of Banjo Paterson and Henry Lawson. How do they express similar themes and attitudes towards country life?

2. Research the work of two female painters, Jane Sutherland and Clara Southern, who were painting at this time. How is their approach similar, but their subject matter slightly different? Why do you think this is so?

MAKING ART

Subjective and cultural frames
Use photography to record an heroic event in your everyday life (for example, an important moment on a sports field, or a solo musical performance).

John Brack

(1920–99, Australian)

Frame: structural
Form: oil painting
Conceptual framework: Brack analyses then represents his view of the world.

Vocabulary

analytical: showing careful thought and planning rather than emotion

ritual: a solemn or serious repeated act

CRITICAL STUDY

John Brack has recorded a social event in *Latin American Grand Final*. The subject is a ballroom dancing competition. It suggests graceful movement and excitement. Brack, however, makes his own interpretation of the event. This relaxing hobby has become an impersonal, artificial **ritual**.

Brack has a unique approach to drawing the human form. His figures are stiff and angular, with false smiles, the men merely silhouettes.

There is distortion. Brack has created his figures in a precise, simplified way. Line as outline, and elegant, flat, simplified shapes are the two elements used in the depiction of the figures. The strong use of diagonals gives a feeling of instability and change.

The vast expanse of red floor acts as a contrast to the detail on the dresses. The floor is tilted, slippery and hostile.

The Battle depicts an historical event, the crucial battle of Waterloo. It symbolises conflict and anxiety within human society as a whole. Brack has depicted the British, French and Prussian troops as pencils and their officers as pens. The combatants raise playing cards as flags or battle standards.

Latin American Grand Final 1969
Oil on canvas, 167.5 × 205 cm
Reproduced by permission of the National Gallery of Australia, Canberra

HISTORICAL STUDY

Brack's reason for painting such new, sharp pencils in *The Battle* was to portray people who have had minimal experience of life, who stagger from one situation to another.

Brack portrays the urban world where people are vulnerable and isolated, usually out of touch with nature and at the mercy of our fast consumer society. His figures are symbols for humanity rather than individuals. Although Brack's approach appears cold and calculated, there is a sensitivity to his **analytical** interpretation. His approach is more from the mind — intellectual rather than spontaneous and emotional.

Of his own working technique, Brack said that he reasoned everything out before starting. He made a watercolour, pen and ink study on paper first, then did a painting on canvas, applying the paint like a signwriter, with a fine sable brush. Brack saw the twentieth-century world as being in a precarious state, an anxious age, where people prefer the artificial to the real — a point of view revealed in his work. Brack saw the irony in everything, and his paintings reflect this irony. He worried about the future of society, particularly city and suburban life. He was also able to see humour in it.

The Battle 1980–83
Oil on canvas, 203 × 274 cm
Gift of John and Helen Brack 1992
Reproduced by permission of the
National Gallery of Australia, Canberra

Discussion

By looking at Brack's works and reading his statements, what do you understand about Brack's opinion and attitude towards life? What can you guess about his personality?

STUDYING ART

Subjective frame
1. The man standing behind the ballroom dancers in *Latin American Grand Final* is actually a self-portrait by the artist. Why do you think he has included himself? Does it add any meaning to the painting for you?
2. Look up the meaning of the word 'irony' in the dictionary and explain how Brack uses irony in his paintings.
3. Can you see any tension in his work? Where and how is it created?
4. Look at the work of Arthur Boyd (see page 154) and describe how his paintings are opposite in approach and technique to those of Brack. From which *frame* does each artist approach his work?

Structural frame
5. Can you see a geometrical shape in the arrangement of the carefully placed figures in *Latin American Grand Final*? What shape is it?
6. Describe Brack's use of colour and the purpose and effect it has.
7. How does Brack use symbolism in his work? Are they Australian symbols or universal ones?

8. Brack actually attended the event of the dancing competition and took photos. Is *Latin American Grand Final* a realistic interpretation? Which parts of the original photographs do you think he might have incorporated and which parts has he altered in his own style?

Historical study
Cultural frame
9. Locate another artwork from a different time to Brack's *Latin American Grand Final* which shows a social occasion or event. What do Brack's artwork and the artwork you have chosen reveal to you about the lifestyle of the time in which each was created?
10. Both *Guernica* by Picasso (see page 146) and *The Battle* by Brack are modern depictions of war. How has each artist communicated his views on war without realistically painting men fighting? What attitudes and values have been communicated?

MAKING ART

Structural and cultural frame
1. Take photographs of a social event or collect images from magazines. Create an artwork, simplifying the images to create your own style. Pay particular attention to the composition — the arrangement and balance of your shapes. Record your research, ideas and preliminary drawings in your Visual Arts Process Diary. Write an evaluation of your artwork.
2. Create an artwork to communicate some of the social activities you are interested in. Present it in an interesting way, such as a sculpture suggesting a dressing table or bookcase, a collection of objects (for example, in a box or suitcase) or a diary. Consider including both images and words.

Wandjuk Marika

(1927–87, Dhangu, Rirratjingu clan)

Frame: structural; cultural
Form: painting — ochres on bark
Conceptual framework: The art object itself has spiritual significance, as the artwork is a visual history of the artist's people, their beliefs and their land. The inner story is not open to a wide audience to interpret.

CRITICAL STUDY

This work is divided into three panels which tell a Dreamtime story of creation. It is obviously about childbirth, but it is not about personal experience as in Davida Allen's painting (see page 143). Marika's artwork is a visual history of a people, their beliefs and culture. The figures have been reduced to symbols. No emotion is shown.

The fine, detailed pattern (the *rrark*) adds to the beauty of the work as well as its spiritual nature. It also identifies the area (the shifting sands on the beach at Yalangbara) and the group of people it represents.

The colours and media used are traditional to the Aboriginal people of Arnhem Land.

HISTORICAL STUDY

This story of the Dreaming concerns the ancestral Djang'kawu who gave birth to the clans in Arnhem Land and who underpin their cultural beliefs and way of life. The Djang'kawu are commonly described as two sisters and their brother who came across the sea from the east and landed at Yalangbara on the eastern shore of Arnhem Land where they made their first camp. They carried with them dilly bags decorated with feathers, conical shaped mats and large digging sticks. They travelled west and, at every place they camped, they made bodies of fresh water by driving their large digging sticks into the ground. The sticks became casuarina trees. The sisters would crouch under the mats and give birth to sacred objects and to the ancestors of the clans who would inhabit that country. The upper panel shows the brother with the dilly bag around his neck, holding two digging sticks, and casuarina trees on either side. The middle panel shows the sisters giving birth to the clans. The lower panel also shows the birth, but now the clans are represented symbolically as the six round shapes of the conical mats. The afterbirth is represented by the dotted forms.

STUDYING ART

Critical study
Structural frame
1. List the colours used in *The Birth of the Djang'kawu Children at Yalangbara*.
2. What does the pattern in the background represent?
3. Draw three symbols from this painting and explain what you think they might mean.

Historical study
Cultural frame
4. What do you learn about Aboriginal beliefs and culture from reading the story of this painting?

MAKING ART

Structural frame
Present a story of your own in three parts using symbols and patterns. Scan the three parts into a graphics program and create a desktop published document of the images, with text explaining the story.

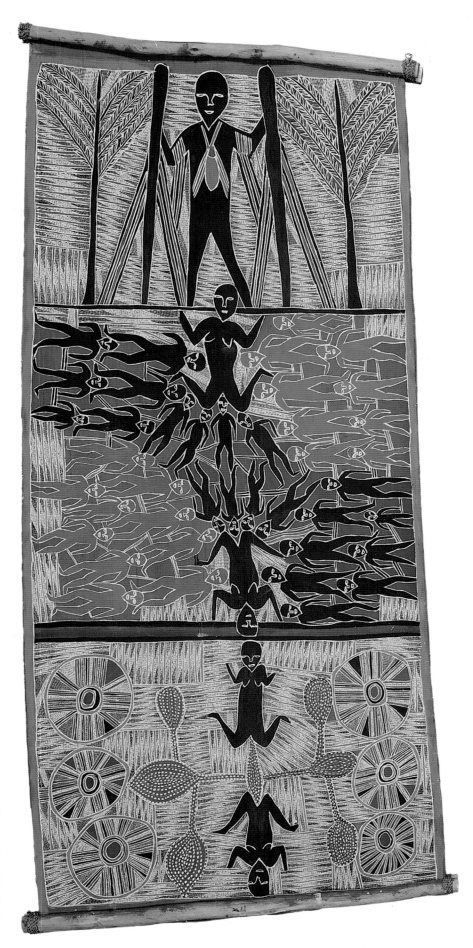

**The Birth of the Djang'kawu
Children at Yalangbara** 1982
Ochres on eucalyptus bark,
147.5 × 66.0 cm
National Gallery of Australia,
Canberra
© the artist, licensed by Aboriginal
Artists Agency, Sydney
Purchased from Gallery admission
charges 1983

Arthur Boyd

(1920–99, Australian)

Frame: subjective; structural; cultural
Forms: painting; ceramics
Conceptual framework: There is generally a personal link between Boyd and his artworks. He expresses his religious ideas based on his life experiences and on reactions to particular places.

Vocabulary

articulate: to clearly express

manifesto: public statement of theories or policy

metamorphosis: transformation of one thing into another, for example one animal becoming another

mythological: belonging to a traditional myth or legend

The Expulsion 1947–48
Oil on hardboard,
101.6 × 122 cm
The Art Gallery of New
South Wales
© Reproduced with the
permission of Bundanon

CRITICAL STUDY

In *The Expulsion* Arthur Boyd has interpreted a religious event that has been recorded throughout art history — the expulsion of Adam and Eve from the Garden of Eden. Boyd is making a religious statement but he is also making an emotional moral judgement. The angel swoops down, yelling at Adam and Eve in anger, whip in hand. Adam hides his head in shame. The wider message here is that in love you are vulnerable to authority. This image of hiding lovers being watched recurs again in later paintings, as does the symbol of the black crow, shown here in the tree.

The landscape of the Garden of Eden is not one we have come to expect from traditional images — this is the Australian bush.

Boyd has used rich, glowing colour. The male and female have been symbolically separated by their flesh colour. Boyd has skilfully applied texture, contrasting the rough rocks with the delicate treatment of the grasses, leaves and hair.

Persecuted Lovers 1957–58
Oil, synthetic polymer paint and
gouache on composition board,
137.2 × 182.9 cm
Art Gallery of South Australia
A. R. Ragless Bequest Fund 1964
Reproduced with the permission
of Bundanon

A social event — a celebration of marriage — is the apparent subject of *Persecuted Lovers*. The bride is in her wedding dress. Boyd has used this event to make a social comment on 'mixed marriages', and the idea of love and guilt. The theme of opposites — good (the bride) versus evil (the hunter) — is also hinted at. The figures have been simplified. There is emotional impact and tension. The use of symbols has developed. Male and female again are of different colours, this time to represent the fact that the bride is a half-caste, the groom a full-blood Aboriginal. The black crow again looks on. The flowers represent both the bridal bouquet and death. The hunter with rifle represents their doom. This painting is about human suffering as well as love.

Referring to an emotional religious event, *Judas Kissing Christ* represents human betrayal. The figures have undergone the same simplification, for expressive reasons, as the figures in *Persecuted Lovers*. The clay has been harshly scratched, taking away any possible decorative quality. Raw emotion is the result.

HISTORICAL STUDY

Arthur Boyd expressed in his work basic human passions, life's struggles, good and evil, life and death. He did this through religious, **mythological** and social events. All were related in some way to his personal views, upbringing (he came from a very religious family) or experiences.

The 'Bride' series represented human conflict, continuing his theme of lovers as victims. Boyd often portrayed contrasts of feeling in the one work, for example passion and suffering, or hiding and being watched. There is generally a sense of tension in his work.

The 'Bride' series, including *Persecuted Lovers*, was exhibited as part of the Antipodean exhibition in Melbourne in 1959. This group of artists believed in using images as meaningful symbols of their feelings and experiences (see the discussion on Charles Blackman, page 16, for further information).

Boyd's lifelong interest in ceramics as a means of expression seems natural given that his father, Merric Boyd, was one of Australia's most gifted studio potters. Boyd used bowls and plates as 'ceramic paintings' as well as expressive sculptures. Merric Boyd's work related to natural forms and the idea of transformations and **metamorphosis**, all influences on Arthur Boyd's artistic themes.

Boyd expressed his personal comments on human affairs and events, the mood being one of inevitable doom.

Judas Kissing Christ 1952–53
Glazed, painted terracotta, 60.9 × 37 × 36.6 cm
The Art Gallery of New South Wales
© Reproduced with the permission of Bundanon

FOCUS WORK
CRITICAL STUDY

James McGrath

(b. 1969, Australian, lives and works in the US)

Frame: Postmodern
Form: digital
Conceptual framework: The viewer is drawn into this image, which hints at the past world yet uses contemporary technology.

ART PRACTICE

Highly recommended in the Blake Religious Prize 2002, this work was created using digital cloth simulation and architectural software to build a viewpoint of a 3D computer environment.

CONCEPTUAL FRAMEWORK

1. This is a new form of artwork — the digital image. What advantages and disadvantages are there in creating digital artworks?
2. Everyone can appreciate the colours and patterns in this work but to take in its full meaning, what is required of the audience?

SUBJECTIVE FRAME

3. What do you actually see in this work?
4. What is the mood? How would the size of this work add to the mood?

STRUCTURAL FRAME

5. How is the sense of drama created?

CULTURAL FRAME

6. How has McGrath melded different cultures and times together?

POSTMODERN FRAME

7. How has technology allowed the artist to manipulate images and create an original, exciting work by borrowing images of a Baroque church, St Ignatio?

CRITICAL WRITING ACTIVITY

Write a short review of this work suitable for a new 'cutting edge' art magazine.

Pozzo's View: Variations on a Baroque Ceiling: 'The Apotheose of St Ignazio'
Giclée (inkjet) print 121 × 200 cm
Courtesy the artist and Michael Carr Art Dealer

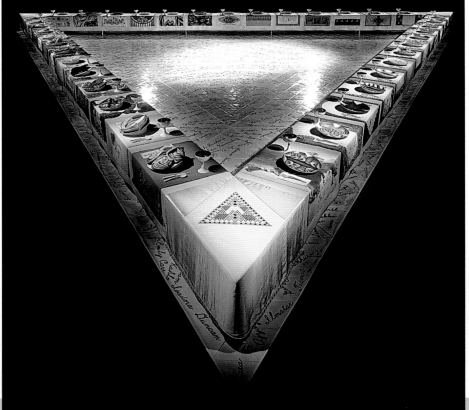

We have received orders
not to move

ISSUES AND THEORIES

DISCUSSION

1. Working in groups of four students, choose from the selection opposite an artwork that deals with an issue that interests you. Discuss the work together. Present to the rest of the class your decisions on:
   - the meaning of the artwork
   - what the attitude of the artist is towards this issue
   - what methods have been used to communicate the artist's ideas and feelings
   - how successful the artist has been in challenging you on this issue.
2. Hold a class debate using the artworks opposite to support your arguments. The topic is: Art should be original and display artistic skill.
3. Look at the artworks opposite and list any that have been created with a medium or technology that would not have been invented before 1930.
4. Which of the artworks opposite are making some kind of political comment?

Kasimir Malevich

(1878–1935, Russian)

Frame: structural
Form: painting — oil on canvas
Conceptual framework: The artist leaves the interpretation up to the viewer (audience).

IMPRESSIONISM

> a modern art movement concerned with depicting light on the surface of objects

FAUVISM

> a modern French art movement that began around 1905, and which was interested in bold, pure colour and decorative line

FUTURISM

> a modern art movement which started in Italy. It sought to represent the dynamic, energetic life of the city and machines.

SUPREMATISM

> Russian abstract art movement in which artworks were limited to basic geometric shapes

CRITICAL STUDY

Here we see a painting based on the theory that art was essentially a visual language of colour, line and form — total abstraction. *House Under Construction* is a dynamic composition of rectangles and squares that lead the eye upwards. The colour is applied in flat areas on a pale background, creating a sense of purity. Malevich was working here mainly in the *structural frame*.

HISTORICAL STUDY

Kasimir Malevich's early work was similar to the art of **Impressionism** and **Fauvism**. His figures then took on the geometry of Cubism. They became further broken up and gained movement, resembling **Futurism**. By 1913 Malevich was seeking a less representational form of expression. His *Black Square* (1914–15), a black square centred on a square white canvas, was the beginning of his totally abstract style.

In the title of *House Under Construction* and in its attitude towards art we see a striving for something new, an optimistic belief in the new age that followed World War I. The war had greatly altered European society. There was a desire to change the world, to make it a better place. Malevich was one of those who believed in the theory that abstract art could turn things around and create new hope. He believed abstraction, like music, could appeal directly to the senses to create a new state of spiritualism. The movement of Russian Modernism was in full swing after the 1917 Russian Revolution and lasted approximately ten years. Malevich called this pure form of abstraction **Suprematism**. By 1930, with the USSR under Stalin's leadership, this modern art was officially banned.

House Under Construction 1915–16
Oil on canvas, 96.6 × 44 cm
Reproduced by permission of the
National Gallery of Australia, Canberra

STUDYING ART

Critical study
Subjective frame
1. What are your reactions to *House Under Construction*?
2. What does it remind you of?

Historical study
3. In what way was abstraction in art a reflection of its time?
4. What are the links between Malevich's paintings and the architecture of the de Stijl group?

FURTHER RESEARCH

Research the way abstraction developed in different countries and through different modern movements, for example Vasili Kandinsky in German Expressionism, Joan Miró in Surrealism, Piet Mondrian in Dutch de Stijl.

MAKING ART

Structural frame
Create an abstract artwork where the main direction is diagonal. You may like to move around torn pieces of paper first to help you decide on your basic composition. You do not need to limit yourself to geometric shapes as Malevich has done in *House Under Construction*. This could be done using a graphics computer program.

Judy Chicago

(b. 1939, American)

Frame: postmodern
Form: installation
Conceptual framework: The idea of the 'master' artist who is the original creator has been challenged, as has the nature of the artwork. These are collaborative works, and involve what were considered craft skills, such as embroidery.

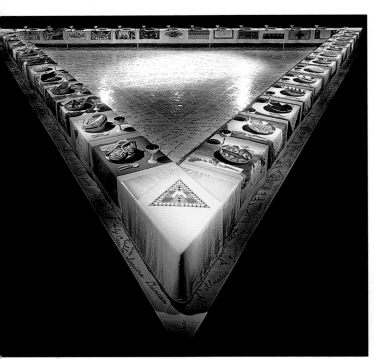

The Dinner Party 1979
© Judy Chicago
Mixed media, 1464 × 1281 × 91.5 cm
Collection of the Brooklyn Museum of Art, Gift of the Elizabeth A. Sackler Foundation
Photograph © Donald Woodman

Emily Dickinson place setting from **The Dinner Party** 1979
© Judy Chicago
Mixed media
Collection of the Brooklyn Museum of Art, Gift of the Elizabeth A. Sackler Foundation
Photograph © Donald Woodman

CRITICAL STUDY

The Dinner Party consisted of a large, triangular table containing place settings for thirty-nine women who had made important contributions to world history. The women come from eras ranging from prehistoric to recent times, and include Egyptian Queen Hatshepsut, American Indian Sacajawea, feminist Susan B. Anthony and writer Virginia Woolf. The project was organised and directed by Judy Chicago in cooperation with a working community of 300 people (mainly women). This joint venture took five years.

Each place setting included a hand-embroidered fabric runner and porcelain plate, chalice (goblet or wine glass) and tableware (knife, fork and spoon) designed in honour of that woman. The names of 999 other notable women of achievement are inscribed in ceramic tiles below the table. The installation was overwhelming in its colour and scale. Some of the oval plates are painted with flat designs. Others have moulded relief (raised) areas, such as that symbolising artist Georgia O'Keefe. Some plates suggest female parts — the erotic nature of many added to their shock effect and general controversy. *The Dinner Party* toured major Australian cities in 1988. It was considered quite shocking at the time. The fact that it cost US$250 000 to complete demonstrates the strength of the women's movement in the United States.

In 1983 Chicago began another large-scale work called *Birth Project*, one section of which — *Birth Trinity* — is seen below. Its theme is childbirth — after all, only a female can comment on this experience in an intimate, personal way, and thus the work is exploring a feminist issue. It consists of approximately 100 individual pieces designed by Chicago. It was made in various types of fibre crafts by 150 volunteer needleworkers, nearly all women. It includes the traditional female crafts of embroidery, quilting, weaving and crochet.

Body parts have been simplified so that they are almost symbols. Curving lines outline the figure and surround it in a decorative way, yet also suggest the waves of contraction pains associated with childbirth.

HISTORICAL STUDY

The feminist movement began in the 1970s and Judy Chicago was one of its earliest 'speakers' in terms of art. She belonged to the women's movement and was co-director, with fellow artist Miriam Schapiro, of the Feminist Art Program of the Californian Institute of the Arts in Los Angeles.

Feminist art focuses on the role of the female, and in particular comments on how women have been shown throughout art history and the power men have had over females. It is also a reaction against the idea during Modernism that all important artists were male.

Birth Trinity, from the **Birth Project** © Judy Chicago 1983
Needlepoint on 6-mesh canvas by Teaneck, NJ Group, 129.5 × 333.2 cm. Collection of the Albuquerque Museum, Albuquerque, NM. Photo: Through the Flower Archives

Feminism is often called the first Postmodern movement. Such female activities as sewing, embroidery, quilting and pottery had traditionally been called crafts and were considered not suitable for display in art galleries. The feminist artists confronted this notion and combined craft media and techniques and an interest in pattern and decoration in their art.

Feminist art is not a unified style; it is more a commitment to a political statement and the use of media and materials long associated with women. It is also an expression of personal female experiences.

STUDYING ART

Critical study
Structural frame
1. Why do you think Chicago chose these lush colours for *Birth Trinity*? Are they symbolic in any way?

Historical study
Cultural frame
2. How is *The Dinner Party* a statement about past cultures? What did it hope to change in the culture of the late 1970s?

Postmodern frame
3. The type of design in *Birth Trinity* can be seen on posters, natural healing books, and CD covers. Why do you think Chicago has used such popular culture imagery?
4. What non-traditional, and thus Postmodern, media and techniques do feminists use?
5. In Postmodern art the process of creating an artwork (the ideas and making of it) is considered as important as the artwork itself. How does this idea relate to *The Dinner Party*?

MAKING ART

Cultural and postmodern frame
1. Create your own table setting based on a female you consider important.
2. Create an artwork which comments on the role of females in your present society. This could be done digitally by scanning in photographs and adding text and layers of various effects.

Barbara Kruger

(b. 1945, American)

Frame: postmodern
Form: photography
Conceptual framework: Kruger comments on her world from a female point of view. She aims to confront and even shock the viewer.

Vocabulary

appropriation: the practice of borrowing images from art, advertising and media and using them in new and interesting ways

context: the circumstances, surroundings or situation of an artwork

feminist: concerned with equality for women, recognition of rights

montage: art technique in which cut-out images are arranged, the images being ready-made; or where several photos are superimposed to form a single image

POSTMODERN

influenced by an experimental, contemporary art movement associated with post-industrial societies

CRITICAL STUDY

Untitled (We Have Received Orders Not to Move) 1982
Photograph, 182.9 × 121.9 cm
Courtesy Mary Boone Gallery, New York

In the artwork below, we read Kruger's message as we do an advertisement on a billboard and we either agree or disagree. We react immediately to her text (words) and images. The messages we see every day in the mass media shape the way we see ourselves — this is what Kruger is reacting against. Her works are generally **feminist** and often political.

The form she uses — large photographic imagery **montaged** with text — deliberately reminds us of billboards, but the message is different. They do, however, refer to the way people are controlled and influenced by the media. She has appropriated her images, using photographs that have already been seen in a different context. This method of **appropriation** is more obvious in her *You Invest in the Divinity of the Masterpiece* overlaid on the image of the creation of Adam (from the Sistine Chapel by Michelangelo). Her slogans are clever, double-edged in meaning, sarcastic, humorous and confronting. Kruger uses sign systems rather than personal expression through paint.

Kruger's images are generally in either seductive or threatening poses. The object being held in *Untitled (Buy Me I'll Change your Life)* is at the same time humorous and threatening. In *Untitled (We Have Received Orders Not to Move)* the figure fills the space, touching the frame on two sides. This gives a sense of tension.

Other examples of Kruger's work include a photograph of a plate of pastries overlaid with the demand 'Give me all you've got'. Kruger makes statements with her works, such as 'Why you are who you are' and 'You are not yourself', which relate to how our culture conditions us.

Kruger, like many **Postmodern** artists, is attacking the power of the media, consumerism, stereotypes of women, and the role of power in a male-controlled (patriarchal) society.

Barbara Kruger at first studied photography, then went into advertising as a designer and picture editor. From poster and magazine advertising she learnt how to tell something quickly through images and words. Kruger develops this device further — she wants you to look at the picture and then disregard the conventional meaning that the image usually carries.

Kruger is regarded as a Postmodernist and a feminist artist. Postmodernism generally questions the idea of the individual. Postmodernist artists appropriate images because they believe identity (what we think of ourselves) is socially controlled. Our self-image is shaped by social images: teenage girls, for example, want to look like the models they see in fashion magazines. Kruger's work *You Thrive on Mistaken Identity*, which has text over a distorted photograph (superimposed with a honeycomb pattern), refers to the lie of the image — you don't really see yourself as you are in the mirror or in a photograph. Her *Your Comfort Is My Silence* is a feminist comment about the way men expect females to be passive and silent. At times Kruger's work can directly confront the spectator, as in her piece *Your Body Is a Battleground*, which is a political statement about abortion. Kruger's work is always thought-provoking.

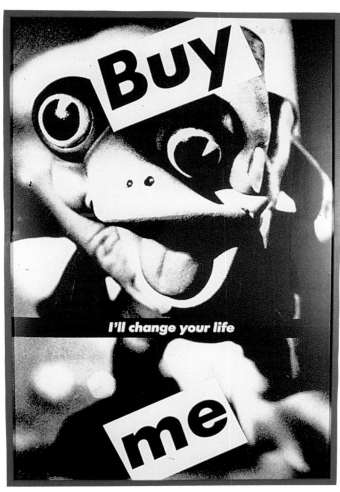

Untitled (*Buy Me I'll Change Your Life*) 1984
Photograph, 182.9 × 121.9 cm
Courtesy Mary Boone Gallery, New York

STUDYING ART

Critical study
Postmodern frame
1. What is non-traditional about the form (media and techniques) that Kruger uses?
2. In what type of roles does Kruger place females in her work?
3. How has Kruger commented on and included popular culture in her work?
4. In what ways does Kruger use humour?
5. List three issues that Kruger has dealt with in her work.
6. How is Kruger's work similar to a poster? How is it different?
7. Kruger's work seems impersonal — there are no individual touches by brush or drawing. It suggests a rejection of traditional notions of art. How does this affect the meaning?

Historical study
Cultural frame
8. What does Kruger's work reveal to us about American society in the early 1980s?
9. In what ways is Kruger's work feminist in attitude?

FURTHER RESEARCH

Lettering has been used in art since the time of the Cubists. Dada and Pop Art also used lettering. Find two examples of modern art with lettering and explain how it adds to the meaning of the work.

MAKING ART

Postmodern frame
1. Choose an image from a magazine. Add lettering and change the **context** to make it a feminist comment.
2. Take an advertisement and alter its meaning by changing the words to make a social comment.

Julie Rrap

(b. 1950, Australian)

Frame: postmodern
Forms: photography; painting; installations; computer-generated imagery
Conceptual framework: Rrap challenges traditional forms of art objects. Her works are confrontational, involve the audience, and are informed by past art.

Vocabulary

conceptual:	concerned with ideas
installation:	an arrangement created for a particular site or gallery
photomontage:	artwork composed of sections of photographs arranged and pasted down

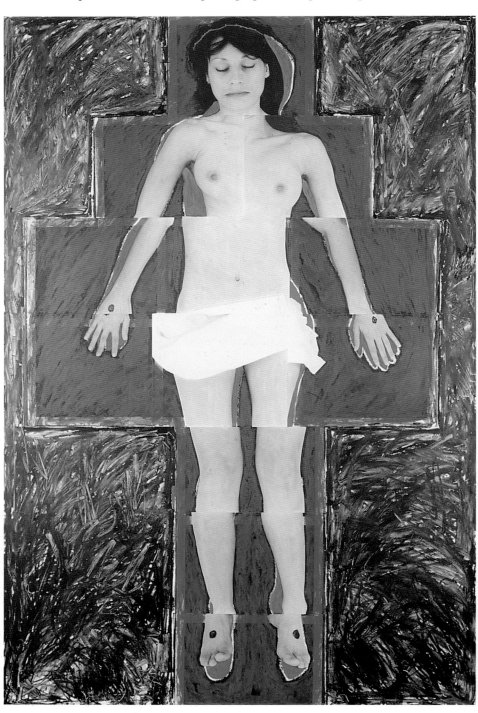

Christ (Persona and Shadow Series)
1984
Colour Cibachrome

Julie Rrap has made a personal and powerful artwork. The image of Christ we are used to seeing is a man on the cross. Here we have a new version.

Photomontage has been used — the image has been divided up into a grid and abstracted. The background has been painted with thick expressive brushstrokes, creating movement. The whole work has then been re-photographed.

The usual symbols of the crucifixion — the cross, nails through the hands and feet, eyes closed, body naked except for a loincloth — are still there. But the differences are that the cross has changed from the neutral wood colour, Christ has been portrayed as a female, and the image is broken up and disjointed.

Christ seems to be a comment on our changing society and its religious values. It is also a feminist statement. The artwork comments on the male dominance of past art. Rrap has chosen an artwork by Munch (see an example of his work on page 140), drawn an outline of the figure and positioned herself within that outline. By doing so, she is slipping out of the stereotype of the female.

Each of the portraits in the *Fleshtones* series was created to suit the individuality of the person. Rrap states: 'I have treated the landscape like an interior.' The skin of the doctor's chest is manipulated to wrap around a rock shape to resemble a pregnant stomach. She took the photographs, then worked on them using Photoshop and a 3-D computer program. The image was then inserted into a landscape and printed digitally. The resulting photograph produces a slight feeling of repulsion, yet it is intriguing. The viewer is left wondering if this is some mutant life force, a comment on contemporary medical science and its attempts to create artificial life, or a joke by the artist. Rrap has certainly 'played games' with the imagery.

Coogee Paul *(Fleshtones series)*
2003
Digital print
150 × 126 cm
Roslyn Oxley9 Gallery

Monument I is one of a series of three works. Each has an imprint or mould of Rrap's body in what appears to be a bronze monument. She playfully invites the participant to not only touch the artwork (normally viewers are asked not to touch artworks in galleries) but to become part of the artwork by placing their body in the same position. This action is recorded on the video monitor. Rrap's humour is evident when we consider the positions of the imprint of Rrap's body and how the participant would look on the video monitor. In the first monument Julie Rrap has been 'caught' on all fours, the imprints being that of hands, knees and feet. In another, the imprint was taken while Rrap was sitting, leaning back with knees in the air (suggesting the position of giving birth); the other is of her lying on her side.

Monument I 1995–96
Fibreglass and bronze dust
Each 141 × 78.5 × 15 cm

HISTORICAL STUDY

Julie Rrap began her artistic career working with her brother Mike Parr (Rrap is Parr spelt backwards) on his performance work.

Her early work, in the 1980s, focused on the representation of the female body. She used photographs of her own naked body against the artworks of the 'great masters', such as Munch, Degas and Rembrandt, to try to change our ideas that have been formed from the way the female has been shown throughout art history. In these works she mimics the poses of the figures in the paintings, placing herself in the historical setting. However, she does not try to disguise herself to fit into them. Her own identity remains as her image slips into, but does not precisely fit into, these past masterpieces. She used several Postmodern processes: the element of humour, appropriation and challenging the precious nature of the original.

Rrap uses a range of media within the one work — photography, photo-emulsion (liquid light), acrylic, oil — which adds to its uniqueness. She also often 'doubles' her image, as in Christ with its blue 'shadow', suggesting reflection or displacement.

Julie Rrap's recent work is mainly in the form of mixed media **installations**. Her work titled *Ten Muses* (1990), which she exhibited in Belgium, continues the use of photography. Here, photographs of feet have been transferred (through the process of using liquid light) onto the top of a group of milking stools. The body has become an illusive fragment. In other recent work, the body's presence has been suggested. In *Untitled* (1994), an installation at the Art Gallery of New South Wales, ballet shoes clumsily move by themselves while a video monitor shows feet attempting to stand on their toes. Other works include human hair, either as photographs in the image of plaited hair, or as the actual substance in unusual situations, such as stuffed into a transparent handrail as part of an installation piece. Her art is **conceptual** in approach. She challenges how the body is represented as an object by art, politics and technology. This is often done with a playful sense of humour working on various levels of meaning and associations. She refers to her artworks as types of 'games', inviting the onlooker to interact and 'play'.

Rrap explores issues of identity and the body.

STUDYING ART

Critical study

Subjective frame

1. What is your first reaction to *Christ*? Do you feel any of these emotions: shock, humour, disgust, alarm, hostility, encouragement? (Include others.)

Structural frame

2. Why do you think Rrap has fragmented (broken up) the image?
3. There is contrast between the figure and the background. How has this been achieved?
4. What symbols has Rrap used in her work? (You might like to consider how she suggests the body in her recent work.)

Postmodern frame

5. How is Rrap's work a challenge to the power of art history?
6. Why do you think the figure in *Christ* seems to be lying down rather than hanging from a cross in a real landscape? How does it add to the meaning?
7. How is her art a comment about power and sex roles?
8. How does Julie Rrap challenge accepted notions of art, such as its serious nature; the purpose of the monument; traditional use of media? (Can you think of any others?)

Historical study

Structural and cultural frames

9. Look at past examples of paintings of Christ on a cross.

How has Julie Rrap changed the image? Consider the form (media and techniques) she has used as well as other structural considerations, such as symbolism and composition.
10. How is Julie Rrap's work similar to that of Kruger (see page 164)?
11. Artmaking practice: List the different media that Julie Rrap has used in her artmaking. What does this tell you about her as an artist?
12. Conceptual framework: Explain some of the methods Rrap uses to attract the interest of and involve the audience.

FURTHER RESEARCH

Postmodern frame

Investigate how women have been portrayed in art throughout history. Find an example of the following roles:

(a) fertility figure   (c) Madonna
(b) mother   (d) naked beauty.

What other roles can you find? How is Julie Rrap trying to break these stereotype roles?

MAKING ART

Postmodern frame

Borrow (appropriate) an image of an important male from a past artwork. Alter its context (surroundings or backyard) and transform it into a female to create a feminist Postmodern artwork.

Jenny Watson

(b. 1951, Australian)

Frame: subjective; postmodern
Forms: painting; installations
Conceptual framework: There is a close relationship between the artist and her artworks, which explore her feelings and responses to her world. The audience can interpret them in various ways according to their own experiences.

CRITICAL STUDY

In *Girl With a Flower* there is a dream-like quality. The girl looks vulnerable. She holds a daisy, reminding us of Alice in Wonderland.

The painting is executed in a direct, simple manner, but its size and brightness of colour give it an importance and meaning.

The overall effect is naive and childlike, from the drawing of the figure to the lettering, as if a child has been practising different letter types. It is as if the painting is a puzzle we are asked to solve.

Dream Palette consists of small, separate canvas boards laid out in an uneven grid. They include images of a clock, a horse's head, a moon face, parts of bodies, and writing. The writings do not seem to connect to the images. The images themselves are an unusual mix, as if they are snippets of dreams, thoughts and memories. The text appears as messy handwriting.

Dream Palette 1981
Oil, synthetic polymer paint, crayon, pastel, pencil and charcoal, 36 canvas boards, 64 × 51 cm each
Courtesy of the artist and Roslyn Oxley9 Gallery, Sydney

HISTORICAL STUDY

Jenny Watson's work is strongly personal and thus difficult to place in a category, although it is Postmodern in approach and does often deal with female issues.

During the 1970s Watson painted portraits, still lifes and horses in a variety of realistic styles, usually directly from photographs. In the 1980s her work became more introspective and nostalgic of her early childhood in suburban Melbourne, for example *Self Portrait of a Little Girl* (1987). Her early love of children's books is evident in her recurring theme of Alice in Wonderland, where she herself becomes Alice. Watson's work shows how our concept of self-identity is influenced by our memories and impressions from childhood as well as our present experiences. We see her experiences of living on a country property symbolised in the horse image which occurs in many of her paintings. Her works are a combination of everyday items and memories.

From 1977 Watson began to include scrawled words and phrases, often taken from television and newspapers, as an important part of her paintings.

In the series of works created for the Venice Biennale in 1993, the text was exhibited separately beside the image. The connection between the two is cryptic and suggestive; the text does not explain the work. In these works she has used the medium of velvet and net to reinforce her role as a female artist.

Watson, by her subjects and techniques, makes art more accessible: expressing female events and dreams that we can appreciate and understand.

Girl With a Flower 1993
Oil on hessian and acrylic on pre-stretched canvas, and text panel, 152 × 91 cm, text panel variable
Courtesy of the artist and Roslyn Oxley9 Gallery, Sydney

STUDYING ART

Critical study
Subjective frame
1. Watson is quite capable of drawing and painting realistically. Why do you think she has deliberately chosen to work in this less formal, more sketchy way? What meaning and mood does it add to the work?
2. Why do you think the girl is holding a daisy? What does it symbolise?

Postmodern frame
3. Watson makes statements in her art about the roles of females. Describe the type of girl she has portrayed in *Girl With a Flower*.
4. Why do you think Watson has included handwriting rather than typed or commercially produced writing? She often includes her own signature in a prominent place, sometimes upside down. What does this add to its meaning?

Historical study
5. Artists are often influenced by other art forms such as music, poetry and novels. Like Jenny Watson, the Australian artist Charles Blackman did a series of paintings inspired by the story of Alice in Wonderland. How has each artist interpreted this story? What similarities can you see between Watson's and Blackman's works? How is each a personal statement by the artist revealing their life experiences?

MAKING ART

Subjective frame
Create an artwork which includes an image of yourself and refers to a story or poem that is special to you. You might like to use the format of *Dream Palette* and do a series of small works, or you could create a video or animation.

Lin Onus

(1948–96, Australian)

Frame: postmodern; cultural
Forms: painting; installations
Conceptual framework: The artist expects the audience to interpret his artworks using their knowledge of Aboriginal and Western art. The artworks reflect Lin Onus's perception of his world.

Fruit Bats 1990
Mixed media
Height 290 cm
© Lin Onus, licensed by VISCOPY,
Australia, 2004

CRITICAL STUDY

In *Fruit Bats* the Hills hoist (clothes line), a symbol of Australian white suburban living, has been combined with traditional Aboriginal colours and linear cross-hatched patterns (called *rarrk*) on the bats. The painted surface of the bats contrasts with the ready-made object — the Hills hoist. The spattering of tiny shapes at the base of the hoist is an Arnhem Land symbol representing bat droppings. There is a strange mixture of symbols and reality in this work — manufactured objects, nature, different cultures. There is also an element of humour.

HISTORICAL STUDY

Lin Onus began painting in 1974 and was basically self-taught. He was heavily involved in the Aboriginal Arts Committee of the Australia Council.

Onus's style was very distinctive, with his photo-realist, non-Aboriginal style converging with traditional Aboriginal techniques. In *Arafura Swamp* rectangles of traditional Aboriginal paintings float in a landscape which reminds us of Monet's *White Water Lilies* (see page 110). Here we have two interpretations of the landscape as expressed by the conventions and beliefs of Aboriginal and Western cultures. In Aboriginal art the representation of the land is through the stories of the Dreamtime. It is symbolic, spiritual, rich in pattern, and has an aerial viewpoint. The traditional Western interpretation of the landscape is as 'a window to the world'; a realistic representation showing depth and atmosphere. By placing the *rarrk*, the spiritual patterning, within the '*Western* landscape' Onus makes a political statement claiming Australia as Aboriginal land.

Each culture has its own visual language. Western culture represents what is seen, whereas the Aboriginal is what is known. Onus has skilfully combined the two — the Aboriginal rectangles float on the surface like lily pads, yet keep their identity. The artwork suggests Onus's experiences in belonging to both cultures.

Onus used to make regular trips from Melbourne, where he lived, to Ramingining, central Arnhem Land, gaining ideas and inspirations for his artworks on the long journey.

Arafura Swamp 1990
Acrylic on Belgian linen, 182 × 182 cm
© Lin Onus, licensed by VISCOPY, Australia, 2004

STUDYING ART

Subjective frame
1. Can you find any humour in Onus's work? Where and how?
2. Why do you think Onus has placed the fruit bats on a clothes line? How has it added meaning to the work?

Structural frame
3. Analyse the two different techniques Onus uses in *Arafura Swamp*.
4. Structurally, what do you think is the reason for including the reflections of the black tree trunks in *Arafura Swamp*? Do they add to the meaning of the artwork?

Cultural frame
5. From the evidence in these two artworks, what do you think is Onus's opinion about white/black relations in Australia?

Postmodern frame
6. How has Onus changed the context, and our perceptions, of the bats and Hills hoist? How does this add to or change their function or meaning?

Historical study
Cultural frame
7. What aspects of traditional Aboriginal art are evident in Onus's work? Look at the painting by Wandjuk Marika (see page 153).

MAKING ART

Cultural frame
Research patterns and visual symbols that represent different cultures: for example, floral patterns on Indonesian batik, patterns on African masks, Chinese calligraphy. Combine at least three of these to make a poster about multiculturalism.

Rea

(b. 1966, Australian)

Frame: postmodern, cultural
Form: digital media
Conceptual framework: This artwork confronts the audience, forcing them to consider social issues.

Vocabulary

Postmodern: influenced by an experimental, contemporary art movement associated with post-industrial societies

CRITICAL STUDY

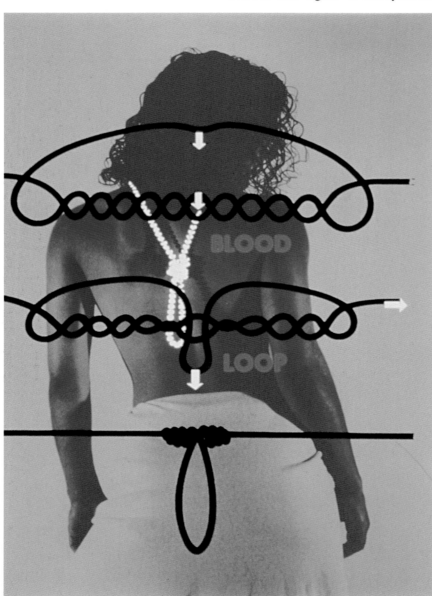

First impressions suggest that *Resistance III* is a comment on black deaths in custody. There are four photographic panels, each image slightly different. The image is of an indigenous person viewed from behind. The figure is anonymous, the face is hidden and it is unclear whether it is male or female. The figure has either a noose or string of pearls around the neck. Overlaid are diagrams showing how to tie a hangman's noose, and the words 'knot', 'blood', 'noose' and 'loop' are superimposed over the image. The images have been manipulated by a computer. Words have been added on top.

The repetition of the image reinforces its power. The central placement of the figure is similar to an advertisement. Red, blue, black and white are the only colours used. The symbol of the noose in the rope diagrams reminds us of an instruction manual. The message of *Resistance III* is a comment on violence, yet the scientific style of noose diagrams is impersonal. The image is a symbol for past and present violent, inhumane treatment of Aboriginal people. The string of pearls is a comment on class and indigenous culture. It calls for a response from the viewer — a social awareness.

The use of technology, text and reference to past art (the figure is standing in a typical S-shape found in classical Greek sculpture) makes this a **Postmodern** work.

Resistance III: I–IV (detail) 1994
Digital C Type, 100 × 60 cm
Photograph courtesy of the artist and
Boomalli Aboriginal Artists Co-operative

Rea is an artist concerned with raising issues relevant to her Aboriginal heritage, with which she identifies personally. She has chosen to work in a Postmodern style. Rea's works are 'readable' by a wider audience because she has presented her ideas using the poster format, photography and words — all elements easily recognised in popular culture.

An earlier work by Rea, *Look Who's Calling the Kettle Black*, explores the influence of colonialism on Aboriginal culture. It consists of ten computer-generated photographic images. The series comments on her memories of her grandparents. With bibles in their hands and dressed in their Sunday best, their Koori culture and spirituality have been taken over. Old photographs of her family are superimposed onto 'Western, white' consumer products such as a toaster and iron. The contrast in images forces us to think about such issues as cultural differences and assimilation policies. It also recalls the way Aboriginal women were placed in domestic service. Rea includes definitions of the words 'black' and 'domestic' in the works.

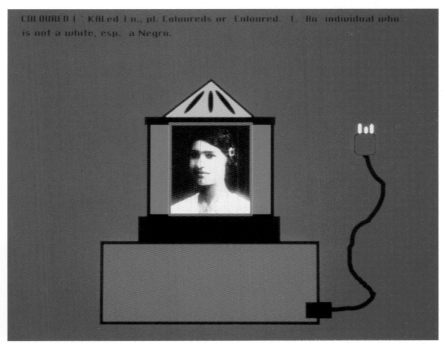

Look Who's Calling the Kettle Black I–X (detail) 1992
Digital C Type, 19 × 25 cm
Photograph courtesy of the artist and Boomalli Aboriginal Artists Co-operative

STUDYING ART

Critical study
Structural frame
1. How has Rea used everyday items as symbols? How have they been simplified and what do they remind you of?
2. Rea uses the structural device of repetition in her work. What effect does it have?

Postmodern frame
3. Postmodernism communicates ideas. What are the main ideas in these two works?

Historical study
4. What similarities in media and approach do you see in the work of Rea and Postmodernist Barbara Kruger? (see page 164). How does their work relate to our present society?

MAKING ART

Cultural frame
Take an existing object (ready-made) which is typically Australian, for example a Vegemite jar, and alter it in some way to turn it into a social comment.

Leah King-Smith

(b. 1957, Australian)

Frame: postmodern; cultural
Form: photography
Conceptual framework: The artwork questions past knowledge, stimulating the viewer to think.

Vocabulary

appropriate: put a familiar image in a new context to change its meaning
archival: contained in historic records

#4, Patterns of Connection 1991
Cibachrome photography
Photograph courtesy of the artist

These images challenge our perceptions of Aboriginal people. We are asked to look again at history, to consider white/Aboriginal relations. The mood is brooding, almost dreamlike. Their impact comes from their large scale, the combination of images and the way the images have been altered. King-Smith has combined portraits of Aborigines and bush landscapes. The figures had been dressed up and posed, and their positions are not natural. By superimposing the landscape over the figures, King-Smith is attempting to place her ancestors back where they belong.

Leah King-Smith is a visual artist living in Queensland. She has used nineteenth-century **archival** portraits of Aborigines from the State Library in Victoria in her art. Her work reflects her personal reactions to her heritage. King-Smith has an Aboriginal mother, a white father and is married to a white person. She originally came from Mundubbera in Queensland and says she has always felt torn between two cultures. Her works are a way of expressing this tension.

King-Smith's work is a personal search for identity but it is also an attempt to gain a wider understanding of the history of white/Aboriginal relations. The contrast of cultures, the attempt to reconcile, in art, Aboriginal traditions with white Western teachings and art images are issues for many Aboriginal artists. We can see this also in such artists as Lin Onus, Sally Morgan and Trevor Nikolls.

King-Smith focuses more on being black than being a female in her photography. Thus she is not a feminist artist, but she does approach her work from a female point of view.

Women have had a big impact on photography since the 1980s. They have used the medium to explore their identity and experiences. They have widened the subject matter and, in doing so, have changed the nature of photography.

STUDYING ART

Critical study

Subjective frame

1. How is the relationship between the people and the landscape in the work from *#4, Patterns of Connection* unusual or confronting?

2. What feelings do you get from this photograph? What does it remind you of?

Postmodern frame

3. How have the images been changed in time and context?

4. What similarities are there in approach, method and content between King-Smith and Rea (see page 174)?

Historical study

Cultural frame

5. How is King-Smith's work a search for identity? How does it communicate ideas on race, gender and power? What historical evidence has been included in her work?

FURTHER RESEARCH

Postmodern frame

Research the work of two artists who have expressed their multicultural background in their art. Discuss how their work relates to traditional Aboriginal art. Have Modernist artworks been **appropriated**? Present your work as a word-processed document with images inserted.

MAKING ART

Postmodern frame

1. Take photocopies of two artworks from different cultures. Cut them up and rearrange them in a humorous way. This could also be created digitally.

2. Consider your own identity and cultural influences. Use Photoshop to arrange and layer images and text.

Imants Tillers

(b. 1950, Australian)

Frame: postmodern; cultural
Form: painting – synthetic polymer (acrylic)
Conceptual framework: Tillers' artworks are his interpretation of the world of the past, as a means of commenting on issues in his contemporary world.

Vocabulary

appropriate: put a familiar image in a new context to change its meaning

CRITICAL STUDY

Imants Tillers has reinterpreted a painting by Eugene von Guérard, *North-east View from the Northern Top of Mount Kosciusko*. Von Guérard created his painting from drawings made during a scientific exhibition. His view is one of the grandeur of nature and its God-given order. The figures are dwarfed by their surroundings, and provide a sense of scale.

In his version of von Guérard's painting, Tillers is challenging the authenticity of the original since it, too, is only an interpretation. *Mount Analogue* is questioning the power of mass media and how it can alter the way we see artworks and the original subject — our environment.

IMANTS TILLERS
Mount Analogue 1985
Oilstick and synthetic polymer paint on 165 canvas boards
279 × 571 cm
Reproduced by permission of the National Gallery of Australia, Canberra

EUGENE VON GUÉRARD
(1811–1901 (b. Vienna) Australian)
North-east View from the Northern Top of Mount Kosciusko 1863
Oil on canvas, 66.5 × 116.8 cm
Reproduced by permission of the National Gallery of Australia, Canberra

In *Diaspora* Tillers has **appropriated** images from a variety of past and present artists including artists from Germany (George Baselitz and Joseph Beuys) and New Zealand (Colin MacCahon), as well as symbols and images from history and international publications and art magazines. *Diaspora* asks questions about discovery and reality. It is a complex work which comments on a wide range of issues: the art world in general, originality and reproduction, identity, multiculturalism and the reinterpretation of history.

Imants Tillers was born in Australia of Latvian refugee parents. He feels a strong connection with his European roots and shares his parents' concern with being detached from Europe, with being displaced persons. This feeling is expressed in *Diaspora*. The painting was completed in 1992 for exhibition at the Latvian National Gallery, where it was shown as a series of paintings exhibited as one artwork. The artwork was a comment on the new political, social and economic circumstances following the collapse of communism in Latvia in 1991.

Tillers studied architecture in Sydney and graduated in 1972 with the University Medal. His earlier artwork included sculptural objects and installations and, in 1972, he participated in a series of events and happenings, for example, *The Joe Bonomo Story*.

The word 'diaspora' comes from a Greek word meaning 'a scattering', but it also refers to the dispersal of Jewish people in Israel in 722 BC. Tillers has extended its meaning in this painting so that it expresses a sense of cultural displacement and longing for a lost homeland. This is an emotion shared by many Australians who come from varied backgrounds.

Tillers is primarily a conceptual painter since his art is heavily based on ideas. The main concept of his work is the manipulation of images through reproduction. The process of his art is quite complex, involving extensive research into writings and images. He explores present and past art as well as history and culture.

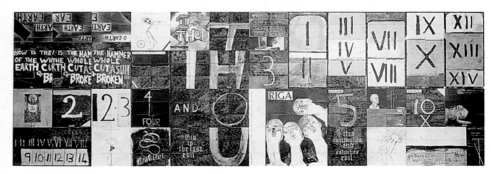

IMANTS TILLERS
Diaspora 1992
Synthetic polymer paint, gouache, oilstick on 288 canvasboard panels, 305 × 914 cm
Te Papa Tongarewa, Wellington

STUDYING ART

Critical study
Postmodern frame
1. What devices has Tillers used in *Mount Analogue* to make us reconsider von Guérard's original? How do these devices reflect our present society?
2. Does the breaking up of the image into squares remind you of anything? Does it add to the meaning of the work?
3. In *Mount Analogue*, Tillers has treated each panel separately so that the colours and brushstrokes do not match exactly. Do you think this was intentional? If so, why do you think he did this?

Art practice
4. *Diaspora* is not a narrative — it does not have a start or finish. How does this affect its meaning? What do you think is Tillers' intention?

Historical study
Cultural frame
5. What references to the past are included in Tillers' work? How is his work a reflection of our present society?

Postmodern frame
6. Find two other artworks in this book that use appropriation. How has this Postmodern method added to the meaning of the work? You may like to work in groups and make a PowerPoint presentation to the class.

MAKING ART

Cultural and postmodern frames
Each student in the class is to investigate their cultural background and contribute an image representing their cultural heritage, which will be combined in a class mural. Include appropriated images from artworks of various cultures.

CHAPTER SIX: ISSUES AND THEORIES

Jill Scott

(b. 1952, Australian)

Frame: postmodern
Form: video installation
Conceptual framework: Jill Scott makes artworks that reflect the impact of technology on our contemporary world. She involves the audience directly in these interactive works.

V·o·c·a·b·u·l·a·r·y

installation: an arrangement designed for a particular site or gallery

Postmodern: influenced by an experimental, contemporary art movement associated with post-industrial societies

FUTURISM

a modern art movement which started in Italy. It sought to represent the dynamic, energetic life of the city and machines.

DADA

a modern art movement that was anti-art and tried to shock its audience (from a French word meaning 'hobby horse')

CONSTRUCTIVISM

an abstract art movement that originated in Russia in about 1914, and which typically used industrial materials

Paradise Tossed 1992
Video art, video drawings and computer graphics, interactive installation and performance
Roxlyn Oxley9 Gallery, Sydney

CRITICAL STUDY

This work deals with the points of view of four young women. The women represent the time frames of the 1900s, 1930s, 1960s and 1990s. By accessing their views, we are able to see the tremendous changes in environmental issues and domestic life which have occurred this century.

Each animation presents a dream home from an architectural style of one of the four periods — Art Nouveau, Art Deco, Op Art and Space Age. We are able to witness the development of the use of household machines as symbols of human–machine relationships since the beginning of this century.

We are given choices and are seduced with advertisement-type slogans. The viewer is asked to 'Step into the technology of Tomorrow'. Other choices allow us to view the development of the means of transport, the technology of mobility, once again accompanied with seductive captions.

Paradise Tossed is an interactive, computer-animated video **installation**. It involves a twelve-minute three-dimensional animation on a Sony laser-disc player. The menus are laid out like pages. The participant (no longer just a spectator of art) can touch the screen and choose segments to be played on another screen, creating associations.

Technological art began with the Industrial Revolution when science and technology came into a much closer relationship. *Paradise Tossed* shows an interest in machines and the acceptance of technology that belonged to the Modernist movements of **Futurism**, **Dada** and **Constructivism**. In the 1950s technology and art moved closer together in kinetic (involving movement) and neon art. In the 1960s video art developed, beginning with the work of Nam June Paik and Wolf Vostell. Recent technology has enabled artists not only to invite viewers to 'participate' in an art event or performance, but to 'interact', requiring a more comprehensive involvement. The artist tries to stimulate a two-way interaction between the work and the spectator, creating situations in which questions by the user are effectively answered by the artwork itself.

Jill Scott's artworks address issues about art and technology, as well as personal issues regarding the role of the female.

The **Postmodern** concern for the interaction of the viewer has been of great importance in Scott's work, and she achieves it through the use of technology such as computer graphics, video and sound systems. By their very form, her installations make a statement about the speed of change in our present society.

Paradise Tossed carries on from Scott's earlier work *Machine Dreams* (1990), in which she dressed up as four members of her family — grandmother, mother, sister and self — to show changes in female roles and their interaction with machinery through time. As spectators moved through the space of the installation they took on an active role by triggering sounds relating to each time frame.

HISTORICAL STUDY

STUDYING ART

Critical study
Postmodern frame
1. The new linking of art with technology, often called electronic media art, has created a dilemma, since the art form is caught in an awkward position between:
   (a) popular culture and experimental art
   (b) art and science
   (c) visual arts and performing arts.
   Which of these apply to Scott's *Paradise Tossed*? Explain how.
2. Do you think interactive art is more relevant to our present society than contemplating a painting on a wall? Why?

Historical study
3. The influence of technology on art goes back to what historical time?
4. Who were the pioneers of video art in the 1960s?
5. What is the common theme which Scott has developed in her work through the 1990s?
6. In what ways is her work Postmodern?

FURTHER RESEARCH

Cultural frame
1. In what ways did the Futurist and Dada art movements glorify the machine or incorporate the new technologies of the mechanical age?
2. How is technology influencing present art?

MAKING ART

Cultural frame
1. Create a video which comments on the various roles of the female or male in our present society. This could be presented as a group installation with accompanying artworks on the theme.
2. Create an animation using machine parts.

Robyn Stacey

(b. 1952, Australian)

Frame: cultural
Form: photo-installation
Conceptual framework: The audience is overwhelmed by the artwork's size, disjointed imagery and bold colour. The artwork represents our contemporary world.

Vocabulary

photo-installation: a series of photographs covering more than one wall, designed for a specific site

Quantel: computer system

Discussion

What images remind you of city life? What aspects of our modern technological world, popular culture and the media are hinted at here?

The Infinity Gardens II 1992
Main panel (Desire)
Eleven matt Cibachrome prints, 105 × 631 cm
Installation view

CRITICAL STUDY

The Infinity Gardens II is a comment on the urban technological environment. The fragmented images arranged in a grid remind us of the images from a television screen that quickly flash before our eyes. The work is a reflection of the speed of technology. There is a dream-like quality to these images created by blurring and glaring lights.

The Infinity Gardens II is a vast **photo-installation**. Our culture is represented as images of the city. Cars, lights blazing, are caught at great speed so that the shapes dissolve. The work includes sections of electronic circuits and power cables silhouetted against an intensely-coloured orange–red background. This background is textured like a television screen in close-up. The word 'desire' is stretched across one panel. Side panels extend into the gallery space and enclose the spectator.

Stacey uses photography, the oldest of the modern forms of technology in art. She has chosen photography as a medium for expressing her ideas because it is reproducible, and thus suits our mediated culture in which we know everything second-hand. But Stacey has introduced new ways of utilising this form. She uses the **Quantel** high-fidelity graphics computer to produce photographic installations.

Stacey began using computer images because they could be manipulated easily and quickly. She begins with her own photographs, video stills or found images from the media. Earlier computer-mediated works included *All Sounds of Fear* (1990). In her work *A Touch of Venus*, Stacey was looking at the depiction of women in painting, the role of Eve, and the Fall (when Adam and Eve were banished by God from the Garden of Eden).

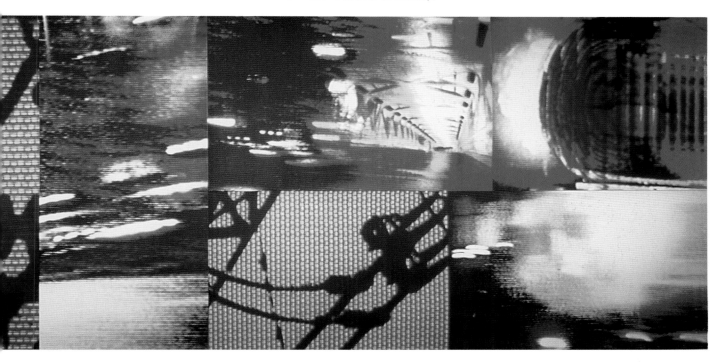

STUDYING ART

Critical study
Subjective frame
1. What does *The Infinity Gardens II* communicate to you? What is your opinion or judgement of this work?

Structural frame
2. Why do you think this work is called an installation rather than an exhibition of photographs? (Look up the definition of 'installation' in the glossary at the back of this book.)
3. Why do you think the images have been arranged in this way?

How does it add to the meaning of the work?
4. Comment on Stacey's use of colour and text (words).

Cultural frame
5. How is this work a comment on our present culture? Look for any evidence of comment on our attitudes, power structures, way of life.

Historical study
Cultural frame
6. What modern technologies does Stacey use in creating her art?

MAKING ART

Cultural frame
Create an installation which comments on the influence of technology on our lives. In your Visual Arts Process Diary record your thoughts, research and the development of this work as well as its documentation in photographs. Write a review of your work for an art magazine.

Phillip George

(b. 1956, Australian)

Frames: postmodern; cultural; structural

Form: digital imagery (as print-outs and CD-ROMs)

Conceptual framework: The artworks are George's response to world issues. He challenges the originality of an artwork and involves the audience.

Vocabulary

digital imagery: images created electronically by points of digital information which are arranged in a two-dimensional grid. Such images appear as points of colour on a computer screen or in a printed version.

ecology: the interrelationship between natural organisms and their environment

Mnemonicon 4 from *Mnemonic Notations* (1992)
Mixed media on paper on canvas, 130 × 288 cm
Photograph courtesy of the artist

CRITICAL STUDY

Mnemonicon addresses several issues including the purpose of technology and its influence on art, and the collision of cultures. Phillip George has combined signs, symbols and imagery from a wide range of cultures, religions and philosophies, and references to **ecology**. Parts of figures are evident, and there is the suggestion of landscape, sea and sky. George breaks down the borders between traditional media (paint) and the new electronic media, in this case **digital imagery** (computers). By doing so, he symbolically breaks down borders of time and culture.

There is a continual encounter in his work between East and West. It is not a confrontation — the images float, at times touching or overlapping, as though part of another world. Many of the images are transparent, placed one on another — interacting but not replacing. The work seems to deal with past, present and future.

Tranzlutions was entered in the Blake Prize for religious art in 2002. The mystical and the everyday are combined in this image of the Madonna and Child floating in the gently lapping waters of an Australian coastline.

Tranzlutions
C-type print 100 × 190 cm

Phillip George's father emigrated to Australia in 1940 from Alexandria; his mother is from country New South Wales. Both sets of grandparents are from Kythera. His artworks make reference to this rich family history, combining imagery from Crete, Kythera, Constantinople, Venice and present-day Sydney.

George's art is about communication and understanding. He uses the freedom and flexibility of computer technology to extend and enrich the forms of art.

STUDYING ART

Critical study
Structural frame
1. George can store his images in computer memory. How does this widen the possibilities for the artist?
2. George has combined both the real and the imagined. Which parts do you think are real and have been scanned into the computer, and which are computer-generated?
3. Draw any symbols you can see in *Mnemonicon 4*. Do you know what they represent?

Postmodern frame
4. In what ways is *Mnemonicon 4* a statement about differences?
5. How does George's work challenge the traditional idea of the originality of the artwork?

Historical study
6. Research the symbols from other cultures that George has used. Explain what country they come from, if they are linked to a religious belief, and their meaning.

MAKING ART

Create an artwork using symbols relevant to your life, interests and family history. Use a computer to scan in and alter the images.

Linda Wallace

(b. 1960, Australian)

Frame: postmodern
Form: video
Conceptual framework: The audience is directly involved in this artwork, which comments on the contemporary world.

Vocabulary

montage: several shots or images partially superimposed to form a single image

CRITICAL STUDY

Eurovision, as the name suggests, is inspired by the Eurovision song contest. The video has been created around four segments of songs sung by the Russian, Swedish, French and German entrants to the contest in the year 2000. To an Australian audience, a range of thoughts may flicker through our mind as the screen changes; we may think about such things as the history and culture of Europe and its languages, foreign 'arthouse' films, migration and globalisation.

Still from *Eurovision* 2001 PAL format video, 19.20 minutes and a DVD interactive Shot, edited and conceived by Linda Wallace www.machinehunger.com.au Sound by Shane Fahey (Footage for *Eurovision* has been sourced from: Jean Luc Godard's *Two or Three Things I Know About Her* (1967) and Ingmar Bergman's *The Seventh Seal* (1957); the *Eurovision Song Contest*, broadcast on SBS in 2000; and images from the Louvre in Paris.)

Linda Wallace has explored many of the techniques available to a digital video artist: splicing images into each other, transforming them, adding text, multiplying and dividing the screen space to create a multi-layered work. Her key devices are fragmentation and repetition. This **montage** of different effects and imagery has revealed a new form for creating artworks using the technology of video — one that is not merely another version of film. It can still tell a narrative but the artistic possibilities have widened. The new-media critic Lev Manovich has termed her work 'digital cinema'.[1]

HISTORICAL STUDY

Linda Wallace is an artist and media specialist and the director of the company Machine Hunger, which has coordinated media projects in countries throughout Asia and Europe. Linda Wallace often acts as the curator for these exhibitions. Clients include the Department of Foreign Affairs and Trade, the Australian Film Commission and CSIRO.

Is it angels, or God, or Satan, or just emptiness?

Still from **Eurovision** 2001
PAL format video, 19.20
minutes and a DVD interactive
Shot, edited and conceived by
Linda Wallace
www.machinehunger.com.au
Sound by Shane Fahey

STUDYING ART

Artmaking practice
1. What have you learnt about the changing nature of the working methods of artists using technology?

Conceptual framework
2. Video art, more than other art forms, needs to be experienced first hand. You cannot gain a good impression of the impact of the work by looking at a still photograph in a book. What other ways can video artists 'exhibit' or show their work? Consider the traditional role of an artwork as a saleable item and precious object. Consider also the problems of copyright in relation to the changing notion of the art object. For example, what is the effect of the availability of DVD versions?

Another of Linda Wallace's video works is *Lovehotel* based on Australian artist Francesca Da Rimini's adventures in cyberspace from 1994–97. This work was assisted by the Australian Film Commission, and premiered at the Sydney Film Festival in June 2000. It has since been shown in Amsterdam, Zurich and Paris.

In 1998, Wallace was awarded a PhD fellowship from the Advanced Computational Systems Cooperative Research Centre, based at the Australian National University in Canberra.

Linda Wallace has said about *Eurovision*:

I ... enjoyed cutting up various narratives into threads and recombining these in novel ways ... playing with the idea of a 'truth to materials' in the digital environment. In terms of its subject matter, *eurovision* is to do with the kind of legacy left by global European culture and science/technology media exports from the late fifties to the late sixties.

... The work is constructed so that you can begin at any point, i.e. any one of the four sequences, and see them in any order. However I am most happy when the work is played as a single screen video, i.e. from start to finish. The DVD interactive mode was an experiment. I think that this work is best when the audience is immersed in it, with the interactivity going on in the viewer's mind.

The sound was engineered by Shane Fahey at Megaphon Studios in Sydney. A band called *Out of the Hat* developed tunes and played along with the projected rough cut of the work. This was added to with loads of layers/samples and then mixed by Shane ... assisted by Steve McMillan.[2]

Phillip George

(b. 1956, Australian)

Frames: postmodern; cultural; structural

Form: digital imagery (as print-outs and CD-ROMs)

The artworks are George's response to his experiences and research into world issues. He challenges the originality of an artwork and involves the audience through the scale of his art and his interactive CD-ROM versions.

ARTMAKING PRACTICE

Phillip George's artworks are hybrid, computer-generated paintings and prints on a large scale. The process is complicated, involving the use of computer graphics packages, hand-painting in gouache, colour laser copies and gilding. George's sources are drawn from transparencies which he scans into his computer's hard disk. He then reworks successive versions, adding colours and shapes, distorting, blending. By transferring the image from computer to copier he is able to blow it up to any size — the works in the *Mnemonic Notations* series are generally three by two metres.

SUBJECTIVE FRAME

1. What ideas, emotions or memories does it suggest to you?
2. Describe what happens to the images from the top to the bottom in this work. What does this suggest to you?
3. What evidence can you see in this work to suggest that George wants us to see more than one meaning?

STRUCTURAL FRAME

4. What methods has George used to suggest the idea of memory and dreams?

5. Describe the use of tone and colour.
6. List three symbols in this work and state what they mean to you.
7. Which areas are in focus (clearly defined), showing the surface texture, and which are blurry? How does this affect the meaning of the work?
8. Which images have been changed or manipulated? How has George done this? (Read the information on Phillip George on pages 184–5.)

CULTURAL FRAME

9. In what way is this artwork a type of diary — a record of George's life experiences and his cultural heritage?
10. What do you see in the artwork to suggest the time period? Is it past, present or future? Or is it a journey from one to another? George calls it 'fluidity of time'. What do you think he means by this?
11. Are all the images Australian? Do you see any images from other cultures or belief systems?

POSTMODERN FRAME

12. How does his work relate to our present society, yet refer to times past?

13. Could this art form have been created fifty years ago? In what way is it new?
14. George keeps his images in the memory of his computer so that he can add to or change them at will. This also means they can be easily reproduced. How does this alter our ideas on what is art?

CRITICAL WRITING ACTIVITY

Write a short review of George's artmaking practice, suitable for a school computer club magazine, to encourage art students to join your club.

ESSAY

In what way is *Memory Stack 2* a 'map of memory'; a build-up of images and experiences?

You might like to refer in your answer to these comments by the artist: 'A bucket of memory is poured down the canvas, compiles itself, sits there and mutates … memory and consciousness, some of the fundamental elements that combine to produce a blueprint of what and how we perceive ourselves and our environment.'[3]

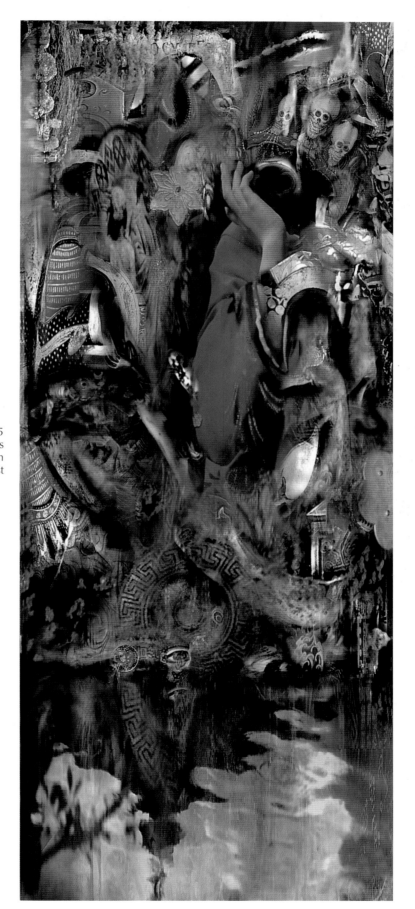

Memory Stack 2 1995
Mixed media on paper on canvas
288 × 130 cm
Photograph courtesy of the artist

Being artwise

What is art?

There is no single definition of art. Individuals have tried to explain their understanding of art, but different people gain different things from a work of art. Art's role and the form it may take are constantly changing. This is because art is always a reflection of society. A tribal society requires special objects for ceremonies and rituals. Art is a way of carrying on traditions and knowledge, particularly of beliefs. Our present society has introduced new forms of art, including video and computer-generated images. Our art comments on such issues as the environment, gender, multiculturalism and the power of the mass media. It is difficult to find one definition to cover all art.

All art involves creativity. It grows from human experience, feelings and thought. Art is something we experience. It adds to our enjoyment or understanding of life.

By looking at art from the past we can gain knowledge and understanding of a society's beliefs, values, attitudes and way of life.

Artists generally have a sharper perception of our world. They experience life deeply, are aware of its beauty, are concerned about its problems. Through their art, artists help us to see more clearly, to be more aware and to think. Artists, particularly recent artists, do not offer us solutions, but challenge us to consider situations. Art is a means of communication — a visual language, a system of conveying ideas and emotions which goes beyond the use of words, similar in a way to music.

In creating art you increase the ways you may explore your thoughts, feelings and imagination. Art arouses your senses.

Functions of art

The functions of art are varied. Art has played many roles throughout history. It is important to realise that it is possible for one object to fulfil several functions at once and that these roles **may change in time and according to context** (the way it is viewed and its surroundings). For example, a Greek pot originally functioned as a storage jar, but it was also decorated, and showed a careful concern for proportion, line and shape. Thus it was also an object of beauty (see chapter 3, page 72). Moreover, the pot explained the ancient Greeks' beliefs by depicting their gods and heroes and their ideas of philosophy, so it was a means of communication. We look at it now displayed in a museum and for us it is a record of a civilisation, helping to explain the ancient Greeks' way of life and values. The same object, redrawn, can also become an advertisement for travel to Greece, changing its function once again.

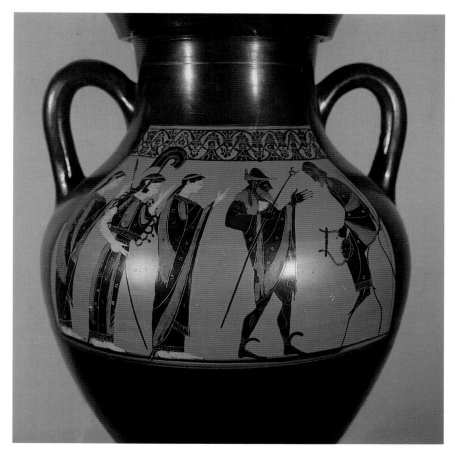

This Greek pot was designed for storage. (It is decorated with images of Hermes bringing Aphrodite, Athena and Hera to Paris for his judgement.) Redrawn in the twentieth century, the pot becomes an image for an advertisement.

Personal functions

Art is a means for people to explore their creative imagination, to express their dreams, beliefs, hopes and desires. Individuals have used art as a means of expressing their emotions (love, grief, anger) and spiritual visions, and of understanding the meaning of life.

Artists also explore their ideas on life and art, expressing their personal theories. Some, for example, show relationships between colour and emotion (see Kandinsky, page 114), and explore ways of representing reality (see Picasso, page 14).

Cultural functions

Art has several important cultural functions, including the following:

Religious/spiritual: Art has the function in various cultures of teaching religion and telling society's stories; of recording important religious events; and of keeping and passing on the culture's rules and traditions.

Narrative: Art can be a means of presenting stories, myths, legends, history, the deeds of a ruler, and so on.

Record: Art records and informs on historical events such as battles and coronations; social events such as celebrations and sport; and natural events such as avalanche and fire. Portraits have the function of recording individual likenesses. Since the invention of the camera, photography has largely taken over this function.

Propaganda: Art has been used as a form of persuasion to glorify rulers, heroes and deities. Political leaders at different times have placed restrictions on art, as a means of controlling information. Art techniques and artworks themselves are also used in advertising to increase its impact.

Social comment: In art we see representations of power, such as portraits of kings. Art also reveals social order, relations between people and the roles they play (race and gender).

Art can reflect a sense of national identity, and create recognisable images or symbols to represent a culture or country.

A function of art can also be to bring about political or social change. This is easily seen in the artworks of feminist artists and in Aboriginal paintings used in court for land rights claims. Art can seek changes in society or affirm changes that are occurring. The Futurists, in their art, glorified changes in society brought about by the Industrial Revolution, the motor car and the concept of speed.

In summary, art serves a variety of functions for a society — it informs and teaches; it explores issues, ideas and emotions. It reflects a culture's beliefs, attitudes, opinions and values, and is an indicator of change.

Written activity/Discussion

1. What is your definition of art?
2. For an object to be called art, what essential features do you think it must have?
3. What do you think are art's most important functions today?
4. How has the art object and the role of the artist changed over time? What do you think has influenced these changes?

Elements of art

The elements of art are what the artist considers when creating an artwork. They are the main components or building blocks of art.

An artist's style is mainly determined by how they use the art elements, what they concentrate on and how they organise the elements according to the art principles (see page 200). The art elements are line, direction, texture/pattern, shape/form, size/scale, colour, tone and mass/space.

Line

A line has several meanings and uses in art. It can be a mark created on a paper with a drawing utensil such as pencil, pen or crayon, or it can be a broad stroke on a canvas made with a large brush. A line may be the meeting edge between shapes or it may divide space. It can define a shape (outline), indicate mood, and create pattern, texture and tone. A jagged, bold line can suggest anger while a free-flowing, curved line indicates gentleness and happiness. Every line has thickness, direction and rhythm. Line is important in both two- and three-dimensional works and is the most common element we use. It has infinite possibilities.

In the Whiteley drawing below, you can see that lines have been used to create texture and contour. Lines have also been repeated to form patterns and free, expressive movements.

BRETT WHITELEY
Interior, Lavender Bay 1976
Pen and ink on paper
76.2 × 57.2 cm
Private collection
© Wendy Whiteley

Activities

1. Explain the different ways line has been used in this artwork by Whiteley.
2. In three rectangles, each 10 cm × 8 cm, express three different emotions just by using lines.
3. Collect examples of lines used in manufactured patterns or advertisements.

The following words describe the way line is used in artworks:

contour	crisp	straight	sensitive
jagged	delicate	spontaneous	wild
swirling	flowing	expressive	soft
broken	broad	aggressive	bold
undulating	narrow	nervous	linear

Direction

There are three main directions:
- vertical — straight up and down
- horizontal — across, parallel to the horizon
- diagonal or oblique — involves angles.

Other directions include spiralling or radiating.

Direction can lead the viewer's eye to a 'focal point' or main area of interest in a painting. It can also indicate movement and mood. The easiest way to understand the emotion or mood associated with direction is to imagine yourself in that position. For example, when you are horizontal you are normally lying down and relaxed. A vertical direction thus suggests height, authority, strength, stiffness, striving. A diagonal direction suggests movement, a split second in time, adding drama to an artwork.

In *Fire Mountain Landscape* below, note the multiple directions of the trees and the curved lines of the mountain tops against the sky.

WILLIAM ROBINSON
Fire Mountain Landscape *(from the Creation series)* 1988
Oil on linen
147.2 × 193 cm
Collection, Art Gallery of Western Australia

Detail from WILLIAM ROBINSON
Fire Mountain Landscape 1988
(see opposite)

Texture/pattern

Texture is used in two ways in an artwork:

(a) The texture of an artwork itself. How does its surface feel? For example, a bronze statue may have a smooth, polished surface. A collage will often have different surfaces; a painting may have thick impasto. A surface is said to be *tactile* if it makes us want to touch it. This is why it is important to see the original.

(b) Texture imitated in artwork. A surface may be drawn to look rough, such as when the bark of a tree looks rough in a drawing but the actual paper is smooth. This is called *visual texture*, and is typical in digital artworks, for example.

A pattern is created when lines, shapes or marks are repeated or organised in various combinations, creating a sense of unity. Pattern is an indispensable part of our daily lives. From earliest times, humans have used patterns to beautify their bodies, utensils, weapons and other possessions.

Pattern may be random, such as autumn leaves scattered on the ground, or repeated, as in checked material or wrapping paper.

Shape/form

We generally think of shape as being a two-dimensional area within an outline, and form as being a three-dimensional object, although these words are sometimes used interchangeably. There is an infinite variety of shapes possible but they can be loosely categorised as geometric or organic. *Geometric* shapes tend to be precise and regular, such as a

Activity

Describe William Robinson's application of paint to create texture.

BRETT WHITELEY
The Olgas ... Soon 1970
Tempera over gesso, enamel,
gold paint, ink, collage, possum
tail, jawbone, boomerang
203 × 325 cm
Art Gallery of South Australia,
Adelaide
South Australian Government
Grant 1977

circle, triangle, square or rectangle. *Organic* shapes are irregular, usually rounded or curved, and seem more 'relaxed' than geometric shapes. They often suggest living organisms, growth or nature in general.

Shapes may also be symmetrical (that is, can be folded or divided equally) or assymetrical. Shapes may be naturalistic and have a realistic appearance, or they may be stylised — simplified to their essential, basic character without details.

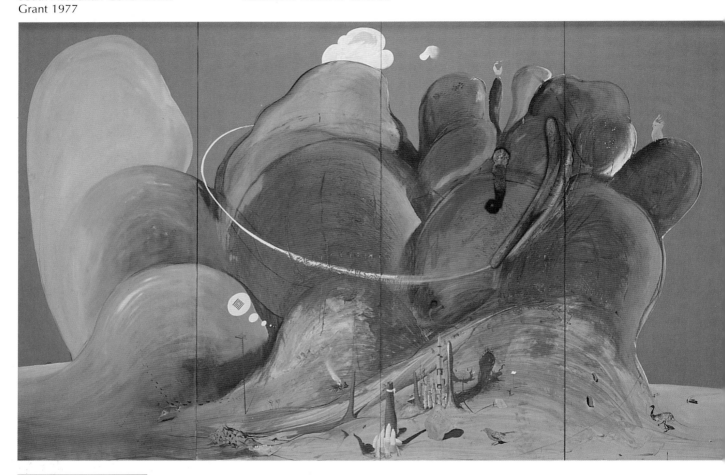

Activity

Brainstorm words that could be used to describe Whiteley's shapes in *The Olgas . . . Soon*.

Size/scale

Size is relative. *Contrast* is created between large and small shapes. A feeling of peace and harmony can be created when shapes are of a similar size. Size is also an important element to consider in creating a sense of unity or balance in an artwork or when trying to create an impact on the viewer. When one size is compared to another, it is called proportion or *scale*. Scale can create a mood — for example, a small boy in a tall, narrow alley — or give importance or meaning, as in Oldenburg's giant sculpture of a gardening trowel in a park.

Activity

Find one example in this book of an artwork in which scale has been an important consideration. How has the meaning or mood been created by the choice of size? How does scale affect the viewer (audience)?

Colour

Colour can give us messages such as 'relax, take it easy' or 'liven up, look here, get happy'. We may not always be aware of this reaction, but we obey these messages subconsciously. Advertising, in particular, uses colour as a tool to affect our mood and reaction to products. McDonald's fast-food chain wants to attract our attention and make us feel happy, so it uses yellow and red for its sign. Have you ever noticed that dental surgeries are usually pale blue, green or grey? They want you to feel calm and relaxed. Colour is important to your daily life and the way you feel. Would you eat Smarties if they were all grey?

Used with permission from Reg Mombassa/ Mambo Graphics

Colours can be divided into different categories:
- *Primary colours* are red, yellow and blue. They are the three basic colours from which all other colours are made.
- *Secondary colours* are two primary colours mixed together; for example,

  yellow + red = orange   yellow + blue = green   red + blue = purple.

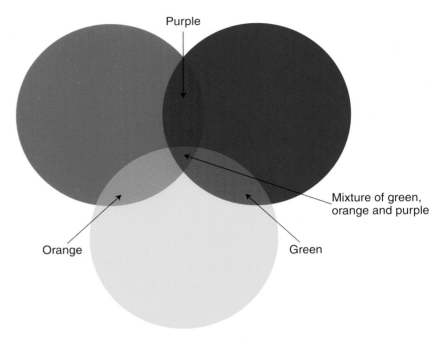

- *Tertiary colours* are a mixture of a primary and a secondary colour.
- *Warm colours* remind us of warm things like fires and the sun. They are yellow, orange, red and pink. In paintings, warm colours tend to jump forward.
- *Cool colours* remind us of cool places like oceans and leafy forests. They are blues, bluish-purples and greens. Cool colours tend to recede in paintings.
- *Complementary pairs* are a primary colour and the secondary colour made by mixing the other two primaries; for example red and green, blue and orange, yellow and purple.
- *Harmonious colours* are colours which are similar and seem to match, such as turquoise, blue and purple.

The following words can be used to describe the way colour is used in artworks:

natural	monochromatic	cool	restricted
expressive	symbolic	bold	dominant
contrasting	warm	dramatic	pastel
harmonious			

Activities

1. Name a video clip that uses colour to suit the mood of the music.
2. Collect examples of advertisements which set a mood by their use of colour.
3. Choose two artworks in this book where colour has been used to suggest a definite emotion or mood.

Tone

Tone is the amount of lightness or darkness; that is, the light and shade on an object. Tone can be used to give the illusion of volume and, also, depth or distance in an artwork. Tone and light can be used to depict weather conditions, time of day and country.

Colours may also vary in tone. Strong contrasts of tone tend to 'come forward' while similar tones tend to 'sit back' in a painting or drawing.

Words used when discussing the use of tone in an artwork include:

dramatic	one light source	soft
diffused	harsh	gradual
contrasting	subtle	chiaroscuro

Activities

1. Make a tonal chart by adding more and more black to white paint in light squares, 2 cm × 2 cm, side by side, so that you gradually go from white through shades of grey to black. Compare this with the tones available on your computer.
2. Make a similar chart using pencil lines closer and closer together and over each other at a different angle (crosshatching).

Mass/space

Mass is the volume or weight of an object or form. A large area of colour or shade can give the feeling of mass in an artwork. Mass is usually associated with sculpture and architecture, and is sometimes referred to as positive space in sculpture.

Space is the distance or depth between people, places, objects or shapes. It is an important consideration in sculpture. The shape of the negative spaces (areas of air) may change as you walk around a piece of sculpture.

As his sculpture below shows, Henry Moore was very interested in the balance between positive and negative shapes.

HENRY MOORE
Reclining Mother and Child 1960–61
Bronze, 228.6 × 90.17 × 132 cm
Collection: Walker Art Center, Minneapolis
Gift of the T. B. Walker Foundation, 1963
Reproduced by permission of the Henry Moore Foundation

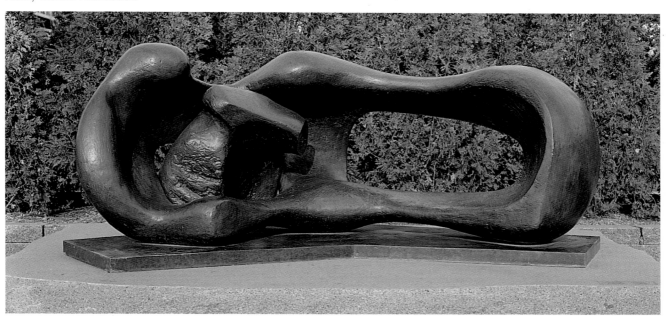

Principles of art

The principles of art are used by artists as guidelines to control the use of the elements of art. They determine how the elements are used, the way they are combined, and their overall effect.

Composition

Composition refers to the arrangement or organisation of an artwork.

Emphasis/focal point

Emphasis is used to draw our attention to an area. If that area is a specific spot or figure we call it a focal point. The focal point is thus where the central action is taking place in an artwork. (See Leonardo Da Vinci's *The Last Supper* (page 37), in which the focal point is the central figure.)

Emphasis is created by the use of the elements of art, for example contrasting colour, tone or directional lines.

Balance/unity

Unity refers to a sense of 'oneness', a feeling of parts belonging, usually created by the balance of the art elements. A unified artwork is one which has its elements skilfully organised into a harmonious whole.

Balance is achieved when the parts compensate each other so well that the result is equilibrium. It creates a sense of 'rightness' in an artwork. Even the depiction of a violent moment with action and drama still needs to be balanced to be convincing and successful as an artwork.

Movement/rhythm

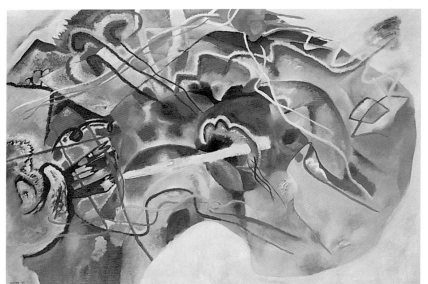

WASSILY KANDINSKY
Painting with White Border (Bild mit Weissen Rand) 1913
Oil on canvas, 140.3 × 200.3 cm
Solomon R. Guggenheim Museum, New York
Gift, Solomon R. Guggenheim, 1937
FN 37.245

Movement in an artwork is the illusion of activity or speed, created by arranging the art elements in such a way that our eye is encouraged to travel across or around the artwork. Diagonal direction is the easiest way of suggesting movement; repetition is another.

Actual movement may also be part of an artwork. This occurs, for example, in mobiles, kinetic art (involving magnets or machines to make objects move), performance work, video art and animation.

Rhythm in an artwork is related to movement. A repetition of units such as lines can set up a rhythm in a variety of art forms. Different types of rhythm include flowing, regular, alternating, progressive and random.

Activity

As a group, look through the earlier chapters in this book to find three artworks with a strong sense of rhythm. Briefly discuss how it has been created.

Writing about art

In order to write a successful essay, you need to:
- explain your understanding of the question in the **introduction**
- refer to artworks to back up your line of argument
- in the **body of the essay** explain both what the artist has done and how
- finish with a strong **conclusion**, stating what you have found and your opinion of the question asked.

Now let's look at these steps in more detail.

Before you begin writing your essay, make sure you have completed the following steps:

(a) Look carefully at the question and *underline key words*.

(b) Have you been asked to argue a point? Will you agree or disagree?

(c) Are you writing art criticism or art history? Have you been asked to write from the orientation of a particular approach (*frame*) such as art practice or the concept?

(d) *Research* information in books and on the Internet — make sure you take note of the book's title, author, publisher, place of publication and date published (also the page number if you are going to use a quote).

(e) Set yourself *limits*. Go through your research and decide what is really relevant to the question, considering the length of the essay you have been asked to write.

(f) Do a *rough*, working out the structure. You may like to do a flow chart or mind map of the key points.

(g) You are now ready to do a *draft*. In doing your draft, consider the following guidelines relating to essay structure.

Essay structure

Introduction

The opening paragraph is where you show you understand the question. Respond clearly to the topic. State your opinion if it has been asked for. This is where you must capture the reader's interest. Start with a strong opening sentence, closely related to the question, and close with an indication of your argument.

Most essays are of the following types:
- **Discuss.** This is asking for a point of view. You must present your knowledge to support your view.
- **Explain.** This means you must give reasons for the cause of, and perhaps the effects of, an event. You may briefly describe first, but an interpretation has been asked for.
- **Describe.** You are being asked to list in order the main facts or points.
- **Compare.** You need to outline similarities and differences between two styles, artists or artworks, and give reasons for the similarities/ differences.
- **Analyse.** You need to explain how an artwork is put together, its meaning, and the relationship of its parts.
- **Evaluate.** This is asking you to determine the value of an artwork and make a judgement on it.
- **Identify.** This requires you to recognise and name things — for example artist, style, period.
- **Interpret.** To interpret an artwork you must draw meaning from it.

The body of the essay

This is where you develop and expand on the question by referring to artists and their work. *Be prepared to discuss at least two examples by each artist to support your argument.* You should:

- use a topic sentence to introduce the main idea of each paragraph
- for each paragraph, refer back to the main essay question (perhaps in the final sentence for each paragraph)
- discuss your artists, artworks or periods chronologically; that is, mention the earlier artist first. This makes more sense, particularly if one influences another or is a reaction to a past style or artist. It helps the flow of your essay if you are not jumping backwards and forwards in time.

You should consider including:

- **What** the artist has created
  - Your reaction to the work, what you see and feel. What is the content or subject? What frame is the artist working from?
  - When was the work produced, where and by whom? What period or style does it belong to? How does it represent the world?
- **How** this effect has been created — its structure/media
  - What is the form of the work, that is mural, relief sculpture, etching?
  - Art elements: line, direction, shape/form, size/scale, colour, tone, texture/pattern, mass/space
  - Art principles: composition, emphasis/focal point, balance/unity, movement/rhythm
  - Use of symbols
- **Why** the artist has created it, the artist's intention, its meaning
  - Is it a reflection or comment on culture — race, gender, power, beliefs, values? 'Historical study' essay questions will require you to give the social background in detail, particularly the influences on the artwork or style (*cultural frame*).
  - What is the function and meaning of the work? Consider its intended function and meaning at the time it was created (for 'historical study'), and if its meaning and function have changed (*postmodern frame*). What does the artwork mean to you (*subjective frame*)? How does it relate to the audience?
  - Has the artist been influenced by others? Has the artist been influential on others?
  - Your judgement of the artwork. This is important for 'critical study' questions but may not be required for an 'historical study' question.

The order you discuss these will depend on the type of question asked — that is, it will depend on whether it is asking about critical or historical study, frames, conceptual frameworks or artmaking practice.

Conclusion

This is where you convince the reader that you have provided sufficient information relevant to the essay question. It should act as a summary of your argument. Remember that the conclusion must be in agreement with your opening sentence and must refer back to the question.

Final copy

Read your draft and check the general flow of your essay. Is it logical and clearly expressed? Are there any points that need further explanation or more information? Have you discussed sufficient examples of art-works as evidence for your argument/opinions? You may like to work directly on the computer so that you can cut and paste and use a spell-checker.

Add your bibliography.

Setting out a bibliography

In setting out a bibliography, you need to follow certain rules:
- List books in alphabetical order by author's surname.
- Encyclopaedias, magazines or newspapers can be listed after the book list.
- Titles of books are in *italic* or underlined.
- The order of each reference is: author, title of book, publisher, place of publication, date, and page number if a quote has been used.
- If listing an article in a magazine, put the name of the article in inverted commas, then italicise or underline the name of the periodical, for example:

> Hughes, R, *The Shock of the New*, Thames & Hudson, London, 1991, p. 26.
>
> Lynton, N, *The Story of Modern Art*, Phaidon Press, Oxford, 1980.
>
> Hughes, R, 'Wallowing in the Mass Media', *Time*, 28 October 1991, pp. 40–46.

- Include any websites. First, list the person/organisation that controls the site. Next, give the date that the site was last revised, or when you visited it. Last, give the URL. For example:

> Philip Bacon Galleries, viewed 9 February 2004,
> www.philipbacon.com.au/artists/GwynHanssenPigott/extract.html

A student sample of art critical writing

Student Sarah Donnelly has given her opinion and analysed two paintings by Fred Williams, taking into account the frames.

Critical writing with short historical introduction

Sarah Donnelly, year 7 student, St Catherine's School, Waverley

FRED WILLIAMS (1927–82, AUSTRALIAN)

Fred Williams was an Australian landscape artist with passion. He is one of the great interpreters of the Australian landscape in the late twentieth century. His main subject is the great and unusual flora in the Australian landscape; only a few times has he painted a seascape.

In this painting, *Upwey Landscape*, Fred Williams interprets his world as dry and barren. We can tell this by his use of colour, paint application and detail. He has used browns, deep reds and oranges for the land, a pale white or very pale aqua for the sky and blacks and greys for the trees to represent a dry, hot climate and vegetation that is scarce. This is compared to the luscious greens and blues that might be used to paint a coastal landscape. By looking at the artist's use of colour we can see and feel what he is seeing and feeling while painting it (heat, dryness etc.).

This painting is almost a flat surface on the hill/mountain (this is described in more detail below), with some very roughly painted trees. We can tell the land is almost flat, as the paint application is pretty even and there don't seem to be any large bumps or obstacles painted. The trees seem to have been painted quickly with a brush with lots of paint on it, but when you look closer you can see small specks of white, blue, green and pink paint strategically placed on the trees. It is quite obvious that they are trees but they aren't delicately painted trees — more a realistic representation of trees. However, after saying this, it is most likely that Williams has studied the landscape carefully and placed the trees in certain positions.

It seems as though the viewpoint is from another mountain about the same height or taller, looking straight across to the other hill or mountain. (It is a hill or mountain, as when looking closely at the trees you will notice they are pointing upwards and so is the hill.)

The painting is an oil painting done on canvas and I think he has used a range of different sized paintbrushes, a palette knife and perhaps even sticks or leaves that he found lying around where he was painting; he might have used these to add texture. As briefly mentioned before, it is most likely he has used a paint-brush to put on a blob of paint and then used different tools to shape and change it, making each tree individual and different.

This painting is quite a serious and sombre painting. It does not create a happy mood; however, it does not create a sad mood. It is a painting that can be interpreted differently depending on the audience and different moods and feelings could be pulled out of it. For example, if you had lived in a place like it when you were a child, you might feel more passionately about the painting.

Personally, I like this painting. I think it is good because it is not a perfect painting yet it isn't abstract. It provided elements of both. Also, it has such a strong sense of the Australian outback and the heat and dryness of the country, which makes it an enjoyable painting to look at. It is also good because it draws your eye around the canvas by the use of colour, and every time you look at it you discover something new or different; something you didn't see before.

It is not in the subjective frame, as it doesn't depict dreams, feelings and emotions but a landscape that the artist is looking at while painting it (whether it is a photo or actually being there). It could be looked at in the structural frame by looking at the way the colour has been used (the shades of red, orange and brown and the colour used on the trees) and the way that the brushstrokes have been applied. It is not a new form of art (landscapes had been painted like that for many years), and it is using traditional materials and techniques. It could also be looked at in the cultural frame, as it is a landscape of Australia (where he lives) and perhaps it depicts where he lives (the bush), his lifestyle and a bit about his identity. Basically, this painting could be looked at in two of the main four frames — cultural and structural; it just depends on how you look at it.

In 1978, Williams moved from Upwey to Hawthorn, Melbourne, and from then on he painted works inspired by suburban sites. In 1974 he painted *Dight's Falls*. It shows bush and vegetation in the front section of the painting, and as your eye is drawn to the top you notice a highly developed city. There is also a dirt track or road which helps lead your eye around the painting as it twists and winds around the painting. I think that Williams has interpreted his world as almost being two worlds: the bush, or outback, and suburbia (the city). This is relevant even in today's society, and I think that he has interpreted it well. Also, notice the different colours used. Earthy greens, browns, greys and blues have been used in the country area whereas quite superficial colours (bright reds, greens and yellows) have been used for the city area. This painting doesn't have particular subject or focus, but it leads your eye everywhere. The contrast between the city and the country has been made obvious and the artist (I think) wants you to notice. As mentioned before, he has made it more obvious by making the road pass where the two meet and naturally your eye always wants to follow the road. This painting has been laid out or put together well so that you look at everything.

The painting was painted using oil on canvas. It seems as though he has used quite fine brushes, as there seems to be a lot of detail in this painting. I think it looks like the artist has waited for the paint to dry and then added more detail and repeated this many times, as it is quite layered (the trees are not just green and brown). He would have used enough paint on his brush to paint quite a big area but not too much so that he could do fine detail and to make sure that it didn't get out of control.

The colours used in this painting and the use of tone are very subtle. Dark greens are used against lighter aquas; creamy oranges are used against slightly more yellow oranges; and light greys are used against dark greys. However, there are some exceptions to this statement. You will notice that the fronts of the main buildings in the city are a very obvious dark orangey red colour and one of the waterholes is a very bright, light shade of blue. Outlines and shadows are not used at all in this painting; it is like a photo with no shadow. Also, it has been blended well. The road and the colour of the road are an example of this. It sort of flows into the bush and it isn't a sudden change from road to bush; the colours have been blended.

As *Upwey Landscape* does, this painting creates a sombre mood. It's not happy, as it isn't bright and colourful (bright reds, oranges, purples, pinks and yellows), but it's not sad, as it isn't all dark, dim colours (dark blues, blacks and greys). It is a painting which can be interpreted differently depending on the audience and different moods and feelings could be pulled out of it.

Again, like *Upwey Landscape*, I like this painting, but for different reasons this time. I like it because it shows the contrast between the city/suburbia and the outback/country/bush. This is close to my heart as I live in the city but most of my family lives in the country, and so I love the country. I am drawn to different places and this painting kind of reminds me of that as it shows both. I also like how it is laid out and how the artist has painted it. I like this style of painting and I like the techniques used to create it.

This painting cannot be looked at in the subjective frame, as the artist has painted something that he has seen, something that he is looking at — not what he dreamed and imagined, and it doesn't express his feelings and emotions.

It could be looked at in the structural frame if you looked at the use of shape, line, and texture and the materials used to create it.

It couldn't be looked at in the post-modern frame as it wasn't painted after 1980, it isn't a new form of art, it isn't mass media and it wasn't created using new techniques.

Finally, it could be looked at in the cultural frame. It shows where he lives and could even tell us a bit about his identity. Perhaps he is torn between the country and the city.

Again, this painting is like *Upwey Landscape*. It can be looked at in either the structural frame or the cultural frame; it just depends on how you look at it.

Fred Williams painted Australian landscapes in the cultural and structural frames. He had a creative mind and suggested rather than described the landscape in his paintings. The result: beautiful paintings depicting the wonderful Australian landscape.

Glossary

abstract: not representing anything from real life; non-representational

abstraction: art that is non-representational, achieving effects through colour, line, form and so on

aerial perspective: technique that makes distant objects lighter and bluer in tone

aesthetic: relating only to beauty, and not to other aspects of art

aesthetically: relating to one's sense of beauty

analytical: showing careful thought and planning rather than emotion

appropriate: put a familiar image in a new context to change its meaning

appropriation: the act of putting a familiar image in a new context to change its meaning; the practice of borrowing images from art, advertising and media and using them in new and interesting ways

aquatint: an etching process in which tiny specks of resin are sprinkled on a metal print plate to protect the metal while in the acid

Archibald Prize: an annual prize set up by a bequest in the will of Jules Francois Archibald in 1919. The bequest stipulated that first prize was to be awarded to an Australian artist for the best portrait of a man or woman distinguished in art, letters, science or politics.

archival: contained in historic records

armature: a framework on which a sculptor builds

articulate: to clearly express

assemblage: a collection of 'found' materials arranged to make a two- or three-dimensional composition

austere: severely simple, without ornament

avant-garde: new, modern, different, experimental

background: area of a painting that depicts the far distance

Baroque: style of art (c.1700s) that set out to impress with dramatic emotional effects and strong tonal contrasts

Bauhaus: an innovative art school, particularly in its methods of teaching design, which originated in 1919 in Germany

bisque: first firing of clay

burin: sharp pointed needle used in etching

calligraphic: containing marks that suggest a type of handwriting

caricature: painting or drawing that exaggerates the features of the person depicted

Classical: describes ancient Greek and Roman art

Classicism: style that refers back to Greek and Roman art, and has a sense of order and harmony

clientele: customers

commission: authorise to be done

composition: the placement of figures and objects; the organisation of an artwork

conceptual: concerned with ideas

Constructivism: an abstract art movement that originated in Russia in about 1914, and which typically used industrial materials

contemporary: belonging to the past decade; modern

context: the circumstances, surroundings or situation of an artwork

contrapposto: sculpture of the human body in which shoulders and chest are turned slightly one way, hips and legs another

controversial: causing argument

cool colours: blue, green, purple

Cubism: a modern art movement. The Cubists were seeking a new way to represent reality by using multiple viewpoints and fragmenting form.

Cubists: a group of artists working from 1907–25 who reacted against the established way of looking at things. They worked from multiple viewpoints, analysing and dissecting parts of items and rearranging them.

Dada: a modern art movement that was anti-art and tried to shock its audience (from a French word meaning 'hobby horse')

digital imagery: images created electronically by points of digital information which are arranged in a two-dimensional grid. Such images appear as points of colour on a computer screen or in a printed version.

distorted: twisted or out of shape

diverse: varied; having many different kinds

domestic: to do with home life

dramatic: exciting; like a play; containing drama, emotion or conflict

ecology: the interrelationship between natural organisms and their environment

elongated: stretched, made longer, distorted

emotive: causing us to feel emotion

etching: a form of printmaking using a metal plate. Lines are drawn through a wax coating on the plate. When the plate is put in acid, the lines are eaten away and ink is then rubbed into the lines. These lines are transferred under pressure onto dampened paper.

exaggerate: emphasise or magnify certain physical aspects

exalted: higher, more powerful

expression: indication of emotion on the face

Expressionism: a trend in modern European art in which the work emphasises emotion and the projection of inner feelings

expressive: showing emotion or personal feeling

Fauvism: a modern French art movement that began around 1905, and which was interested in bold, pure colour and decorative line

feminist: concerned with equality for women, recognition of rights

foreground: part of a painting that depicts the area nearest the observer

foreshortening: drawing/painting technique in which parts of the body that are closer to the viewer appear larger, and limbs appear shorter

form: shape or solidity, volume

Futurism: a modern art movement which started in Italy. It sought to represent the dynamic, energetic life of the city and machines.

glaze: a liquid painted on before the last firing to make a ceramic object waterproof. It can add colour, a dull shine (matt finish) or a glossy finish.

gouache: opaque water-based paint, similar to poster paint

humanism: belief system that stresses human, not spiritual, concerns

hybrid: made from many sources; composed of different things

icon: a well-known, respected image (originally meaning a sacred image)

idealised: presented in a perfect or ideal form, without imperfections

idiosyncratic: unique to a particular person; distinctive, unusual

impasto: thick, obvious paint

impregnated: saturated, thoroughly mixed with, absorbed

Impressionism: a modern art movement concerned with depicting light on the surface of objects

Impressionists: a group of French artists intent on showing the passing effects of light and atmosphere on everyday scenes and landscapes. They used short brushstrokes of pure colour.

innovative: new, different, ahead of its time

installation: an arrangement created for a particular site or gallery, creating an environment in itself

in the round: describes a three-dimensional sculpture that you can view from all sides

irrational: not what is normally expected; unreasonable, illogical

kiln: large 'oven' capable of creating high temperatures, used to fire clay

kinetic: relating to motion; moving

kitsch: pretentious, sentimental or in bad taste

leather hard: semi-dry, but still capable of being worked on

linear: containing lines as an important feature of a work

linear perspective: technique that represents depth by drawing lines going to a vanishing point

lithograph: a print created by using wax crayon on stone. The principle is that water is repelled by wax.

manifesto: public statement of theories or policy

Mannerism: style of sixteenth-century European art, mainly current in Italy

mediated: not direct or immediate; conveyed through a second or third medium, such as television

medium: the material used by an artist

melancholy: gloomy state of mind; sadness

metamorphosis: transformation of one thing into another, for example one animal becoming another

minimalism: style that doesn't have unnecessary detail or adornment, but instead has refined simplicity

minotaur: mythical creature that was half-bull, half-man

model: to blend light to dark to create solidity

Modernism: a twentieth-century art movement that broke away from the traditions of realism, eventually reaching abstraction. It included many different styles, such as Cubism, Fauvism, Expressionism and Surrealism.

monotony: sameness, uniformity

montage: art technique in which cut-out images are arranged, the images being ready-made; or where several photos are superimposed to form a single image

monumentality: grand scale, solidity and impressiveness

motif: ornament or distinctive feature

mundane: ordinary, everyday

mutation: the process of changing form, creating a new type of organism

muted: toned down, softened

mythological: belonging to a traditional myth or legend, usually to do with gods and goddesses

naive: childlike, simple

narrative: a story

naturalistic: presenting nature in an accurate, lifelike way

non-figurative: not containing likenesses of objects, places or people

organic: based on nature, on living things

palette knife: a very thin, bendable metal blade used for mixing or applying paint

parody: a humorous, exaggerated imitation

pastiche: art that borrows from different styles and combines them into a new artwork

patina: green coating that occurs on aged metal

performance art: art in which the artist is part of the work, the action of creating is important, and which is presented to an audience

perspective: way of making objects appear to recede into the distance. In *aerial perspective* distant objects are lighter and bluer in tone, with softer edges. *Linear perspective* is a geometrical method of representing depth on a two-dimensional surface by drawing lines going to a vanishing point.

photo-installation: a series of photographs covering more than one wall, designed for a specific site

photomontage: artwork composed of sections of photographs arranged and pasted down

plein-air: painted out of doors, directly from nature

Pop Art: an art movement of the 1950s and 1960s originating in London and New York. It used images of popular culture and consumer society and often borrowed techniques from commercial art.

portrait: individual likeness of a person

Post-Impressionists: included Cézanne, Gauguin, Van Gogh and Seurat. They went on to create a unique style of their own.

Postmodern: influenced by an experimental, contemporary art movement associated with post-industrial societies. It usually breaks the boundaries of art, challenges the idea of originality, and often draws on several art traditions.

prestigious: regarded as important; bringing success and fame

printmaking: general art term for the process of creating multiples of an image, each one being unique

propaganda: biased information that aims to further one's cause or damage another cause or group

Quantel: computer system

rationalism: the principle of taking a sensible, reasoned approach

ready-made: a selected object in its unaltered state which is exhibited as a work of art

recontextualise: to change the way objects/materials are normally seen

Renaissance (art): art in which the emphasis was on humankind and nature. 'Renaissance' means rebirth. It was a time of rediscovery of Roman classical ideals, and covers the period from about the fourteenth to the sixteenth century.

ritual: a solemn or serious repeated act

Rococo: style of art and architecture that began around 1700 and which was typically playful, lighthearted, ornamental, delicate and less sombre than Baroque art

Romanticism: nineteenth-century art movement that emphasised emotion and tended towards dramatic or exotic themes

scale: relative size, proportion

schematic: simplified like a diagram

semi-abstract: not quite abstract; containing some reference to the real world

silk-screen print: print made by forcing ink or paint through unmasked areas of silk

site-specific: designed for a particular place

slip: liquid clay of fine texture

slurry: semiliquid mixture of clay and water

spontaneity: quality of being quickly done, unplanned, instinctive, unconstrained

spontaneous: quickly done, unplanned, instinctive, unconstrained

still life: arrangement of lifeless things such as ornaments, fruit, flowers and musical instruments

subjective: exhibiting personal feelings; not objective

Super-Realism: style of art influenced by photography, and characterised by sharp focus and precise realism

Suprematism: Russian abstract art movement in which artworks were limited to basic geometric shapes

Surrealism: a modern art style interested in dreams and the subconscious

symmetrical balance: way of structuring an image so that each side has equal weight, equal balance

symmetrical: able to be divided into parts of equal shape and size; same both sides

tableau: (plural — tableaux) group of people or objects arranged to represent a striking scene

tactile: relating to the sense of touch; inviting the viewer to touch

text: words of a document

thrown: made on a potter's wheel

tonal contrast: light against dark

transcend: rise above or beyond; exceed

transitory: temporary, impermanent; description often associated with Postmodern work

translucent: allowing some light to pass through

unify: work as one, bring together

universal: relevant to all

urban: to do with towns or cities

utilitarian: having a use or purpose; for example a jug or cup

vibrancy: quality of being lively, thrilling, energetic

vibrant: rich, thrilling

voluptuous: well-rounded, sensuous

woodcut: print created from block of wood on which unwanted parts are cut away from the surface and the remaining areas printed

Notes

Introduction

1. Terry Barrett, *Criticizing Art: Understanding the Contemporary*, Mayfield Press, California, 1994, p. 16.
2. Ibid., p. 16.
3. Ibid., p. 16.
4. Concepts and terminology are derived from Board of Studies, New South Wales, *Syllabus: Visual Arts (Years 7–10)*, 2002.

Chapter 1

Henri Matisse

1. John Russell, *The Meanings of Modern Art*, Thames and Hudson, London, 1981.
2. Harold Osbourne, *The Oxford Companion to Twentieth Century Art*, Oxford University Press, Oxford, 1988.
3. Norbert Lynton, *The Story of Modern Art*, Phaidon Press, Oxford, 1986, p. 31.
4. Herschel B. Chipp, *Theories of Modern Art*, University of California Press, Berkeley, 1968, p. 132.

Pablo Picasso

5. Norbert Lynton, *The Story of Modern Art*, Phaidon Press, Oxford, 1986, p. 54.

Charles Blackman

6. Felicity St John Moore, *Blackman: Schoolgirls and Angels*, National Gallery of Victoria, 1993, p. 98.
7. Bernard Smith, *Australian Painting: 1788–1990*, Oxford University Press, South Melbourne, 1991, p. 308.

Jenny Sages

8. Jenny Sages, *Sydney Morning Herald*, 16 September 1994, p. 20.
9. Jenny Sages, *Look*, Art Gallery of New South Wales, March 2001, p. 38.
10. Bruce James, *Sydney Morning Herald*, 31 March 2001.
11. Edmund Capon, A report on the judging of the 1994 Mosman Art Prize, 22 July 1994.

William Robinson

12. Lynn Fern, *William Robinson*, Craftsman House, Sydney, 1995, p. 54.

Brigiat Maltese

13. Julieanne Campbell, 'Brigiat Maltese', in *Ceramics: Art and Perception*, No. 15, 1994.
14. Ibid.
15. Ibid.

Tintoretto

16. Graham Hopwood, *Handbook of Art*, Graham Hopwood, North Balwyn (Vic.), 1987, p. 97.
17. H. W. Janson, *History of Art* (3rd ed.), Thames and Hudson, London, 1986, p. 467.

Chapter 2

Margaret Preston

1. Margaret Preston, 'From Eggs to Electrolux: The Black Swann of Trespass', in *Art in Australia*, 1927.
2. *Woman's Budget*, 16 December 1931, p. 5.
3. M. Preston, 'From Eggs to Electrolux: The Black Swann of Trespass', in *Art in Australia*, 1927.

John Wolseley

4. Lee Fergusson, 'Wolseley and Majzner Read the Land', in *Artlink*, Vol. 15, No. 1, Autumn 1995, pp. 40–5.
5. Press release, Roslyn Oxley9 Gallery, www.roslynoxley9.com.au, 6 September 2001
6. Lee Fergusson, loc. cit.

Franz Marc

7. Herschel B. Chipp, *Theories of Modern Art*, University of California Press, Berkeley, 1968, p. 182.

8. A. Z. Rudenstine, *The Guggenheim Museum Collection: Paintings 1880–1945*, Harry N. Abrams Inc. Publishers, New York, 1976, p. 493.

Joan Miró

9. Jack A. Hobbs, *Art in Context* (2nd ed.), Harcourt Brace Jovanovich, Orlando, Fla., 1979, p. 260.

10. Herschel B. Chipp, *Theories of Modern Art*, University of California Press, Berkeley, 1968, p. 432.

11. Ibid.

Jeff Koons

12. Martha Buskirk, 'Art and the Law: Appropriation under the Gun', in *Art and America*, June 1991, pp. 37–39.

13. Pamphlet from exhibition: *A John Calder 25th Anniversary Art Project*, 1996 Sydney Festival, Museum of Contemporary Art.

14. Robert Hughes, *Nothing If Not Critical*, Collins Harvill, London, 1990 (and in United States by Alfred A. Knopf, Inc.), p. 15.

Bronwyn Oliver

15. Graeme Sturgeon, *Contemporary Australian Sculpture*, Craftsman House, Roseville, 1991, p. 72.

16. Ibid., p. 71.

John Davis

17. Graeme Sullivan, *Seeing Australia*, Piper Press, Sydney, 1994, p. 17.

Richard Goodwin

18. Graeme Sturgeon, *Contemporary Australian Sculpture*, Craftsman House, Roseville, 1991, p. 25.

Chapter 3

Richard Sapper

1. C. Burchard, 'Richard Sapper — Shaping the Modern World', Goethe Institute, Feb. 2003, www.goethe.de

Vincent Van Gogh

2. From a text wall display, Van Gogh Exhibition, January 1996, Yokohama Museum, Japan.

3. Ibid.

4. Herschel B. Chipp, *Theories of Modern Art*, University of California Press, Berkeley, 1968, p. 40.

Max Dupain

5. Edmund Capon quoted in S. Ellis & S. Hawkins, 'Photo Maestro Dupain Dies, 81', in *Daily Telegraph Mirror*, Thursday 30 July 1992.

Margaret Olley

6. Anna Maryke, 'Margaret Olley', in *Oz Art*, December 1995, p. 9.

7. Ann Loxley, 'Margaret Olley', in *ITA*, September 1990, pp. 23–25.

Janet Fish

8. John Arthur, *Realists at Work*, Watson Guptill Publishers, New York, 1983, p. 70.

Marcel Duchamp

9. Arturo Schwarz, *The Complete Works of Marcel Duchamp*, Thames & Hudson, London, 1971, p. 469.

10. Hans Richter, *Dada Art and Anti-Art*, Thames and Hudson, London, 1965, p. 65.

11. Norbert Lynton, *The Story of Modern Art*, Phaidon Press, Oxford, 1986, p. 127.

Rosalie Gascoigne

12. *Sense of Place*, exhibition catalogue, Ivan Dougherty Gallery, 1990.

Andy Warhol

13. Norbert Lynton, *Landmarks of World Art: Modern World*, Paul Hamlyn Press, London, 1965.

14. Alan Solomon, in Gregory Battcock, *The New Art*, Dutton Paperback, New York, original version 1963, pp. 67–82.

15. Gregory Battcock, 'Anti Art and Criticism' by Allen Leepa, *The New Art*, Dutton Paperback, New York, 1973, p. 127.

16. *America and Europe: A Century of Modern Masters from the Thyssen Bornemisza Collection*, educational leaflet to accompany Australian tour, October 1979–August 1980.

Claes Oldenburg

17. M. Amaya, *Pop Art and After*, Studio Paperback, Viking Press, New York, 1965.
18. Robert Hughes, 'Wallowing in the Mass Media Sea', *Time*, 28 October 1991.

Jean-Siméon Chardin

19. Robert Hughes, *Nothing If Not Critical*, Collins Harvill, London, 1987, pp. 75–76.
20. David Piper, *An Introduction to Painting and Sculpture Vol. 1: Understanding Art*, Mitchell Beazley Library of Art, London, 1981, pp. 74 and 117.

Chapter 4

J. M. W. Turner

1. L. Hermann, *Turner*, Phaidon, London, 1975, p. 44.
2. A. Wilton, *The Life and Work of J. M. W. Turner*, Academy Editions, London, 1979, p. 162.
3. W. Guant, *Turner*, Phaidon, London, 1981, p. 21.

Maurice de Vlaminck

4. M. Carra, *Vlaminck*, Park Lane Publishers, Grange Books, London, 1991, p. 3.

Wassily Kandinsky

5. Robert Hughes, *Nothing If Not Critical*, Collins Harvill, London, 1987, p. 159.
6. Ibid., p. 160.
7. Ibid., p. 158.
8. Herschel B. Chipp, *Theories of Modern Art*, University of California Press, Berkeley, 1968, p. 347.
9. Alfred H. Barr Jr, *Cubism and Abstract Art: New York 1936*, Museum of Modern Art, New York, Catalogue, p. 66.

Fred Williams

10. Patrick McCaughey, *Fred Williams: Fred Williams Landscapes 1969–1974*, Fisher Fine Art Ltd, London, 1979.
11. Sasha Grishin, 'First Attempt to Assign Fred Williams a Place in History', in *Canberra Times*, November 1987.

John Olsen

12. Bernard Smith, *Australian Painting 1788–1990*, Oxford University Press, Melbourne, 1991, p. 315.

Robert Dickerson

13. Robert Hughes, *The Art of Australia*, Penguin, Ringwood (Vic.), 1970, p. 241.
14. Bernard Smith, *Australian Painting 1788–1990*, Oxford University Press, Melbourne, 1991, p. 306.

Jeffrey Smart

15. Robert Hughes, *The Art of Australia*, Penguin, Ringwood, 1970, p. 204.

Donald Friend

16. Robert Hughes, *The Art of Australia*, Penguin, Ringwood, 1970, p. 172.

Brett Whiteley

17. Bernard Smith, *Australian Painting 1788–1990*, Oxford University Press, Melbourne, 1991, p. 389.

Chapter 5

Davida Allen

1. Graeme Sullivan, *Seeing Australia: Views of Artists and Artwriters*, Piper Press, Sydney, 1994, p. 45.

Pablo Picasso

2. Norbert Lynton, *The Story of Modern Art*, Phaidon Press, Oxford, 1980, p. 190.

Arthur Boyd

3. Bernard Smith, *Antipodean exhibition catalogue*, 14–15 August 1959.

Chapter 6

Linda Wallace

1. Lev Manovich, *The Language of New Media*, MIT Press, Cambridge, Mass., 2001.
2. Linda Wallace, www.machinehunger.com.au/eurovision/

Phillip George

3. Writing by Phillip George to accompany exhibition and publication of *Memory Stack 2*.

Further research

Modern painting

Chipp, Herschell B. *Theories of Modern Art*. University of California Press, Berkeley, 1968.

d'Harnoncourt A. & McShine, K. *Marcel Duchamp*. Museum of Modern Art, New York, 1973.

Kandinsky, V. O. *On the Spiritual in Art*. (Trans. and ed. Hilla Rebay.) Solomon R. Guggenheim Foundation, New York, 1946.

Lippard, Lucy R. *Pop Art*. (4th printing.) Praeger World Art Series, New York, 1973.

Ratcliff, Carter. *Warhol*. Abbeville Press, New York, 1983.

Shapiro, Meyer. *Modern Art: 19th and 20th Centuries*. George Braziller, New York, 1968.

Ferrier, J. L. *The Art of the 20th Century*. Chêne-Hachette, Paris, 1999.

Australian art

Burke, Janine. *Australian Women Artists: 1840–1940*. Greenhouse Publications, Richmond (Vic.), 1980.

Caruana, W. *Aboriginal Art*. World of Art Series. Thames and Hudson, London, 1993.

Eagle, M. & Jones, A. *A Story of Australian Painting*. Macmillan, Sydney, 1994.

Germaine, M. *A Dictionary of Women Artists of Australia*. Craftsman House, Sydney, 1991.

Haese, R. *Rebels and Precursors*. Penguin Books, Ringwood, 1988.

Hughes, R. *The Art of Australia*. Penguin, Ringwood, 1970.

Isaacs, J. *Australia's Living Heritage: Arts of the Dreaming*. Lansdowne Press, Sydney, 1984.

Kirby, Sandy. *Sightlines: Women's Art and Feminist Perspectives in Australia*. Craftsman House, Sydney, 1992.

Klepac, L. *Australian Painters of the Twentieth Century*. Beagle Press, Sydney 2000.

McCulloch, A. *Encyclopaedia of Australian Art*. McCulloch Publishing, Melbourne, 1988.

Roslyn Oxley9 Gallery, www.roslynoxley9.com.au/artists

Ross, P. *The History of the Archibald Prize*, Art Gallery of New South Wales, Sydney, 1999.

Scarlett, K. *Australian Sculptors*. Nelson, Melbourne, 1980.

Smith, Bernard. *A Place of Taste and Tradition*. Oxford University Press, Melbourne, 1979 (reprinted 1988).

Smith, Bernard. *Australian Painting, 1788–1970*. Oxford University Press, Melbourne, 1971.

Sturgeon, Graeme. *Contemporary Australian Sculpture*. Craftsman House, Sydney, 1991.

Sturgeon, Graeme. *The Development of Australian Sculpture 1788–1975*. Thames and Hudson, London, 1978.

Sutton, P. *Dreamings: Art from Aboriginal Australia*. Viking Press, Melbourne, 1988.

Electronic media art

Zurbrugg, Nicholas. 'Electronic Arts in Australia', *Continuum*, Vol. 8, No. 1, 1994.

Charles Blackman

Amadio, N. *Charles Blackman: Lost Domains*. Reed, Sydney, 1980.

Blackman, B. 'The Antipodean Affair', *Art and Australia*, 5 April 1968, pp. 607–616.

Haycraft, D. 'The Making of a Manifesto', *Art and Australia*, 26 February 1988.

St John Moore, F. *Charles Blackman: Schoolgirls and Angels*. National Gallery of Victoria, 1993.

University of Western Australia, Lawrence Wilson Art Gallery, www.arts.uwa.edu.au/LW/waywewere/blackman.html

Arthur Boyd

Gunn, Grazia. *Arthur Boyd: Seven Persistent Images*. Australian National Gallery, Canberra, 1985.

Hoff, U. 'The Paintings of Arthur Boyd', *Meanjin*, 17 February 1958, pp. 143–147.

Mollison, James. 'Arthur Boyd', *Art and Australia*, 3 (1965), pp. 114–123.

National Gallery of Victoria, www.ngv.vic.gov.au/collection/australian/painting/b/boyd.html

Pearce, B. *Arthur Boyd: Retrospective*. Art Gallery of New South Wales, 1993.

Philipp, F. *Arthur Boyd*. Thames and Hudson, London, 1967.

Savill Galleries, www.savill.com.au/html/aboyd03.htm

John Brack

Grishin, Sasha. *The Art of John Brack*. Vols 1 and 2. Oxford University Press, Melbourne, 1990.

Lindsay, Robert. *John Brack: A Retrospective Exhibition*. National Gallery of Victoria, 1987.

Monash University Arts Faculty, Visual Culture section, www.arts.monash.edu.au/visual_culture/projects/diva/jbrack.html

Grace Cossington Smith

Department of Education and Training Victoria, Teachers — Gender Education, www.sofweb.vic.edu.au/gender/projects/gaw/bioLY/cossingtonsmith.htm

Eva Breuer Art Dealer, www.evabreuerartdealer.com.au/cosssmith.html

James, B. *Grace Cossington Smith*. Craftsman House, Sydney, 1990.

Thomas, D. *Grace Cossington Smith*. Exhibition catalogue, Art Gallery of New South Wales, 1973.

Thomas, D. 'Grace Cossington Smith', *Art and Australia*, Vol. 5, No. 4, March 1967.

William Dobell

Adams, B. *Portrait of an Artist: A Biography of William Dobell*. Hutchinson, Richmond, 1983.

Hylton, J. *William Dobell: Portraits in Context*. Wakefield Press, Adelaide, 2003.

Pearce, B. *William Dobell, 1899–1970: The Painter's Progress*. Art Gallery of New South Wales, Sydney, 1997.

Waldmann, A. 'The Archibald Prize', *Art and Australia*, 20 February 1982, pp. 213–266.

Rosalie Gascoigne

MacDonald, V. *Rosalie Gascoigne*. Regaro Press, Sydney, 1998.

Massy, J. *Rosalie Gascoigne: Diverse Visions*. Queensland Art Gallery, Brisbane, 1990.

Roslyn Oxley9 Gallery, www.roslynoxley9.com.au/artists/

Joy Hester

Adams, B. *Portrait of an Artist*. Hutchinson, Melbourne, 1983.

Burke, J. *Joy Hester*. Greenhouse Publications, Richmond, 1983.

Eva Breuer Art Dealer, www.evabreuerartdealer.com.au/hester.html

Reid, B. 'Joy Hester: Draughtsman of Identity', *Art and Australia*, Vol. 4, No. 1, June 1966.

Edvard Munch

Boe, A. *Edvard Munch*. Ediciones Poligrafa, Barcelona, 1989.

Georgia O'Keeffe

Georgia O'Keeffe Museum, Santa Fe, www.okeeffemuseum.org

Margaret Preston

Ambrus, C. *Australian Women Artists: First Fleet to 1945 — History, Hearsay and Her Say*. Impressible Press, Woden (ACT), 1992.

Butel, E. *Margaret Preston: The Art of Constant Rearrangement*. Penguin Press in association with the Art Gallery of New South Wales, 1985.

McQueen, H. *The Black Swann of Trespass*. Alternative Publishing Co-operative, Sydney, 1979.

North, I. *The Art of Margaret Preston*. Art Gallery of South Australia, Adelaide, 1980.
Topliss, H. *Modernism and Feminism: Australian Women Artists 1900–1940*. Craftsman House, Roseville (NSW), 1996.

Jenny Sages
www.kingstreetgalleries.com.au
Video *Two Thirds Sky: Artists in Desert Country*, Film Australia 2002.

Jeffrey Smart
Art Galleries Schubert, www.art-galleries-schubert.com.au/www/Jeffrey_Smart/smart.htm
McDonald, J. *Jeffrey Smart: Paintings of the 70s and 80s*. Craftsman House, Sydney, 1990.
Savill Galleries, www.savill.com.au/html/smart.htm

Linda Wallace
Linda Wallace, www.machinehunger.com.au.

Brett Whiteley
Brett Whiteley Studio, www.brettwhiteley.org, © 2003.

Fred Williams
Grishin, S. 'Fred Williams and Australia's Landscape', *Hemisphere*, 26 June 1982, pp. 370–374.
McCaughey, P. *Fred Williams*. Bay Books, Sydney, 1980 (1987).
McCaughey, P. *Fred Williams: The Pilbara Series 1979–81*. Exhibition catalogue, CRA Ltd, Melbourne, 1983.
Media Equation Pty Ltd, South Melbourne, www.me.com.au/williams/
Mollison, J. *A Singular Vision: The Art of Fred Williams*. Australian National Gallery, Canberra, 1989.
Mollison, J. *Fred Williams: Etchings*. Rudy Koman Gallery, Sydney, 1968.
Topliss, H. 'Fred Williams', *Art and Australia*, Autumn 1990, pp. 401–403.

Index